Keeping in Touch

Marjorie Burke

authorHOUSE™

1663 LIBERTY DRIVE, SUITE 200
BLOOMINGTON, INDIANA 47403
(800) 839-8640
WWW.AUTHORHOUSE.COM

First published by AuthorHouse 10/25/05

ISBN: 1-4208-5326-0 (sc)
ISBN: 1-4208-5325-2 (dj)

Library of Congress Control Number: 2005905228

Printed in the United States of America
Bloomington, Indiana

This book is printed on acid-free paper.

Acknowledgements

Without Jane's letters, this book would not exist. So, I must thank her for being the faithful correspondent, and allowing me to use their contents.

I also must thank Linda for her FBI file, Wanda for my old letters, and Anne for her stories. During the course of my research, I bugged and prodded my old friends, and called up former agents with whom I hadn't spoken in over 30 years. Former Agents Mike Hennigan, Jack Keith, Stephen Gaughan and Dick McCormick were most helpful in substantiating, or providing additional information on matters discussed with them.

Finally, it would be an injustice if I did not thank my former husband, John Burke, who made available the directory, which enabled me to contact the ex-agents. He also gave me the computer on which this book was written. This should exempt him from any derogatory remarks. However, I believe I have been kind!

Ay, there are some good things in life,

that fall not away with the rest.

And, of all best things upon earth, I

hold that a faithful friend is the best.

Last Words of a Sensitive
Second-Rate Poet by
Edward Robert Bulwert Lytton
Earl of Lytton

From Familiar Quotations by John Bartlett, Thirteenth Edition, Published 1955 by Little Brown and Company, Boston, Massachusetts.

PART ONE

Reception Room, San
Diego FBI office, 5th
and Spruce, circa. 1962

It was a week or so after Christmas. I had taken the ornaments from the tree – lacy snowflakes and angels crocheted by my mother, crystal icicles passed down from my dad's mother, and the little houses I made from milk cartons, aluminum foil, and red and green paper, the year I was pregnant with my son. They were back home in their boxes – some of which have become fragile over time.

The cards were next. I untaped them from the doorways, and read them each one more time. It was then that I realized there was no card from my oldest and dearest friend. I went back through the stack. Jane never missed my birthday or Christmas, not ever in the 40 years in which we had corresponded. Not getting a card from her could only mean one thing. Something was wrong. I dialed her number in Bonita, California. Her answering machine came on, so I left a message. After a day or so, when I did not hear back from her, I tried again. She wasn't answering.

It was time to conduct a little investigation.

I "telephonically contacted" a mutual friend, Anne Sarris, with whom Jane and I worked in the San Diego office of the FBI in the 1960s. (Agents were always "telephonically" contacting people.) Anne was the security clerk. I can still picture her scurrying to and from the vault with mysterious "en code" tapes. Over the years, Jane kept in touch with her, passing along news of her family in letters to me. She sometimes joined Jane and me for lunch when I was in San Diego. Jane thought of us as her daughters, she had said, having no children of her own.

While Anne was looking into Jane's whereabouts, I took out a box of her letters, which I have saved. I wondered just when we had become such good friends. And, what made her continue to write

1

to me long after my younger friends became mere Christmastime correspondents.

My memory ticked back to June 13, 1960 -- the day I entered on duty as a GS-4 stenographer for the FBI – the day I first met Jane.

My mother worked downtown, so I rode to work with her in the family's 1958 Chevrolet.

"Good luck. I'll pick you up here at five," she said, as she dropped me off in front of the Walker Scott Department Store on Fifth Avenue. The Bureau offices were in the San Diego Trust and Savings Bank Building at Sixth and Broadway, a location with which I was familiar, having spent the last four years a few blocks away attending Cathedral Girls' High School at Third and Cedar Streets.

My best friend, Lana Ludlow, and I strolled many an after-school hour up and down Broadway, checking out the cute sailors. Our fetching brown jumpers, bobby sox and saddle oxfords rarely aroused the attention of the U.S. Navy, however. It wasn't until the FBI called me up to join its ranks that I realized the Bureau's offices were located there. Once I accepted the job, Lana dropped me like a hot potato. I suspected it had something to do with her family's attitude toward the Federal Government. During the 1960 census, her grandmother had commented that, "the number of toilets in a person's home is none of the government's business!"

It felt good to be out of the old brown uniform. I wore a dark blue gingham dress with a large white collar, white gloves and freshly polished white pumps.

As I pushed through the brass-framed revolving door of the bank building, I was too young and nervous to notice the lobby's marble floors and walls, iron teller's cages, and a ceiling so high that its chandeliers appeared to be suspended in space. I found my way to the elevators. An outer door of scrolled brass opened to reveal its dark wood-paneled interior.

"Seven please," I said to the uniformed operator. When the doors opened, the words "Federal Bureau of Investigation" stenciled in gold on the glass, gleamed in front of me. I entered the office. From her desk behind the counter, a tall, stern-looking woman approached. She wore a straight, dark dress. Her glasses had rhinestones at the corners, and her black hair was pulled back tightly into a chignon.

"You must be Marjorie McClintock," she said. "I'm Jane Esther Campbell."

Jane was a 20-year veteran, and the secretary to the Special Agent in Charge.

"Did you bring the results of your physical examination?"

I handed her some paperwork, which she quickly scanned, then turned back to me.

"This form must be completed by your doctor," she said, pointing out a couple of blank lines.

"Do you have your work permit?"

I must have looked perplexed, because she then explained in what seemed a very official manner:

"The law requires that you obtain a work permit if you are not yet 18."

My knees began to knock and I felt faint. "I have to call my mother," I gulped. "I don't have my own car."

When sufficient time had passed for mother to arrive at Electric Supply Distributors on Market Street, I called and asked if she could take me to get a work permit and to the doctor's office. Fortunately, she was able to leave work to run me around town.

This mission accomplished, we returned to Sixth and Broadway, where, once again, I took the elevator to the seventh floor. I handed the paperwork over to Miss Campbell.

"SAC Price will see you now," she said, apparently satisfied that all was in order. She led me into his office. A distinguished looking man, with thick salt and pepper hair, approached with his hand extended to shake mine.

"Frank Price," he said, with a smile. "Pleased to meet you, Miss McClintock. I'm sure you'll find working for the FBI both rewarding, and enjoyable. I think you'll also find we are like family here. Welcome aboard."

I began to feel somewhat at ease.

"Miss Campbell will show you around and introduce you to everyone."

First, Jane took me to a large squad room for the criminal agents. She introduced me to a few of the agents who were typing or dictating. They smiled and welcomed me. We proceeded down the hall, where she pointed out the switchboard/radio room and the Chief Clerk's office, on our left, and then the Steno Pool, on the right. Here, I was turned over to the Chief Steno.

Helen Kilgore was, how does one say this kindly, a school-marm type. Her hair, which was neither blond nor brown, was cut Buster Brown style, with bangs topping her round face. She wore glasses and was rather large breasted. She reminded me of the nuns I had all through school, minus the habit. Her manner was not unlike the gym teacher at school, who was a former member of the U. S. Army.

I was introduced to the other stenographers – Sandie, Jeanine, Monica, Sharon, Margo, Pat, and a few others whose names I have forgotten. They were all busy typing, but stopped a moment to welcome me. I was assigned a desk, bare except for the IBM electric typewriter, a steno pad, a couple of pens and a calendar.

A handbook was issued to me. "Familiarize yourself with this," Miss Kilgore said. "It's our bible. If you refer to it, you won't need to ask a lot of questions."

She assigned me a couple of "rough drafts" – simple letters – to get me started.

Before I had a chance to type a thing, it was lunchtime.

"Come on," my neighbor steno, Pat Meaney, said. "I'll show you the employees' lounge."

Pat entered on duty the previous Monday. With a whole week under her belt, I thought she'd be a good person to connect with.

I grabbed my brown bag lunch and tried to look nonchalant, as we headed down the hall. Pat's hips swayed from side to side as she maneuvered the hall in spike heels. I tottered alongside in my one-and-a-half inch pumps. We passed a small room with a half dozen or so desks.

"That's the security agents' room where they work the CP,USA cases," she said, as I pretended to know what she meant. I would soon realize that there were many all cap abbreviations to learn.

An attractive brunette, Pat seemed much more self-confident than I.

"I just started last week. It's a lot to get used to and Helen can be kind of a pain, but the other girls are really nice. Where did you go to school?"

"Cathedral Girls' High," I answered.

"An all girls' school," she choked. "How awful. I'd hate to go to school where there are no boys."

"I've been dating this guy, but it's nothing serious," she said.

"Do you have a boyfriend?"

"Kind of," I said. "I've been sort of dating a sailor who one of my girlfriends fixed me up with for the senior prom."

By this time, we had reached the lounge, where the girls were chattering away. They tried to include me by asking questions, but after getting one and two word answers, they went back to whatever it was they were discussing, and I mostly listened.

That afternoon I studied the sample book which contained different types of correspondence – airtel, memo, letter, report, and the famous "302" (interview report form). Agents constantly dictated results of interviews, which ultimately were incorporated into a report to "the Bureau." Airtels always went airmail, except to Los Angeles – something I forgot once and was duly chastised by Miss Kilgore. Reports often went out to numerous field offices, so when typing a "302" we always had to make the maximum number – eleven. More copies required use of the mimeograph.

"This is your production sheet," Helen said, at the end of the day.

"Each time you are given an assignment, you enter it on the sheet, with the date received and the estimated number of pages. Nothing is allowed to remain on the sheet over five days. As each item is completed, you draw a red line through it. By 4:30 each day, you are to hand in a copy to me so I can schedule shorthand assignments for the following day. Any questions?"

"Not right now," I answered, thinking that I shouldn't have any trouble typing things up in five days. Little did I know how full that production sheet would become, and how often letters or reports would need to be expedited, forcing routine correspondence to wait.

Memories of that afternoon are vague, except for being introduced to a lot of people and a lot of rules and regulations. Five o'clock rolled around and it was time to sign out. All my nervous anxiety had left me mentally and physically exhausted. My feet were killing me as I walked to Fifth and Broadway to meet my mother. I gave her a rundown on my day, which continued over dinner with my dad and sister. Afterwards, I collapsed on the sofa in utter exhaustion, and fell asleep – a practice which continued for some time. My dad told me years later that he never thought I'd last.

~

Within a couple of weeks, I began taking my breaks later than the others – maybe because of my shyness and being overwhelmed with all the chatter in the lunch room. It was a custom of Jane's, also. Before long, we began to get acquainted.

Jane lived with her parents in Chula Vista, a city south of San Diego, close to the Mexican border. She was an only child, and had enjoyed a wonderful relationship with her mother, who now was quite ill. Some days Jane was exhausted from having to get up during the night to tend to her, and she worried about the efficiency of the homemaker who came during the day.

The relationship with my mother, on the other hand, was tense. She was strict, and now that I was working and feeling independent, we were battling on a daily basis.

I asked Jane if she had always lived in Chula Vista.

"No. But, I was only six years old when we moved here from Florence, Alabama. My parents were originally from St. Paul, Minnesota.

"My father's family moved to Alabama, for the warmer climate. I think my grandmother had tuberculosis. By the time that he and mother married, he had a good job in the insurance business there, and was well-liked, so he brought his bride to Florence.

"After a few years, my father decided to move the family to California, because he didn't like the way his wife was being treated."

"What do you mean," I inquired.

"The southern women wouldn't invite her out because they felt she was too outspoken. She taught school in Minnesota. Also being from the north, there were still strong feelings from the Civil War."

"What made your dad chose California?"

"He told me that he had seen Chula Vista from the train on his way to or from Mexico," Jane explained. "He thought at the time that it was such a pretty place and that he wouldn't mind living there."

"We moved to San Diego when I was only seven. I was born in Pittsburgh," I responded.

"My dad started up a small appliance store after returning from World War II, but couldn't make a go of it. His old job wasn't available, and he had to take another one with the same company, but he wasn't happy. One day when he returned from work, my mother was reading a letter from her sister, who lived in San Diego. They had heard about a job driving a school bus and working as a janitor at a school, which my dad could have if he was interested. So we moved here."

Another time, Jane and I discovered that we both had Scottish backgrounds.

"My father's ancestors belonged to Clan Campbell," she said, "headed up by the Duke of Argyll." My mother sang Irish songs to me when I was a child, but I think her ancestors were from Scotland too. I also think there was a Pennsylvania Dutch connection on my mother's side."

"I think my dad's mother was Pennsylvania Dutch, or German," I said, "and my paternal grandfather was Scotch-Irish."

(Years later, a cousin of mine on my father's side, discovered that our family was from the Clan MacDougal.)

～

My first days at the Bureau were often intimidating. Men, in general, made me nervous, and here I was thrown into a world of G-men. Imagine how startling, while taking dictation from one agent, another removes his belt and tosses his .38 caliber Smith and Wesson across the adjacent desk! The agents, as a whole, were quite handsome. One in particular caught my eye almost from the start. A few enjoyed embarrassing, or startling the young clerks and stenos. One day as I took dictation from Mike Hennigan, Bill Fields approached and asked me, "Do you know what virgins eat for breakfast?"

Dumbfounded, I answered with a meek "No."

The agents roared with laughter.

The desks were gray metal, the tops of which contained a simple blotter, desk calendar, and phone. Everything else was locked in the desks. Very little decoration adorned the offices, other than the FBI emblem or a photo of J. Edgar Hoover.

Agents were required to wear conservative suits and ties. Only white or light blue shirts were permitted. Some of the men routinely wore hats, but others didn't. There were spares in the coat closet, for which a mad scramble would ensue in the event of an arrest. An agent wouldn't want to be caught hatless if his face was to appear in the paper or on the news.

The stenos were mostly high school graduates who had scored high on their shorthand and typing tests. A rookie steno's abilities were not only challenged by the unique language used by the agents, but by their various regional accents. Take Mike Hennigan for instance, with a thick Boston accent. One day when I was taking his dictation, he described a school of dance as "maudin." I asked him to repeat the word, which he did. I still did not recognize it. "Are you old-fashioned, or something?" he quipped, as he spelled "m-o-d-e-r-n." Agent Paul Stapleton was from New York. I remember thinking that he sounded like Bugs Bunny. Southern boys, like Billy Bob Williams, were another kind of challenge. At times it seemed they were speaking another language all together!

One morning, shortly after my entrance on duty, I entered the Steno Pool and heard a steno exclaim: "Five hours!"

A tiny, blond, chain-smoking young lady named Monica, described by some of the agents as a "crackerjack" steno, was reacting to her daily shorthand assignment. And to think how I had groaned over five-minute timed writings in shorthand class. It wasn't long before I grew accustomed to taking two to four hours of dictation a day, however.

The investigation into the Mary Lou Olson kidnapping was underway at this time, and a top priority in San Diego. The body of this young, pre-teen, was found in Mexico. The belief was that she had been raped and murdered before being transported across the border. While the FBI's jurisdiction didn't include murder, the fact that her body was found in Mexico brought San Diego office into the case. Sadly, the case was never solved in those days before DNA was used to solve crimes.

Special Agent Frank Sullivan was the case agent. He died a few months after I began working for the Bureau. Fellow agents and others believed that his around-the-clock work on the Olson case killed him. The entire office, except for a skeleton crew, attended his funeral. A strong sense of family was evident among the employees, and being driven in an official Bucar to the funeral made me feel like a celebrity.

Monica, dressed entirely in black, sobbed hysterically. She had been assigned to Mr. Sullivan during the Olson case. She left the Bureau shortly thereafter.

Another, more well-known kidnapping was that of Frank Sinatra, Jr., from the Lake Tahoe area. That case was solved.

It was in this time-frame that Jane lost her mother. I was so busy making new friends and having some fun, that I wasn't tuned into Jane's needs. I do remember her telling me, though, that she could feel her heart breaking when her mother died.

I had become friendly with Pat Meaney, who sat next to me in the steno pool. We started out going to dinner, or taking in a movie, but eventually spent a lot of time together. My new friend was quite different from my best friend in high school. Pat walked on – what I considered at the time – the wild side. The words to a popular song then, "The girl can't help it, she just can't help it," ring in my head when I think of her. She must have appealed to my inhibited, shy self.

Her hair was curly dark brown, cut short. She had large dark, brown eyes and long eyelashes, loaded with mascara. Freckles peeked out from beneath her makeup. At dinner one evening, a young man at a nearby table commented, "I've never seen so many beauty marks in one place!" Her skirts and sweaters were tight, showing off her curvy figure, and her ability to flirt drew men to her, both inside and outside of the Bureau. I latched on to her, hoping that the guys she left by the wayside might notice me.

"We need to do something about your wardrobe," she instructed. "Your dresses look like they belong on an Iowa farm girl. Don't you ever wear straight skirts?"

"I always thought my hips were too big for them" I answered.

"Your hips aren't too big, silly. You have a nice shape. And no one would ever know that you have a bustline from the way you stand. Throw those shoulders back and your chest out."

I never wore straight skirts – always fully gathered ones, and I was self-conscious about my "bustline." Pat certainly got me to change the way I thought about myself and had me wearing straight skirts and sweaters in no time. She also introduced me to makeup. We got carried away with the heavily arched eyebrows, however.

She also didn't like my choice of music – rock and roll all the way. I loved Elvis.

"That's so immature," she'd say. "You should listen to something more sophisticated, like Ray Coniff." So I listened to Ray Coniff.

Her very favorite song was "Always" -- "I'll be loving you, always, with a love that's true, always....not for just an hour, not for just a day, not for just a year, but always" – which I found to be ironic as I got to know her.

We spent many weekends together. I stayed at her house, where she lived with an aunt and uncle and her adorable grandmother.

"It's a great life if you don't weaken," Grandma Meaney would say. "Praise the Lord and pass the ammunition," was another of her expressions.

Somewhere along the line, Pat came up with the bright idea that we should dress up and see if we could get a drink at a fancy bar.

"Maybe we'll meet a couple of nice men with money."

Hair teased and sprayed, nails painted, and rhinestone jewelry in place, we'd slip into our "cocktail" dresses and five-inch heels. Pat drove us, in her little Renault, to a lounge at a swanky hotel. We always were served a drink, but I don't ever recall meeting any rich men.

Early the next morning, grandma would stick her head inside our bedroom door, calling for us to "Rise and shine."

"You two don't exactly look like you're ready to fight big, bad tigers," she's say as we sat down to breakfast.

I don't believe that I shared these adventures with Jane. I certainly would not tell her about going to bars when we were only eighteen. My mother wasn't happy with my new friend, but Jane felt that she must be an upstanding person since she had passed the Bureau's investigation.

As it turned out, before long, Pat's shenanigans got her fired. She had taken a sick day to look for another job.

By this time, I was trying to attract the attention of Agent Joseph Scallini. And, Pat had taken up ice skating. I think she enjoyed wearing the tights and short skirts that allowed her to show off her shapely legs. I did not accompany her to the rink, as I have never been inclined to attach blades or wheels to my feet. She began dating a young sailor who she met at the rink, but her eye was on his older friend, a Lieutenant Commander.

One day, as I took dictation from an agent, Joe approached. My heart began pounding.

"Are you planning to attend the party at the Admiral Kidd's Club?" he asked of the agent, who said yes. Then he looked at me.

"I didn't know anything about it," I said.

"You should come. You'll have fun. Everyone has fun at our parties."

I took Joe's asking as a personal invitation.

"Okay, I guess I'll go, if the other girls are going."

I arranged a ride to the party with two other stenos, Margo and Sharon. Trying to look sophisticated in a straight aqua dress with belted waist, accented with crystal earrings and pendant, I hoped to attract Joe's attention.

When we arrived at the club, Bill Fields, approached and asked, "Whatcha girls drinking?"

"We're not old enough to drink," Sharon said.

"Ah, come on. You don't want to be a bunch of party poopers, do you?" How about a vodka gimlet? Young gals like those fancy drinks."

Margo and Sharon declined, but I decided to try one. When he brought it to me, I took a sip, thinking it was very strong, but good. I liked the fact that it had a green cherry.

I looked around and finally eyed Joe. He was without a date. He was talking and laughing with Jane, and they sat next to each other during dinner. I was jealous, and kept looking their direction.

After dinner, a group congregated in the lounge.

"Come join us," Joe said when he saw me at the door. I took a seat on a sofa with some of the others.

"What are you drinking?" someone asked.

"Vodka gimlet," I said, hoping to sound sophisticated.

One of the agents was telling stories. When a group of musicians began to play, Joe rose and extended his hand to me.

"May I have the pleasure of a dance?"

I rose from the sofa, and took his hand.

"Relax," he said, as he pulled my stiff body close to his. I thought I had died and gone to heaven.

"Are you having a good time," Joe asked.

"Oh yes, I am so glad I decided to come to the party."

The music stopped, but we stayed on the dance floor. And when the band played another slow song, we danced again. He asked if he could take me home.

"This is too good to be true," I thought to myself, as I nervously told him I'd have to find the girls, to tell them I had a ride. Upon relaying this fact to Margo and Sharon, the latter chastised: "Margie, you came with us, and I think you should go home with us."

There was no way I was going to take her advice. On the way home, Joe pulled the car over along the harbor where the lights were dancing on the water. He put his arm around me, and pulled me toward him. His kisses were soft, then more intense.

Even though we made conversation, I don't remember any of it. I just remember his wonderful kisses.

"I really need to get you home," he said eventually. "And what happened here must stay between you and me and those fenceposts."

"Okay," I said, although I was dying to tell someone about my dreamy evening.

We arrived at my house much too soon. I didn't want the night to end.

"All good things must come to an end," he said, as he walked me to my front door. "See you tomorrow."

Inside the house, I leaned my back against the door and swooned. I didn't fall asleep until the wee hours – going over every second of the evening in my head.

~

In the fall of 1960, the office moved to a three-story box-shaped contemporary structure, with lots of glass – quite different from the old architecture of the bank building. The address was Fifth and Spruce.

Jane didn't like the new location.

"I miss being able to walk to the department stores on my lunch hour," she said. "And, there's no place to pick up things for sewing."

I thought the building was beautiful – so modern. The large windows allowed the girls in the steno pool, located on the west side of the building, to view the vibrant autumn sunsets of red, orange, gold and purple, as we tallied up our production sheets at the end of the day. Inspectors, visiting from the east coast, usually came in October or November, and often remarked about the spectacular sunsets.

The arrival of the dreaded "Inspectors" – a team from headquarters – turned the office into a frenzy. Every file was reviewed, and the secretaries and stenos were deluged with dictation, which had to be transcribed promptly, in addition to our usual workload. We were always glad when they left.

The office was only a block away from Balboa Park – home of the world famous San Diego Zoo. My high school friend Lana and I spent lots of weekends there, viewing not only the animals and exotic flowers, but also the cute sailors. The museums in the park are housed in buildings originally constructed for the Panama-California exposition of 1915. The Old Globe Theater, famous for Shakespearean plays, is there, as well as a botanical garden and lily pond. Those of us who worked at Fifth and Spruce often enjoyed the park during our lunch hour.

Before Director J. Edgar Hoover's annual visit, the office had to be shipshape. When he was seen approaching the building, a designated agent made sure that the elevator was ready and waiting for him on the first floor. Hoover whisked through the office, shaking everyone's hand.

"Pleased to meet you," he'd say over and over.

"Yes, sir," we'd reply. We were forewarned to give him a firm handshake, since he considered a limp grip a sign of weak character.

Once, our Chief Steno, Sandie Marchand, greeted the Director with "I hope you are having a nice vacation." She was duly corrected. The trip was business!

After all the frantic preparation, Mr. Hoover was gone within minutes – most likely headed for the Del Mar Race Track. He and Clyde Tolson always stayed at the Hotel Del Charro in La Jolla.

Upon first meeting Mr. Hoover, most of us were surprised by his short, stocky stature. No one could deny his dynamic personality, however.

Occasionally, I filled in for the Assistant Special Agent in Charge's secretary, which meant working side by side with Jane in the reception room.

She was still living in the house with her father in Chula Vista – the little town which had caught his eye on a train from Mexico many years before. I vaguely remember attending the funeral when he passed away. When Jane eventually sold the house, she moved to a garden apartment in Bonita. She was so happy to have a place of her very own, and talked with me about decorating it. When she was ready for the "unveiling," she threw a little party for the girls from the office. We had some drinks and swapped stories. Jane told us about a fellow who said he wanted to "screw" her! I was dumbfounded to hear this. As I got to know her, however, I found that she loved to laugh and often giggled as she told me the latest "off-color" joke. We constantly had our ears open for a new one to share on our next break.

Working in the front office with Jane meant dealing with the local crazies. Without fail, whenever a full moon appeared, they'd come to the reception area with their odd complaints about flying saucers or voices from beyond. The Agent on Duty, during those times, would have to become creative to satisfy the complainants.

"Simply attach a string of paperclips to your belt. This will ward off the aliens," some were told. Others were instructed to put tin foil over their windows "to thwart the rays from outer space."

A panic button, under the counter, could be used if the girls felt threatened – like the time a man, carrying a shoebox, tied with twine, ranted that he hated women.

"I think you girls should start an aberrant box," SAC E.C. Williams suggested, "so we'll have a card on these people. That way the agent on duty can check to see what instructions the complainant was given on his last visit."

We agreed that was a good idea.

"Long ago, there was an agent here by the name of Dave Fish," Jane told me with a gleam in her eye. "He was 6'4," very handsome, and a lot of fun."

"One time, when confronted with a nut, he grabbed a raincoat from somewhere, threw it over his shoulder, put on a hat, and introduced himself as the Attorney General. That particular guy never came back."

"I think you liked him," I commented. She said she would have been "enamored with him if he hadn't been married." She loved hearing about my amorous pursuits, but when I hinted to her that I liked Joe Scallini, she cautioned:

"I'm not sure, but I think he has been dating a girl – a divorcee. I'm pretty sure he's been seeing her for quite awhile."

I was not happy to hear this news, but figured that since Joe was Catholic, he would think twice before marrying her.

"But, he didn't bring her to the party last month," I said.

"You're right. He doesn't always bring her to office parties. I'm not sure why. I just think you should keep your emotions in check."

It didn't do any good for her to warn me. I was smitten with this dark, handsome Italian, with brown puppy-dog eyes. Anything Italian fascinated me. I had painted-by-number scenes of gondolas in Venice hanging in my bedroom. And, I thought the Chianti bottles, dripping with candle wax, in Italian restaurants were romantic.

Besides, he seemed to like me. He told me he was from Pennsylvania. I interpreted that as having something in common. When he told me he had worked for the Bureau in Washington, D. C. in the "mechanical section," I assumed he worked on Bureau cars.

"No," he laughed. "The mechanical section was where reports were printed and assembled. It's where we put together the *Investigtor* – the Bureau employees' monthly magazine.

Joe organized a bowling league, and asked if I would like to join. I listed bowling as a hobby on my application, and Joe had conducted my applicant investigation. I joined with my dad. The end of the season was celebrated with an awards banquet, to which I wore an emerald green satin dress, long black gloves, and black patent leather "Springolators" (five-inch heels with just a strap across the top of the foot.) After dinner, Joe came around to my side of the table.

"Do you mind if I ask your daughter to dance," he inquired of my father.

"No, go ahead," dad replied, as he looked at me. I had a big "yes" written all over my face.

"See," I said to myself. "He does like me." I swooned for days. But, I wondered why he didn't ask me out on a date.

One night when we both worked late, he finally asked me out. I was glad I had worn my hot pink sweater and matching skirt.

"Would you like to grab some dinner. I know a great place that serves up a mean steak."

I couldn't believe my ears. I didn't like steak, but there was no way I was going to turn down the invitation.

The restaurant was dark, with a red carpet. Tony Bennett was singing an Italian lovesong in the background. Perfect!

When the waitress came to take our order, Joe ordered a T-bone.

"I'll have the ground sirloin," I said.

"You're going to order hamburger!" He seemed disappointed.

"I don't really like steak," I replied.

I wasn't much of a conversationalist in those days, and probably just grinned at him all night. He had conducted my background investigation, so he knew about my sheltered Catholic life. I was madly in love with him, even though he kept telling me he was too old for me. Nothing could dampen my efforts.

I managed to get myself invited out for a drink, or a bite to eat on a few occasions, staying to work late when I knew he was still at the office. One evening during the holiday season, after I had been out with one of my girlfriends, I drove by the office. I saw Joe. I pulled up next to the curb, and wound the window down.

"Working late, again?" I inquired.

He leaned into the window and started talking.

"Why don't you get in," I said.

We exchanged small talk; then I asked the question I was dying to ask.

"Have you been dating someone?"

"Yes, I have been," he said, "but I plan to break it off after the holidays."

I was ecstatic, but acted cool. We talked for a little while, and he kissed me goodnight.

A few months went by, and one day, I realized he had been away from the office for a couple of days. I missed him terribly. That evening,

I drove around in my 1956 Chevy, trying to get up the nerve to call him.

"What have you been up to?" I asked when he answered the phone.

"I just added to my family," he replied.

"What did you do, get a dog?"

"No, I got married."

My heart sank. I fell against the back of the phone booth. Somehow, I managed a weak, "Oh, well, I guess I'll see you at the office."

Tears streaming down my face, I drove to Pat's house. She wasn't home, so I went to see my new friend, Wanda. She was sitting on her bed, listening to Johnny Mathis, scooping ice cream from the carton.

"Would you like some?"

"How can you eat so much and stay so skinny?" I sassed. She weighed all of 89 pounds!

"Can't you see I'm too upset to eat anything," I said, fidgeting at the edge of the bed.

"What's the matter with you?"

"Joe got married."

"Well, Margie, you knew that he was practically engaged. What did you expect?"

"I certainly didn't think he would just up and get married like that." I was having trouble breathing.

"You're just going to have to keep yourself busy and get your mind off him."

Since adequate sympathy was lacking here, I drove back to Pat's house. She was still out, so I visited with her aunt, while I waited.

When Pat got home, she rambled on about her adventures at the skating rink.

Finally, I blurted out, "Joe got married."

'There are plenty of other fish in the sea. Do you want a drink?"

"That won't help," I said. "Besides, I already have a splitting headache. I better go home. Mother will be pacing the floor, waiting for me."

"Okay, but if you want to go out tomorrow night, call me."

I sobbed myself to sleep that night. My heart was broken and I was sure I would never recover.

The next day, I could barely wait to see Jane. Of course, she already knew, because Joe had to apply for leave and advised her of his plans.

"I know this will be hard for you, Marge, but he is a good bit older than you are. You're so young, and attractive. You'll meet lots of young men. I know that probably doesn't help, and I am sorry."

She was right. No one could say anything that would help. I truly felt I would never meet anyone else that I would love as much.

~

Wanda O'Dell was working as a teller at the San Diego Trust and Savings Bank when she was recruited. She entered on duty in February of 1961 as a file clerk.

Pixie-like in appearance, with big brown eyes, she was a conservative dresser, wearing mostly beige, navy blue, or gray. Pat got me to wear straight skirts and sweaters, and I talked Wanda into wearing red!

She eventually became switchboard operator and radio dispatcher. Having been born in Bristol, Tennessee, where she lived until she was 15, she had a strong southern accent. We all teased her for the way she came up short on the "I" in FBI when answering the phone.

Wanda and I often went to the movies, or out shopping. Afterwards we'd talk until one or two in the morning. We both had troubles with our mothers. Wanda's father died when she was in high school, and left her mother with Wanda and a younger brother and sister.

"My mom wants me to babysit Christie again," she'd say. "I had a chance to go out Friday night, but now I can't."

My mother was very strict. Even though I was working, and considered myself an adult, she continued to pose lots of rules.

"Don't worry about her so much," I overheard my dad say. "She has a good head on her shoulders."

But, it seemed that my mother and I fought whenever I was home. One night at the dinner table, I announced that I was going to fly to Las Vegas for Pat's wedding. Pat had been dating the Lieutenant Commander, and when he received a transfer to Washington, D.C., they decided to get married.

"I absolutely forbid you to go," were my mother's words.

Shortly thereafter, Wanda and I rented a two-bedroom apartment. I was 19 at the time; she was 21.

Several agents expressed surprise over our move.

"Girls don't move out on their own," they said. "You're supposed to live with your parents until you get married."

But, we had already rented the apartment.

Wanda was a morning person, so she made breakfast.

"Margie, get up!" she'd call repeatedly. I could hear the wire whisk hitting the sides of the glass bowl, scrambling the eggs. My clock radio blared with Ray Charles belting out "Hit the road, Jack," or Leslie Gore crying, "Its my party and I'll cry if I want to," but the noise had little effect on rousting me from my warm bed. We barely made our 8:15 sign-in, especially on mornings when my 1956 turquoise Chevy choked up and I had to get out, pop the hood, and adjust the flap on the carburetor. (This impressed the hell out of an agent named Gerald Mahoney.)

Gerry was the office photographer for a time, and as such attended FBI parties. When Wanda had a date to a party and I didn't, I asked if he would escort me. He was eager to do so, and later, asked me out. We attended a stage production of Carrousel, and a Charger football game. For a time, he was on limited duty after being diagnosed with a type of hepatitis. Once given the okay to return to work, he asked me out to celebrate. He told me he had serious feelings for me. But, I did not feel the same toward him. Shortly afterwards, he was transferred to San Francisco. Wanda insisted on inviting him over for dinner. He gave me a card -- Ziggy with a tear in his eye. Now, here was a very nice gentleman, who would have treated me well, but was I interested? Of course not!

Since Wanda made breakfast, the evening meal was my responsibility. That plan worked in my favor. We went to my parents for dinner and to watch *The Virginian* on Wednesdays, and usually to Wanda's mother's another night. Friday nights, we went to Consuelo's Restaurant for Coors and Mexican food. Cheese quesidillas were complimentary with drinks in those days.

The two of us got along great. She washed and waxed the kitchen floor, and I scrubbed the tub and toilet -- while listening to her Johnny Mathis and Jerry Vale records.

On November 22, 1963, we were at work when word came that President Kennedy had been shot in Dallas. Security Clerk Dave Guyer, entered the steno pool, signaling us to be quiet.

"The President's been shot," he announced, as he directed our attention to the report coming over the intercom.

All typewriters stopped, and we listened to the confusion in utter shock. We sat speechless, shaking our heads, not believing our ears.

We parked ourselves in front of the televisions the entire weekend – not a common practice in the 1960s. The streets were eerily quiet. Then, unbelievably, we witnessed Jack Ruby shoot Oswald.

Our first day back to work, Anne Sarris told us how she had scheduled the baptism of her baby daughter that weekend, and her priest questioned whether they should go through with it. Anne had made all the arrangements for a traditional Greek ceremony, so she pleaded with him, saying:

"It's a little baby's christening, not a wedding." The priest finally agreed to perform the ceremony.

During the Cuban missile crises, we feared that we would be going to war when we heard President Kennedy's report on the intercom. The threat of Communism was serious business. We studied all about its evils in high school, with *Masters of Deceit* by J. Edgar Hoover, being required reading. Now, taking dictation from agents who worked CP,USA cases made it all the more real.

Wanda and I took a Greyhound Bus across country to visit a woman she met the year before on a bus trip home to Tennessee. "Kat" lived in Charleston and just happened to have a brother, who was single. At the bus station in Birmingham, Alabama, I headed for the restroom designated for "colored." Wanda grabbed my arm.

"You can't go in there," she told me. "Use the restroom for whites."

What did I know. I'd never been through the south before.

While Wanda visited Kat and her family, I continued on to Washington, D.C., to see my friend Pat. We'd kept in touch by letter and were anxious to get together. She and Bob lived in Rockville,

Maryland, where she worked at a law firm. Shortly after she was married, she wrote of having sex with her boss on the floor of his office. Her husband wasn't taking care of her needs, she said. I think she looked to me for approval of her actions. The way she explained it, she had me convinced that the affair was justified.

She took me to the White House, Capitol Hill, the Smithsonian, the National Gallery of Art, and to see all the monuments. We went to Arlington, where we visited President Kennedy's grave. I was very impressed with the Nation's Capital, and all the men I observed there. We also went to the best department stores, and I bought my first pair of Italian leather shoes!

On Wanda's return to San Diego, a letter from Tom Garrett awaited her. Letters came two or three times a week, and Wanda wrote him back. She'd push me aside to run to the mailbox on our return from work each day.

A day or so before Christmas, 1964, Wanda received a package from Tom. It was a larger box than she was expecting. She looked at me with disappointment in her eyes as she tore into it. Inside was a smaller box, inside which was still another box.

"Oh, Margie," she said, "There better be a ring in here somewhere." Finally, she reached a tiny box deep inside which held the diamond she was looking for. Her eyes were wide with excitement.

"Isn't it the most beautiful ring you've ever seen?" she said, flashing it at me. Then she ran for the telephone to call Tom.

Wanda and I spent a lot of time together in those days, since she was engaged to a man across country. They were both big baseball fans. She often listened to the games on the radio, and even had me rooting for the Los Angeles Dodgers. We drove to Los Angeles often, stayed with friends of hers, and attended Dodger ballgames during the reign of that awesome pitcher, Sandy Koufax, and notorious base-stealer, Maury Wills.

On occasion, we visited Wanda's predecessor (San Diego's switchboard operator/radio dispatcher). Trinky, she was called, married a police officer and moved to St. Thomas, where they ran a restaurant on the beach for a year or so. We kept in touch by letter. They returned to the States and opened a pizza house and bar in Los Angeles, which was frequented by local police officers. Wanda likes to remind me about celebrating my 21st birthday there, a tale best left untold – although I vaguely recall considerable drinking and partying with a couple of members of the LAPD.

The highlight of Wanda's days at the FBI was her special assignment to El Paso, Texas, to work on the interstate fraud investigation involving Billie Sol Estes. Today, she only remembers that it "had something to do with his selling property which he did not own." Former Assistant Director Cartha DeLoach's book on the Bureau reveals that the property was grain elevators.

In 1964, Bureau Headquarters requested volunteers to staff a new office in Jackson, Mississippi, being opened due to the upheaval following the death of Medgar Evans, riots which erupted after James Meredith's enrollment at the University of Mississippi, and finally, the murder of the three civil rights workers. Wanda and I volunteered to go, but our supervisors denied our requests.

Years later, when watching the movie, *Mississippi Burning*, I could understand why our boss had considered the assignment too dangerous for two young women.

The highlight of my career, and that of my fellow steno, Linda Berdeen, was the time we took part in the arrest of a spy.

At the beginning of this project, as I downloaded my memory bank into my computer, I "telephonically" contacted Linda Anderson, nee Berdeen, to ask for her help in recalling the episode.

We were summoned to the SAC's office – E. C. Williams, at the time. The case agent Richard McCormick, and a few others, including our "dates" were present. The "pitch" went something like this:

"We would like your permission," McCormick asked of Williams, "to use these two lovely young ladies as decoys – as dates -- in a parked car with Mitchell and Waters. Agent Mitchell is a former minister, and Waters is the son of a minister, so we think the girls will be in good hands."

"If you think it will help catch this guy," Williams said, "then you have my approval."

On the night of the arrest, we took our places, with our dates. I was in the front seat with Mitchell; Linda in the back with Waters. They obviously enjoyed the authorization to snuggle up with us girls. Before long, the windows fogged up.

Then, the words "Move in and take pigeon," came softly over the radio.

Simultaneously, the headlights of the Bucars, which had formed a wide circle, flashed on. Linda and I witnessed Agent McCormick in the middle of the parking lot putting the handcuffs on the spy. Linda volunteered to return to the office with the agents to take the subject's statement.

"I couldn't believe it," she told me the next day. "The guy was shocked that he was caught. He kept mentioning that he had a sick daughter."

In an effort to dig up more details, (while writing this book) I tracked down former Agent McCormick. He recalled the details.

The spy was in the Navy and had contacted the Russian Embassy in Washington, D.C.

"The 'cover' on the phone notified the Bureau office in D. C., which in turn passed the information on to San Diego. That's how we first heard about it," he said.

"When a fellow, who answered an ad in the newspaper for someone to make a pickup, became suspicious because of instructions involving a travel route, and meeting a contact, he called the San Diego FBI Office. It was a totally lucky break," McCormick related, "that the guy called direct and didn't go to the local police. The office was small enough, that we put two and two together."

Former Agent McCormick said that his resemblance to the man who answered the ad was the reason he was selected to take his place.

"The contact turned his car over to me and gave me instructions to go to the northern part of the city, then move to another place – a church parking lot. A package was picked up somewhere along the line which contained the money for the Russians."

"I had to determine whether the guy was the actual 'subject' or just a messenger," Mr. McCormick told me. "The 'subject' was believed to be armed, so nearby backup was necessary. We thought using you girls as decoys was a great idea."

Linda has kept a file from her FBI days. It contains a photograph of the two of us, along with several agents, receiving letters of commendation for our part in the arrest of the spy. A letter, dated August 19, 1964, signed by J. Edgar Hoover, states: "Your services in connection with a matter of great importance to the Bureau in the security field were of the highest caliber...The alertness and effectiveness you demonstrated ...were indeed superior and your performance was vital in insuring success to the operation." (I don't know what happened to my copy.)

Linda's file contains an Outstanding Performance rating, given to her by Assistant Special Agent in Charge, Jack Keith; a photo clipping from *The Investigator* (our monthly magazine), August, 1962 issue, of the clerks and stenos taken outside "the Valley Ho Restaurant following the semiannual clerical conference;" and still another from the September, 1962, issue of a group of us with our bowling trophies.

∼

In 1962, an ex-Navy man by the name of Larry Feldhaus, reported to the San Diego Office. Larry was tall – about 6'2 or 3" – sandy haired and blue eyed. He drove a little red 1956 Thunderbird – the one with the porthole window. "What's the poop?" he'd ask, when looking for

From left: SAC E.C.Williams, ASAC Jack Keith, Marjorie McClintock, Agent Dooley, Linda Berdeen, SAs Dick McCormick, Norm Gray and Jean Gray.

information on a case. I always had a soft spot for a sailor. When Larry first asked me out on a date, I hesitated -- still in love with Joe. I told him, hoping he'd object – why, I do not know. Instead, he encouraged me to go out with Larry. I had mixed emotions, but agreed to a double date with his roommate and Linda.

Of course, I talked over the prospect of dating Larry with Jane.

"See, I told you someone else would come along," she said. "He's very handsome."

The guys had rented a rustic cabin hideaway with a fireplace. Sometimes, we'd have dinner there, listen to music, and talk. Eventually, when Larry and I were alone, I would remove my dress, but never the lacy black slip or undergarments. The necking I had started with Joe, advanced to petting with Larry. But all the warnings by the Monsignor and the nuns about sex before marriage still rang in my head.

San Diego was Larry's first office, and after the customary year, he received a transfer. On his way out of town, he stopped by the front office, where I was working with Jane.

"I guess it's time to bid farewell," he said. "I really had a good time here. Thanks for everything."

Then he gave a salute, and off he went.

"What a nice young man," Jane commented. "I'm sure you haven't heard the last of him."

Larry answered a couple of my letters. The last one I received from him informed me that he was getting married – to his old college girlfriend. I read the letter over a couple of times. I felt totally rejected. Once again, I cried on Wanda's shoulder, and then Jane's the next day at work.

There was a long dry spell, with no available single agents. But then, Tony Scarborough – the most controversial fellow with whom I became enamored -- arrived on the scene. He had a law degree, and was the son of a judge in Santa Fe, New Mexico. He had no car – didn't see the need when the assignment to San Diego would last but a year. He rented an apartment in walking distance to the office. I drove him to guitar lessons, where he learned to play flamenco music.

I was 22, and in a complete state of sexual frustration. I literally threw myself at him, and he obliged. After one passionate evening, he talked of an old girlfriend. "Was there ever to be any hope for me?" I thought. Jane assured me there was.

Tony was Spanish speaking – reason enough for Jane to like him. He enjoyed Mexican food, as did I, and introduced me to Huevos Rancheros. He was thought to be "odd" – not the usual FBI type – but Jane understood my attraction. She loved the Spanish language and had a fondness for Mexico, probably inherited from her father, who lived there in his early 20's, after his mother died.

(Years later, when my teenage son was watching MTV, Steve Tyler of Aerosmith was screaming out "Walk This Way," I remarked about his uncanny resemblance to a fellow I used to date – Tony, minus the long hair and outrageous attire!)

~

Marjorie with Mr. and Mrs. Thomas Garrett, May, 1965

In May of 1965, I accompanied Wanda, via Greyhound Bus again, to Mullins, South Carolina. Our SAC – E. C. Williams – met us at the station to bid her farewell. When the bus pulled into the El Centro terminal, the Resident Agents there met us to bid goodbye. During our "tour of duty" in San Diego, one of the El Centro agents had taken us fishing on the Salton Sea, and another had invited us to an onion ring party, thrown due to a bumper crop of Bermuda onions.

Wanda and I got off the bus in Dallas, to stay overnight with a friend of hers there, and also in New Orleans, where we stayed with her sister.

She and Tom were married in a quiet ceremony by a Baptist minister. It was a beautiful day and, of course, the bride looked ravishing. The next day, I boarded the bus for Washington, once again, to visit Pat.

On my return to San Diego, I figured my love life was going nowhere. It was inevitable that Tony would be transferred soon. So, I asked the SAC if he would allow me to transfer to New York.

"Absolutely not," he said. "New York is no place for a young girl like yourself." Agent friends of mine backed him up.

"How about Washington, D.C.," I persisted. Looking for greener pastures, I figured D. C. was a good choice. While on vacation there, I had noticed a large number of men. The Bureau was always looking for clerks and stenos at headquarters. And, Pat was in favor of it. She had encouraged me to transfer to D. C. in her letters.

"We would really hate to see you go, but if you insist, Washington is probably a better choice," SAC Williams said. So we put in for a transfer for me.

While I was awaiting approval, Tony was transferred to San Juan, Puerto Rico.

When my transfer came through, I immediately contacted Pat.

"You can stay with me, at least for awhile," she said. "Bob will be in Nevada on assignment for several months."

I packed my bags, bid farewell to my San Diego family and friends, and hopped a jet for National Airport.

Thus, there came an end to my 15-minute (ahem) breaks with Jane. I promised to write and keep her posted on my activities.

Washington, D.C.

I arrived at the "Seat of Government" in August of 1965. I described the place as "greener pastures," because it was the greenest place I'd ever seen – trees everywhere. I was used to the "Golden" State of California.

Pat greeted me at the airport with her husband and another couple.

"I thought Bob was going to be in Nevada," I inquired of Pat.

"Oh, he's leaving in a couple of days," she said.

Their apartment was a one bedroom, so I was curious about the sleeping arrangements. "We have a rollaway bed," Pat said when I asked. The hall closet would serve as my temporary quarters.

I would soon learn these were the least of the surprises in store for me.

The next morning I boarded the express bus. It took an hour to get to D. C. August means hot, humid weather in Washington – not good climate for teased hairdos, which required massive quantities of hairspray. I debussed at Ninth and Pennsylvania and crossed the street to the Justice Department building.

"What in the world am I doing here," I asked myself as I stepped onto the elevator. "I hope to God I haven't made a big mistake," I thought. "I'll have to stick it out at least six months to save face."

I reported to the Training Division, where I was to supervise the stenos. The workload was nothing like it had been in San Diego, but everyone was friendly and helpful. Details of that day are not etched in my mind like the first day in San Diego.

When I returned from work, Pat was preparing dinner. She was sipping a scotch and soda.

"Want one," she said as she lifted her glass.

"Might as well," I answered. We spent our nights gabbing into the wee hours.

A week or so after my arrival, Bob left for Nevada. All of a sudden, Pat had someplace to go after dinner, sometimes not returning until morning.

"What are you doing," I asked. She told me that she was "entertaining" a friend of theirs, whose wife was out of town. She acted as though this was perfectly normal!

By the time October rolled around, I thought I would freeze while waiting for the express bus out on the parkway. Fellow bus-riders kidded me, asking, "What are you going to do, come winter!" The song "California Dreaming" by the Mamas and the Papas often rang in my head. "All the leaves are brown, and the sky is gray."

Evenings were lonesome, since Pat was out a lot. Occasionally, we did go out to a nice restaurant or club – Blues Alley, where there was great jazz, or a place called Good Guys on Wisconsin Ave. (Their red matchbook features the Marx Brothers). The holidays approached and I found myself homesick. I wrote lots of letters home to my parents, and to Jane, and to Wanda in South Carolina.

One Friday night, on returning from work, I could hear music and voices as I approached the apartment. When I opened the door, there was a party going on. Pat was in the kitchen, lip-locked with some guy.

When she saw me, she merely said, "I decided to have a few people in from work."

I didn't have a car, so I hung around and tried to mingle. Then the doorbell rang.

"Would you get that, Margie," Pat said. I was dumbfounded when I opened the door to find Bob standing there, briefcase in hand.

"What are you doing here," I asked stupidly. "I happen to live here," he answered.

"Pat invited some people from work," I explained, hoping that she had disengaged herself from the man in the kitchen.

"What do you think you are doing," Bob asked her. "And why didn't you pick me up at the airport?"

Pat made some excuse, and Bob went into the bedroom. People immediately began to leave. The rest of the evening was spent in awkward silence.

Sometime later, I returned late from work to find Bob sitting in the dark. Pat wasn't home, so I went to bed. By this time, I was sleeping in the bedroom, and Bob was sleeping on the roll-away. A fistfight in the parking lot outside my window woke me up.

Bob and Pat's date were having a punching match. "I have to get out of here," I said aloud to myself.

The next morning, I contacted the housing unit at the Bureau, to get a list of girls looking for roommates. Then I called Howard Johnson -- a college buddy of my former beau. Tony had written and given me Howard's number. He was a lawyer for the National Labor Relations Board.

I was working on Capitol Hill, on loan from the Bureau, the first time I met Howard. When he picked me up for dinner in front of the Rayburn House Office Building, I took note of his slight build, wispy light brown hair, and glasses. He was pleasant, but definitely not my type. I could tell he liked me, however. He said he was impressed, because I always had a book tucked under my arm. We went out to dinner and nightclubs; then to his office Christmas party. He gave me Avon's "Rapture" – my fragrance of the day. I eventually told him it wasn't fair to continue letting him take me out, because he was looking for my affections and I wasn't willing to reciprocate. He told me to call him if I needed anything. After the fistfight at Pat's, I took him up on his offer. He agreed to drive me around to check out prospective new living quarters.

I found a place on South Capital Street, where three girls were looking for a fourth roommate. I liked the place, and they liked me, so I had a new home.

Two of them – Sharon and Barbara --dated District policemen. Sharon's fiancé, Larry, was in the habit of cleaning his gun at our dining room table, which I found unsettling, even after years of watching the G-men unstrap their guns from their belts. I often retreated to the bedroom, which I shared with "Babs," to watch *Peyton Place*. Babs had no eyebrows, so she painted big arches in their place. She also wore huge hair rollers to bed. We got along fine. She and her fiancé introduced me to a cousin, yet another District policeman. I dated Buzzy for a time, but he was too immature for me. I especially disliked his throwing beer bottles out of the car window. Sharon and Barbara eventually married, and other Bureau girls took their place.

Frances was from Bardstown, Kentucky, which garnered me an invite to her home in May, 1967. It was the first and only time I attended the Kentucky Derby. Too bad, it rained. I, in turn, invited her to join me on a visit to Wanda's in South Carolina.

One of my roommates was the daughter of an SAC in Los Angeles. Stephanie made me laugh. She dated a young man who was working as a clerk while awaiting his appointment as a Special Agent.

"I've decided to have Bill call me Daphne," she announced one day, for some reason I didn't understand. But she insisted when he called that he ask for "Daphne." I wasn't to turn the phone over until he did.

At one point, she started wearing a wig. "I'm so worried about the way my hair just keeps falling out. I'm going to be bald."

"I don't think your hair is falling out any more than anyone else's," I said, trying unsuccessfully to console her. She had a beautiful, thick head of hair, and I couldn't figure out why she thought it was falling out.

When she became Mrs. Bill Brannon, she had a full head of hair.

There were a couple of other girls, one named Ellen, who invariably got sick after being out on the town, and another named Claudia, who called agents who had left Washington, running the phone bill sky high. Eventually, I decided to take a smaller place on my own.

The Training Division was where all new agents reported for duty. In the 1960s, classroom instruction was conducted at the Washington Field Office, and only two of their 14 weeks were spent at Quantico, Virginia. Many of these young men were "spoken for," but that didn't stop me and other Bureau females from showing them around the Nation's Capital when they were off duty. Of course, new agents were on their best behavior, some commenting that we were probably "plants" to make sure they were fine, upstanding moral fellows.

Assistant Director Joseph J. Casper (known as "Jumping Joe" – reportedly because he was rather excitable) headed up the Training Division. A steno's ability was put to the test when taking his rapid dictation.

Summoned to his office one morning, he instructed: "We are sending you up to the Hill. The Chairman of Appropriations, George

Mahon, needs temporary secretarial help, and Mr. Hoover asked that I select a top-notch girl. You fit the bill, and I know you'll do what is expected."

"Okay," I answered, even though I did not understand exactly what was going on. Congressman Mahan was the Representative from Lubbock, Texas. I enjoyed clipping news out of the local papers and writing letters to the new brides, people celebrating anniversaries and birthdays, but even more, I enjoyed the opportunity to be creative when answering constituents' letters regarding pending legislation.

Being assigned to the Training Division, enabled me to visit with agents from San Diego who were back for "in-service" training. When Mike Hennigan was in town, he took me to the Mayflower Hotel for lunch. Mr. Hoover was known to frequent the Mayflower for his meals, but we did not see him. Mr. Hennigan must have thought I turned out okay, because he'd often ask my opinion with regard to his young daughters.

Eventually, I was assigned to the Crime Records Division, headed up by Assistant Director Cartha "Deke" DeLoach. My immediate boss was a rather flamboyant character by the name of Hobson Adcock, who gave me great Christmas presents from Neiman Marcus. Another secretary, by the name of Pat Ruzich shared the office with us. She told me about a young man by the name of John T. Burke, Jr. She wanted me to meet him.

In December, 1966, I flew home for Christmas. I was anxious to visit the FBI Office to see my old friends. Jane was excitedly planning her marriage to Will Brown in the spring of 1967.

"Now, where did you meet this man?" I asked.

"Oh, I've known him since high school. He's a few years older than I, but our fathers knew each other quite well."

"Has he ever been married?"

"Oh, yes, but his wife died. He has four grown sons," she said with a giggle. "Marty Carlson says that means he must like sex."

I was shocked by this remark from a woman in her fifties!

She was close friends with Marty and his wife.

Mr. and Mrs. Will O. Browne,
May 21, 1967

"Have you been in touch with Will over the years?" I asked.

"No, not really. I didn't know him well enough to grieve for him when his wife died, but after my dad passed away, I wrote to him, because I always felt he liked me. We started dating, and he asked me to marry him."

"That's wonderful."

"I'm altering my mother's wedding dress. I was beginning to think I'd never have a chance to wear it. It's almost done, but I have so much to do, I'm in a dither."

"Knowing you, Jane, everything will turn out beautifully," I assured her.

I wandered through the office. Many of the agents were not in, as I expected, but it was fun to see my old friends in the steno pool and clerks' office. They expressed amazement at my talkativeness. Something about Washington turned me into a storyteller. Even my dad asked, "What happened to our quiet little Margie." I think I was just excited to be home.

During my visit, I traveled to Los Angeles to attend a Christmas party at the home of my Washington roommate, Stephanie. Since

I'd be in the area, I contacted Sandie Marchand. I had been her replacement as the supervising steno in San Diego when she and her husband moved to Santa Monica. (I kept her apprised, in 30-page letters, of all the goings-on in the steno pool after she left.)

"We're going to be out of town, but you can use our apartment, if you'd like."

As it turned out, I didn't need to take Sandie up on the offer. A handsome Italian lived across the hall. He invited me to a Christmas party, and I ended up spending the weekend with him. When I told him I had worked on "the Hill," and wouldn't mind leaving the Bureau, he told me that a friend of his was the field representative for Congressman H. Allen Smith, and that he'd put a word in for me.

Working at the Seat of Government just wasn't as exciting or rewarding as working in the field. I grew weary of constantly retyping letters so that they would meet with Mr. Hoover's approval. I thought it was a big waste of time.

After a couple of wonderful weeks in sunny California, it was time to return to Washington.

As the plane approached Dulles Airport, I remember thinking, "This looks like a scene from a black and white movie." San Diego had been alive with color, even though it was January. Could this mean that I was homesick? The feeling did not last long.

Shortly after my return, I agreed to meet this John Burke. He was a handsome fellow with black hair and blue eyes. "He works in the Reprint Room with Bob," Pat said as she introduced us. After a few minutes of idle chatter, he had to run to his part-time job at the Safeway, but asked me to lunch the next day.

Pat was dating Bob McCarthy, who was from New York. He had gone to college with one of John's friends from Clinton, Massachusetts. They hit it off immediately. John and Bob were working as clerks awaiting acceptance into the FBI Academy. My preference in those days of husband-hunting was that the young man be educated and on the road to his life's career. I also "required" that his military obligation had been fulfilled. John Burke met the criteria.

It was raining, at noontime, so we opted for the Justice Department cafeteria.

John told me that he was from Clinton, Massachusetts, a place I had never heard of. He was Catholic and had two sisters. That's about all the information he was able to impart, as he later recalled when relating the story to others.

"I wondered what I would talk about with a girl from California," he said. "But once I asked where she was from, she launched into her 'I was born in Pittsburgh, but moved to California when I was seven' dissertation, and before I knew it the 45-minute lunch break was over."

Despite my tendency to take over the conversation, he asked me out again – and again, often admonishing me for talking too much.

We lived in apartment buildings with a shared parking lot – unbeknownst to me until John came to pick me up for our second date. We walked for quite a long time around the parking lot.

"Where is your car?" I finally asked, thinking we were going to be late for the movie.

"Oh, I don't have one," he answered.

"Why didn't you say so? Mine is out front."

We saw Dr. Zhivago, which I thought was a great movie. John didn't comment, so I asked if he enjoyed it.

"It was worth coming out for," he replied, which I assumed meant he liked it. When I met him, John had spent most of his time hanging around his apartment or sleeping when he was not working.

At times, I had difficulty interpreting his expressions, and he joked with me when my pronunciations reverted to Pittsburghese.

One Monday morning on our busride to work, I mentioned going to church on Sunday.

"I attend Our Lady of the Mattress," he responded. Still naïve, I had to stop and think about that one.

Before long, he started attending Mass with me, and talked lovingly about his parents, sisters, and his sixth-month old nephew. I got the impression that he would be good husband material.

We often double-dated with Pat and Bob. Our weekends were full of parties with Bureau friends, or dinner out at an inexpensive restaurant, since the guys made very little and were paying off college loans. I had scouted out plenty of good, cheap places to eat on my own. Sometimes, we would splurge and go to Blackie's House of Beef for a good steak. If we were in the mood for lobster, we went to the Market Inn ("2nd & E Sts. SW at the Freeway," according to the matchbook). Occasionally, on a Sunday, we'd take a ride to Normandy Farm in Potomac, Maryland, for a great homemade chicken dinner.

Before he met me, John had not taken advantage of Washington's many monuments and museums.

"I can't believe you haven't been to the Jefferson Memorial," I said – one of my favorites.

One night after he finished his shift at the Safeway market, I picked him up, picnic dinner in tow, and took him to see the cherry trees in blossom. They looked beautiful with the spotlights on them. On weekends, I took him to the National Gallery of Art, the Smithsonian, the Lincoln Memorial and Reflecting Pool. I wanted to make sure he saw all D.C. had to offer – most of which was free!

≈

During this time, I was asked to fill in as a relief in the Director's Office, when a secretary was on leave. I took over Alice Denning's job. Her office was the farthest away from Hoover's in the row which made up the Director's suite. Alice moved up the line, but was next door if I needed to consult with her. Like Jane, she was a single career woman who looked after her mom and dad. When her father passed away, I bought his 1965 Plymouth Valiant. I was tired of depending on public transportation, especially on weekends when I wanted to explore areas beyond the Capital.

My assignment in Mr. Hoover's office required calling downstairs to "Records" to run a name check. I identified myself as "Miss McClintock, substituting in the Director's Office." When John, or Bob especially, answered the phone, they teased me about my introduction. I would then explain that I did not want to misrepresent the fact that I was only filling in and not permanently assigned to the Director's Office.

One day, while I was working in Mr. Hoover's office, a call came from Tony (the lawyer from Los Angeles).

"Were you serious about wanting to work on the Hill?" he asked.

"Yes," I said ecstatically.

"Well, Congressman Smith is looking for a girl. Why don't you give him a call?"

So I did. We set up an appointment at his home, and as soon as I told him that I worked for the Bureau, we clicked. He had been an agent back in the 1940s. He offered me a job with an increase in salary. I jumped at the chance.

Thus, my "career" with the FBI came to an end, in February, 1967.

Working on Capitol Hill was a wonderful, educational experience, but turned out to be short-lived. I enjoyed exploring the halls of Congress during lunch breaks, and having a famous bowl of bean soup in the Capitol Hill Dining Room, hoping to see a famous Senator or Congressman. Once, Senator Everett Dirksen was dining at the next table. Sometimes, I walked across the street to the Botanical Gardens.

~

I wrote to Jane, and other friends, all about the young man I had met, and eventually about my wedding plans. I wanted to get married in December since one of my favorite songs was Ray Coniff's, "Santa, Make Me His Bride for Christmas." We thought about getting married in Washington, but I really wanted to get married at home. San Diego seemed the better choice given the time of year and the fact that my parents hated to fly.

I called my former roommate Wanda in South Carolina.

"You have to come out for the wedding," I told her. "We are getting married in San Diego, and I want you to be one of my bridesmaids."

"Of course, I'll be there, and I'd be hurt if you didn't ask me to be a bridesmaid! What kind of dresses do you have in mind?"

All of us still sewed at the time, so I had Wanda and another friend, Mary Lou Mark, make their dresses – gold satin -- from a simple pattern. My sister, the maid of honor, would wear green.

As for my wedding dress, being the ever frugal girl, I opted to rent one. I described it in great detail, however, for the write-up in Clinton's little hometown paper.

John's parents, sister, Mary Ann, and best man, Bill Walsh, flew out for the wedding. His sister, Patricia, had just given birth to a baby girl, so she and her husband weren't able to make the trip. My cousin Earl

McClintock and his wife Alice came down from Oxnard. Earl was an usher, and their daughter Louise was my flower girl. A fellow who John and Billy knew from Massachusetts was living in the Los Angeles area, so he filled in as a second usher.

On December 30, 1967, John and I were married at Our Lady of Grace Catholic Church. The church was already decorated for Christmas with poinsettias – no need to spend money on flowers -- and it was a beautiful 72-degree day. What more could one ask for? Well, a priest who could carry a tune, maybe!

We had a simple reception afterwards, returned to my parents' house with a few relatives and close friends, after which John and I drove to La Jolla, where we spent our first night as husband and wife. We had dinner at the Marine Room, which sits directly on the edge of the ocean – a very romantic spot. John, however, was preoccupied with getting his hands on the tickets for the Rose Bowl. The next morning we drove to the Glendale/Pasadena area, in time to see the Tournament of Roses Parade, and afterwards, the Rose Bowl game – compliments of Congressman Smith. The next day we visited Disneyland. Photographs show John dressed in a suit and tie, and me in a white coat with white fur collar!

Once we were back in D. C., John moved into what had been my apartment on South Capital Street – the one I moved into to get away from all the headaches my younger roommates were causing me.

The Vietnam War coverage was on television every night as John called for his hors'd'oeuvres, (horses' ovaries, as he referred to them). I tried serving elaborate meals – many times from recipes in my Congressional Cookbook, but they took too long, and John preferred meat and potatoes. (The Cookbook contained recipes of President and Vice Presidents' wives, Congressmen and Senators' wives, and some Congressmen and Senators.)

One night, as I was slaving in the kitchen, I heard the television announcer say that President Johnson had a message to deliver. I ran to the living room to hear him tell the country: "I will not seek, and will not accept your nomination for another term as your President."

One Saturday morning, after the murder of Martin Luther King, as I went out to do the grocery shopping, National Guardsmen were posted along the streets due to the outbreak of riots. I returned to the apartment to inform my husband.

"That's it, we're moving!" he said.

John was in new agents' class, which meant we would be making a move shortly.

"I don't want to move now, and then again in a couple of months," I pleaded. But he insisted that we needed to move out of the District. So, we moved – to Alexandria, Virginia.

Another morning, we woke to the shocking news that Robert F. Kennedy had been shot in Los Angeles. Like everyone else, we could not believe what we heard, especially since it had only been a couple of months since the death of Martin Luther King. It seemed the whole world had gone mad.

~

The day finally came that John had been waiting for -- his first office assignment. It was Dallas, Texas.

Before we headed west, Tom and Wanda Garrett drove up from South Carolina to bid us farewell, since we didn't know how long it would be before we'd see each other again.

During those couple of years in Washington, D. C., I occasionally flew – puddle jump would more accurately describe the trip -- via Piedmont Airlines, to visit Wanda and Tom. The flight made two stops before arriving in South Carolina. On those weekends in Mullins we visited Tom's sister's farm, where we picked vegetables and gathered freshly laid eggs. A southern fried chicken dinner was always a treat. Sometimes, Tom drove us to Myrtle Beach for a fish dinner. Wanda and I stayed up to the wee hours talking about "old times." After I met John, he accompanied me to Mullins a time or two.

Dallas/Fort Worth, Texas

The 1965 tan Plymouth Valiant, which I had purchased from Alice Denning, carried John and me to Dallas. I was expecting our first child by this time.

"I suggest you fly ahead," the doctor said, warning that a long car trip may not be wise.

"I think that's a good idea," my husband agreed.

I wouldn't hear of it. I loved car trips, and I wanted to be with my husband. Besides, I didn't want to miss a thing.

Shortly after arriving in Texas, I spotted a sign for a Mexican restaurant.

"John, we have to stop there. I want some Mexican food."

"Are you crazy," he said. "You'll be suffering for sure, with all the heartburn you've had."

"I don't care. It will be worth it. I'm dying for some real, honest to goodness Mexican food."

"Okay, but don't expect any sympathy when you get indigestion."

We only had a short time to find an apartment, since John had to report for duty. We chose one in a small complex, with a pool. The apartment was dark since it was under an outside stairway, but since first office assignments were only for a year, we didn't mind.

John's first day as an agent left him somewhat "disenchanted." The veteran agent, to whom he had been assigned, started the day off taking a ride to pick up a goat for a barbecue. He couldn't imagine spending his valuable training on such a mission. In due time, however, his workdays turned to investigations.

Dallas was a training office, which meant there were other new agents. Many were newlyweds like us. We socialized regularly, getting together for holidays, which made being away from family a little easier.

Carole Gibson was one of the other wives with whom I became friendly.

"I'm going to enter a pie in the State Fair. Want to join me?"

"I'd love to go the fair," I told her, "but baking isn't one of my strong areas, so I think I'll forego an entry."

We had a wonderful time, listening to the country music, checking out the cowboys, and, of course, the exhibits.

Since I was now living a bit closer to San Diego, my parents drove over for a visit, first chance they had. They wanted to get to know John, and make sure I was okay, being pregnant and all.

After only two months in Dallas, John was re-assigned to the resident agency in Fort Worth. So, we packed up our belongings and moved again.

We rented a new apartment in a brick complex, which surrounded a beautiful pool. By this time, I was over the sleepy stage of my pregnancy. I took up the art of decoupage and had a great time "hacking" up pieces of wood to which I glued prints of old maps and country scenes, which I aged by burning their edges. Our walls were filled with my artwork. I also spent many hours writing letters to family and friends.

On March 28, 1969, our son was born, at Harris Hospital. I thought he was the most beautiful baby I had ever seen.

"He looks just like your mother!" my husband exclaimed, after informing me that he thought I was dead when he saw me after giving birth. He had chosen to go home and get some sleep while I was in labor, telling the doctor to call him when the baby was born! Since the doctor decided to put me out for the delivery, I was still unconscious when John arrived.

This new world of motherhood threw me for a loop. My sister, Donna, came to "help," but she was as inexperienced as I with a new baby.

"I don't know whether to change him first, or feed him," I'd say as he woke up screaming, in a diaper that was soaking wet. It wasn't until John's parents came for a visit, and I handed my screaming child over to his grandmother, that he calmed down.

Eventually, I got the hang of caring for my new baby. I loved taking him out in his stroller and watching him as he enjoyed his swing. I wrote down every new thing in his baby book.

It was exactly one year after our arrival in Texas that John received his second office assignment:

Newark, New Jersey

It was August, and it was hot. The 1965 Valiant was not air-conditioned. John wanted me to fly ahead with the baby, but I wanted to make the trip by car. Tommy didn't think it was a good idea, however, fussing a great deal of the way. By the time we reached the Garden State, we were frazzled.

Upon receiving the transfer to Newark, I wrote to a former steno, who was then living in New Jersey with her husband and children. I had been corresponding with Jeanine, who referred to Newark as "the bowels of the country."

"Sounds enchanting," I wrote back.

The first time I laid eyes on the place, I knew what she meant. It was August, 1969, and evidence of the riots in Newark the summer before left the place looking like a war zone.

For a time, Jeanine rode to work in San Diego with my mother and me, and a few others who paid us something like five dollars a week.

"Sounds like you're running a wildcat taxi," my friend Mike Hennigan jokingly accused.

Jeanine didn't drive, and was married to Joe Batis at the time. Everyone thought they were happily married since they always seemed to have such a good time at office parties. They were great dancers. But when people expressed surprise at her decision to get a divorce, I remember her saying, "Why do people assume they know what goes on behind closed doors?"

After getting settled in Edison, New Jersey, I visited Jeanine, who lived nearby. When Wanda came for a visit, we drove over to see her.

"She still doesn't drive," I told Wanda, in a letter later on. I eventually lost touch with Jeanine.

~

For the first six months, John and I rented an apartment in Edison, New Jersey. The apartment bordered a nice park, with a pond. The park was nearby when we moved to our first home, so I took Tom there often. He loved to toss stale bread to the ducks, and play on the swings and monkey bars.

149 East Chestnut Street

In February, 1970, we purchased our first home in Metuchen, New Jersey – a three bedroom colonial with a center stairway, living room on one side, dining room and teeny kitchen on the other, bedrooms upstairs. I was certain we could not afford it.

Jane at her desk, as she retires, after 30 years with the FBI

"I'm glad you worry so much about money," my husband would say, "so I don't have to."

It was then that Jane wrote that she had more addresses for me than anyone else on her mailing list. In fact, she had to start a new address card for me!

It was also about this same time that Jane and Will purchased their home in Bonita, having lived the first few years of their marriage in an apartment Jane rented after her father passed away.

In March, 1970, Jane retired after 30 years of service. If I had planned better, I could have attended her retirement party. But I was wrapped up in my new home and taking care of my baby. I had flown to San Diego in July, 1969 (at the time we all watched man walk on the moon) before leaving Texas. So, between lack of finances, and the recent move, I guess I couldn't justify the trip. I am sorry now that I didn't.

Jane's retirement party was held at the San Diego Police Range. The Agents arranged for a Mexican theme, since Jane always loved the Spanish language and Mexico.

Jane Sent Me a Copy of Her Retirement Speech.

"When I walked down that long hall at 728 San Diego Trust and Savings Bank on Friday, March 1st, 1940, little did I think I would be working there for thirty years for a total of 16 SACs.

"The San Diego Office was opened the October before that by SAC Percy Wyly and one clerk. By the time I arrived five months later, the office had added a night clerk, a receptionist, one steno, and eight Agents!

"Mr. Wyly was there long enough to write my 45-day efficiency rating, then so-called. During that first year, while trying to learn formats, procedures, etc., of the Bureau, I had also to get used to four different SACs, each of whom made changes in the office according to the way they wanted it operated. SAC Richard B. Hood was sent down from his post as LA SAC to get the office administratively set up. He was followed by Horace Duffy. Then, in the early part of 1941, Assistant Director Harold Nathan told Mr. Hoover he wanted to retire, but Mr. Hoover did not want to lose him, so told him he would transfer him to the 'quiet little office of San Diego.' As you know, in December of that year Pearl Harbor was attacked. I had been to Hawaii that summer and made quite a few friends among the Hawaiian people. Was listening to the radio that morning, heard the news, got dressed and ready to go to work. About that time, I received a phone call from the office. We worked until 2:30 a.m., and then were back to work at the usual hour; worked until sometime after midnight, and the next night until about 11:30. All during World War II, we worked nine hours a day, six days a week, and the Agents put in 100 hours a month voluntary overtime!

"All of the clerical employees those first few days worked mainly on compiling and double-checking lists we had of those considered dangerous Japanese, Italians and Germans, to be picked up. After those pickups, there were countless reports to be written of their apprehension and then later reports listing all contraband found, sometimes pages and pages.

"In connection with the translation of some of the contraband items picked up in Japanese homes, there was hired by the Government a trusted middle-aged Japanese man from Chula Vista, who, incidentally, my Father had also used as an interpreter in court when he was Judge in Chula Vista. This man worked under the supervision of a first office Agent. The Agent's name was Gil. He was from Mississippi. One night, after working a long day, he was fooling around and pointed his supposedly unloaded gun at the ceiling and it went off. He was subsequently transferred to Kansas City, but SAC Nathan didn't want to lose him, so he intervened. He called Mr. Hoover and convinced him to allow this young man to stay, commenting that he was 'dangerous' and it would be better if he shot an old SAC than a new one.

"You might be interested in how little we were ready for this from a security standpoint. Steno pool was off the main public corridor – doors left unlocked all along the hall, although not standing open. For the protection of the female employees, there was left standing in a corner of the steno pool behind some telephone equipment, a loaded shotgun. We were given no training, and I remember once asking how to use it. The Agent from whom I inquired said, 'Oh, just pick it up and shoot – you can't miss anything within 50 yards.'

"Also, at the beginning of the War, when a message had to be decoded in a hurry, all the Clerks worked on it at once, each one being given a certain number of lines of the message to decode by hand.

"My first years in the Bureau, there was no such position as Secretary to the SAC in San Diego. Each SAC picked whatever girl from the pool he wanted to dictate to, and she would do that work as a Grade 4 Steno. When the position of Secretary to the SAC was established in Grade 5, I had been taking Mr. Nathan's dictation, and was chosen for the position. Incidentally, taking his dictation was no mean trick. First, I would write the word (with which I was unfamiliar) as completely as possible in shorthand; then if I had time, would go back and write it in longhand. If I didn't know the word or how to spell it, I would then get out my dictionary. If there was no luck there, I would go to the big dictionary. If still no luck, I would ask everyone in the pool, then the Agents, and finally the Number One Man, as the ASAC was then called, rather than ask Mr. Nathan. He had a terrific vocabulary. When he dictated, he sometimes strode around the room with his hands folded behind his back and his ever-present pipe clutched between his teeth. This, of course, was a great aid to understanding the unfamiliar fancy words. He always dressed in black. He had a very sarcastic sense of humor. Sometime after he retired, he moved to San Francisco and lived in a small hotel there. On a trip I made to San Francisco, I was out late one night and decided to sleep in, as we worked long and hard in those days and didn't get the chance to sleep in often. I called him at 11:00 a.m. and he asked me to lunch. I said I hadn't yet had breakfast, so when I met him downstairs, he told all the help that I was his former drunken secretary from San Diego.

"Other SACs I have worked for are Mr. CC. Erwin Piper, now City Administrator of Los Angeles; Frank Price, who is present tonight; Thomas E. Bishop, now an Assistant Director at the Bureau, and Richard J. Baker, now an SAC at New York. As I said, there have been a total of 16; however, this is probably one reason I have continued to enjoy my work over a thirty year span, for, due to the changes, not only in SACs but the entire personnel, it has been a different office each year.

"All in all, it has been a wonderful thirty years, but now I am ready to turn my desk over to a new, most capable hand in the lovely Marie, and I am sure that with the wealth of Bureau experience held by Marguerite, this new team will be a first-rate one.

"At this time I want to thank each and every one of you for making my last days in the Bureau happy, memorable ones – so many memories I can cherish in the days to come. You cannot possibly know how much it has all meant to me. Thank you one and all from the bottom of my heart. I'll not say Adios – just Hasta La Vista."

∼

"There were only eight Special Agents," Jane told me, when she first started working at the Bureau. "That number grew to 100, with the attack of Pearl Harbor. There was so much closeness at that time," she reminisced.

After Mr. Nathan retired, he moved to New York. He invited her to lunch at Grand Central Station, when she visited the City. He introduced her to Melvin Purvis.

"You know who Mr. Purvis is, don't you Jane?" The name wasn't ringing a bell with her, so she answered, "No."

Mr. Nathan then asked, in his often sarcastic manner, "Do you remember John Dillinger?"

Jane nodded – of course she did!

(Mr. Purvis was Chicago's Special Agent in Charge when Dillinger was shot.)

Investigative Clerk John R. Baker, a 25-year veteran of the Bureau, wrote Jane an eight-page typed letter on her retirement. He also had some interesting stories about "Pop" Nathan.

During IC Baker's training period, he had taken dictation from an Agent William A. Robinson. "I remember his name because his initials spelled W.A.R." Baker wrote. When he took the teletype to "Pop" Nathan for approval, "the boss scanned the message, puffing on an ever-present pipe, saying nothing as he raced through the text. Suddenly and with added smoke, he screamed, 'What is THIS!'" Baker, who thought he had transcribed his dictation perfectly apparently had never heard of "modus operandi," and had butchered the words. Needless to say, he never made that mistake again.

Baker recalled an agent by the name of L. B. Allen, who had a "mind of his own to be sure." When called into Mr. Nathan's office to receive instructions on handling a case, "the boss spewed words through his tight lips as he drew repeatedly and puffed away on his pipe. When he finished, he looked up at Allen and said, 'Is that clear?' Allen replied, 'Frankly, no! If you'd take that confounded pipe out of your mouth, maybe someone could understand you,' at which time the boss removed his pipe; repeated the instructions, and Allen departed."

Baker also recalled "a male clerk by the name of Weeter Pond, who had cut tapes on about 50 teletype messages for the Bureau. After sending one or two messages, the Bureau operator broke in and advised that the 'form' being used for these messages was 'unacceptable.'

"'Pop' Nathan was there; told Pond to continue, and again the Bureau operator broke in with the same refusal to accept the messages in that form. It was a busy night; everyone was at the office working and tension was high. Mr. Nathan told Pond to tell the Bureau: 'SAC says messages are to be accepted in form being sent.' It was obvious that even the teletype operator at the Bureau knew who our SAC was, and the messages were continued until completed."

Baker's letter also contained some interesting history from the 1940's.

"The Chief of Police in San Diego was Clifford E. Peterson, and the Sheriff of San Diego County was Bert Strand. Robert E. Ware was Sheriff of Imperial County. Mr. Nathan used to always eat at the Grand Central Café on Broadway, just east of Sixth Avenue. Mr.

Dorward wouldn't miss having his meals downtown at Mannings. Just below the SAC's office was the old Botsford Hotel and Grill, a hangout for agents at mealtime. Streetcars were still running in some parts of San Diego; the bus had taken over other routes. There were no 'one-way' streets. The El Cortez was the highest point in town and the biggest buildings were the Bank of America; First National Bank; San Diego Trust and Savings Bank and the Medical-Dental Building. A number of the single agents resided at the San Diego Club, and the married agents were spread around the outlying areas. Highway 101 was the main artery between San Diego and Los Angeles. Also popular with gourmets in those days was the U. S. Grant Coffee Shop and the Rendezvous, and for the penny pinchers, there was Keith's Waffle Shop and Leighton's Dairy Lunch."

At the end of Baker's "missive," as Jane would refer to it, he adds:

"We have served God; our beloved country, and a man in whom we have always had, and still have, the utmost faith, respect, trust, confidence, and loyalty, the Honorable J. Edgar Hoover."

About Jane, he said, "she is, has always been, and will always be the type of person who typifies the old saying which reads, 'I expect to pass through this world but once. Any good therefore that I can do, or any kindness that I can show to any fellow creature, let me do it now. Let me not defer or neglect it for I shall not pass this way again.'"

Among Jane's old papers is an office roster dated November 15, 1947. The SAC was W. A. Murphy; there were 27 agents, which included those assigned to "resident agencies" in El Centro, Riverside, and Santa Ana. Eventually Riverside and Santa Ana were made a part of Los Angeles' jurisdiction. There were 12 clerks and stenos and 12 operators between two radio stations – the transmitting and receiving sites. Telephone numbers looked something like this: Woodlawn 7-1914; Main 2659; Franklin 0673 and Humbolt 8-3064!

Included at the bottom of the roster were the following instructions:

"To Call Kirby by Radio: Dial Franklin 1101 (SD PD), ask for Radio and request them to relay a call through Station 90 for SD 711 to 1021."

SD PD refers to the San Diego Police Department.

Marjorie and Jane at ex-FBI gals' luncheon, Oct. 1971

Further: "Agents having 2-way cars will be advised via Radio Station when they have messages and will call the office when advised to that effect."

Post J. Edgar Hoover Days

During the 1970's, Wanda and I were still exchanging newsy letters. She saved several of mine. (Without doubt, I wrote to Jane with the same news.) A letter postmarked: "Metuchen, NJ Sep 21 1972," relates a visit by my parents. While we traveled to Pittsburgh to visit relatives, John took a "week's duty in Atlantic City."

"Soon there will be an opening for a man from John's squad," I wrote, "and he wanted to get an idea of what the place was like, thinking maybe the taxes wouldn't be so terrifically high. The idea of an RA (resident agency) appeals to him and there's a lot of talk that the Agents will be able to use the Bureau cars for commuting, especially out of the RA's." We were looking at ways to cut expenses since I wanted to work on my education in the hopes of "eventually doing some sort of writing."

My letter continued: "I haven't really heard any more rumors as far as Bureau changes, except there is some talk of giving agents in Newark and New York a cost of living allowance."

The FBI had added two women to its ranks – a first. Reportedly, one was an ex-marine and the second an ex-nun, which drew some wisecracks from the men.

A 16-page handwritten letter to Wanda (and in all likelihood, Jane too) dated Nov. 10, 1972, announced that I was expecting our second child.

"We are hoping for a girl -- at least Tommy and I are – don't know about John, but I think a baby girl would soften him up!"

"Tommy is listening to *Perspectives in Percussion* on the stereo. Remember when Dave Guyer borrowed that record when he bought a stereo? What a long time ago it seems that Dave visited us at the apartment on University Place!" (Dave had been a friend of Wanda's and was a clerk in the San Diego office.)

On the subject of the Bureau, I wrote:

"It will be curious now to see what happens to the Bureau as Mr. Gray will undoubtedly get his permanent appointment. One of the gals I worked with in the Director's office recently celebrated her 30th anniversary. It was perfect occasion to write and congratulate her, but also ask for the scoop on the new Director's office. In a prompt reply, she said she had never thought of the Bureau without Mr. Hoover, and that just as she was coming up for her 30th anniversary, there was indication that she might lose her job. One Assistant Director told her, 'Hell, Alice, you don't want to stay here with this new crew coming in.' She said she really felt wanted. As it turned out, Mr. Gray asked her to stay, even though he brought in his own staff, the average age of which was about 30 – just as she was about to celebrate her 30th anniversary. She said that 'didn't exactly make me want to jump for joy.' Her job has been somewhat changed, but she says she's really enjoying the new system. Mr. Gray drops in and says, 'Hi Alice, what are you up to?' when Mr. Hoover didn't even know her name after she had worked in his office for 10 years.

"Anyway, Alice said she was never told that her position was permanent, so she was wondering what would happen when Mr. Gray got his permanent appointment. I'm sure he'd keep her as she is a real conscientious but regular type person.

"Alice wrote of how 'Miss Gandy (Mr. Hoover's secretary) handled everything and arranged for the office staff to ride in the funeral procession directly behind Mr. Hoover's body. We were allowed to sit where normally the family would sit, at the service.'

"There's a lot of talk about a lot more transferring around – Gray being a Navy man and all. If John wishes to pursue administrative advancement, he'll eventually be made a supervisor, but instead of staying in Newark, he'll be sent to Washington for awhile, then out to another field office as a supervisor. On the other hand, if he chooses not to become a supervisor, he could remain in Newark for a number of years. Right now, he really isn't sure what he wants to do. He enjoys being a street agent and does not enjoy 'desk' work, but we don't relish the thought of bouncing around the country.

"While on the subject of the Bureau, did I tell you that Jane wrote awhile back that the Scallinis were expecting? Well, they had a girl a couple of months ago – and Joe celebrated his 20th with the 'B.'"

In a ten-page handwritten letter to Wanda in January, 1973, (mailed with an eight cent Eisenhower stamp) I talked about our indecision about adding a room to the house.

"We'd just go ahead and add the room and half bath, but John feels the Bureau is in such a state of flux, with Gray not yet permanently appointed, and a thousand and one rumors going around about relief supervisors, after two years, going to Washington, Agents being able to transfer out of Class A offices after 5 years to their OP (office of preference), etc., that we just are'nt at all certain how long we may be here – not that we ever were – but when Hoover was alive, it was a pretty sure thing we'd remain in Newark for years. Now, we may possibly go to Washington in the next year or so. We just don't know. So anyway, our latest decision (they change daily, believe me) is to try to save some money so if we do get transferred, we'll be able to afford a larger house."

In a 14-page handwritten letter dated Friday, April 27th, I mentioned that "John just called to say he has to fly down to Washington with some loot which has to be checked out. There is some doubt as to it's ownership. A bank robber's mother claims it is hers, so they are going to check it to see if the robber's prints are on it." John was working bank robberies in Newark at the time.

"A couple of weeks ago, John called me to say he had just talked to an old friend of mine – couldn't imagine who – Jack Keith! He was in the office for a conference," I wrote. "I called and left a message for him to call me if he had a chance. He called back in about 15 minutes and talked to me a good half hour. I deliberately didn't keep him on the phone, but he didn't rush the call at all. He was in Newark on a visit from Washington, D.C., where he heads up the organized crime unit. Just as he was preparing to retire as ASAC in Atlanta, L. Patrick Gray came for a visit and asked if he would come to Washington. Mr. Keith said, 'How could I say no.'"

"He inquired about 'that little gal, Wanda,' and I informed him how we keep in touch and that you had been up here for a visit, and I down to South Carolina last May. He said he 'really felt bad' that he never looked you up while he was stationed in Atlanta. He passed along some news of other agents I knew and mentioned he had been back to San Diego two years ago for his son's wedding. He didn't have much to say about the changes in Washington, stating that his transfer there was unexpected." I told Wanda that I "didn't think anyone knows what to think about it all, especially with all the Watergate mess." The last page of the letter, which was written a few days later, stated, "Since I wrote page 12, Gray resigned."

I undoubtedly wrote Jane about my "telephonic" visit Jack Keith.

In a letter to Wanda, dated Feb. 27, 1973, I commented:

"It must have been a surprise hearing from Jean Gray. I had no idea that he was the Legal Attache in Manila."

She and Jean became friends in San Diego, after their tour of duty in El Paso, Texas. After Wanda married, they exchanged Christmas cards, but it had been a few years since she heard from him.

∾

A Christmas note from Alice Denning in 1974 or 1975 stated:

"Hasn't this been a year for the Bureau! We seem to be settling down a little now with Mr. Kelly. He seems very nice – but then I said that about Mr. Gray. Mr. Kelly brought two law enforcement men with him as Executive Assistants and I am their secretary, but still handling the mail. It's really more than one person can handle, but I enjoy working with these men a great deal and the work is very interesting."

At Christmas, 1977, she asked, "Do you think they will ever come up with a new Director for us? I really don't envy anyone who would take the job – it is a thankless one."

In a letter dated January 20, 1978, Alice wrote:

"We are all sitting back wondering what the new regime will bring. Webster seems to be highly respected – I hope he can give the Bureau the lift it needs. None of us know just what will happen to us. The office is overstaffed and has been for years. If Judge Webster brings his secretary that will mean Mr. Kelley's secretary will be surplus also." She added that she "would very much like to retire, however, the Bureau has never gone the early retirement route. My former boss is doing consulting and wants me to come with him. He is located at Dulles and it would be so much more convenient for me, and, frankly I am tired of the Bureau."

By Christmas, 1978, Alice had taken an "early retirement." She wrote:

"I had inquired earlier of the possibilities, but they said – no way. Then Judge Webster was bringing secretaries from St. Louis and we were well-stocked to begin with, so they asked if I was still interested. I jumped at the chance and have never regretted it."

My fascination with interior decorating got into full swing with the house in Metuchen. I became a regular customer at Metuchen Hardware, and probably drove the men there crazy with my ideas and questions about paint and wallpaper. I drew some raised eyebrows over wanting to paint the living room ceiling with a semi-gloss of pale yellow, and the hall a sour apple green. I hung a gold foil paper in the dining room to go with our Spanish dining room set, and papered a bedroom/den with an English hunt scene. I didn't realize then that I was preparing for what has now been 18 years working in a wallpaper and paint store.

Our finances were such that there often was less than $5.00 in the checkbook, leaving me to resort to redeeming my Green Stamps for something new for the house -- a shower curtain, for instance.

My curly-haired toddler occupied a good bit of my time, and as much as I loved him, and being home with him, I wasn't content with my life. I tried to keep myself occupied with various projects, about which I always wrote to Jane. I wrote more to my mother and mother-in-law about my frustrations with motherhood. Growing up, I believed that a girl's ultimate goal was to be a wife and mother. No one ever put the idea into my head that there were alternatives to marriage and children, but the onslaught of the women's liberation movement had me questioning my choice. Being a stay-at-home mom just wasn't doing it for me. When Tommy was three years old, I began calling around to lawyers' offices to see if I could get part-time employment. One lawyer took pity on me and hired me to research natural vitamins vs. artificial ones, a venture in which he was interested.

Tom suffered with ear infections and invariably came down with one on the days I was scheduled to work. After less than a year, I decided to stay home.

During our vacation in York Beach, Maine, in the summer of 1972, I became pregnant with our second child. The due date was May 18, 1973. By the first of June, John came home each night, asking, "Anything yet?" It seemed that our darling baby girl was not at all anxious to enter this world. I passed the days watching Watergate hearings on our black and white television. Finally, on June 7, Sarah Kathryn was born – at the JFK Hospital in Edison, New Jersey.

Prior to her birth, I wrote the following to Wanda:

"I guess this new baby will have a real old-fashioned christening in Massachusetts. John's first cousin who is a priest will baptize the baby, and John's mother is planning a party for all the relatives. I don't know whether she intends an open house type thing, or if she plans to hire a place like they seem to do for showers, receptions, etc. She came from a family of nine children, all of whom had married and had children."

Before long the old frustrations set in again. John worked long hours and was no help around the house when he was home. I began to take writing classes at a nearby community college and submitted a few articles to magazines, but when John came home from work to find me propped at my typewriter, he admonished.

"Do you have to do these things on my time?" he'd say.

Frustrated, I complained about my life – to my mother, to Jane, and to John. Meeting other young mothers, once Tommy entered nursery school, helped. I also became friendly with an elderly neighbor, Roslyn Halvorsen, who had a wonderful garden, planted with flowers which bloomed all through the spring and summer. Peonies bordered her sculpted garden. She introduced me to beautiful perennials such as columbine, foxglove, and bleeding heart, and fun things like the "money plant" and bittersweet, which made attractive dried arrangements. When her day included thinning out her flowerbeds, I'd be summoned. "Get over here," she'd command, "with your shovel and wheelbarrow!"

John and I became very good friends with an English couple, who lived across the street -- Kath and Stuart Beech. In 1974, when I returned after a three-week visit home to San Diego, Kath informed me that John had barely been home during my absence. It was after that, that I began to notice suspicious activity on his part – leaving for work earlier than usual, with a new aftershave trailing after him; mysterious hang-up phone calls, and lots of late nights at "work." The most obvious sign was that he no longer seemed interested in me sexually. Granted, I had lost a lot of my sexual drive after the birth of each of my children, but I didn't expect my husband to turn to someone else. When I was at my wit's end about my marriage or my kids, I cried on Kath's shoulders.

I also began to confide in Jane about my husband's unfaithfulness. I felt I had my own "Master of Deceit." The name of an old television show, *I Led Three Lives,* frequently popped into my mind. Being an FBI agent -- with secret assignments and all -- John was able to dupe and deceive me, even though I had worked for the Bureau. As Jane would say, "Back in our days, an agent would be transferred to someplace like Butte if he was suspected of having an affair." Butte, Montana, was a disciplinary transfer for agent who got out of line.

She would enclose a separate "Personal" note inside her regular letters, with her comments.

During this time, I submitted a story to Redbook entitled, "My Battle to Find Contentment as a Housewife and Mother." (How dumb is that? – although at the time it was a battle). The editors thanked me for submitting same, adding that they were "grateful" that I took the "time and trouble to write" and wished "it could have been selected for publication." I related in that story how my husband said he did not understand why I had waited until I was married and had children to decide that I'd rather be doing something else with my life. I admitted that when I was single, my goal was to find a husband to share my future with, adding that I had no way of knowing beforehand how keeping house and caring for babies would affect me. My story also related that I had often talked to my husband about my dilemma and that he was agreeable to anything I chose to do "as long as it was going to make me happy." At other times, however, he would make comments such as, "When you can go out and make $50,000 a year, I'll stay home and take care of the kids!"

The Women's Liberation Movement made me rebellious and I am certain now that John had no idea how to deal with me.

When Sarah turned three, I felt I had to get out of the house. I asked a friend, who knew a local lawyer, if he needed a secretary. As it turned out, he didn't, but a friend of his did. So, I went to work for Henry Gurshman. I enrolled Sarah in nursery school. The poor child went double session – morning and afternoon. By the time John received his transfer to Massachusetts, I had Gurshman's office so organized and running so efficiently, he almost cried when I left. He said I was the best secretary he ever had and pleaded with me for months afterward to come back.

~

My letters to Jane were filled with my incessant frustrations, attempts at writing, latest decorating adventures, and our social activities. Hers described elaborate dinner parties that she and Will hosted, car trips they took, and the latest addition to their lovely garden. Birthday cards from Jane were always special -- often handmade and decorated with pressed flowers.

She was sympathetic, always supportive of me, and praised my efforts in all that I tried to do. It's no wonder I kept writing to her.

PART TWO

Letter writing is the only device
for combining solitude with good company.
-- Lord Byron

For the first two years of their marriage, Jane and Will lived in the apartment which she rented after her father died. In 1969, they purchased a beautiful hacienda – Spanish style, with red tile roof -- in Bonita, California. Jane named her house "La Casa de las Chuparrosas," which is imprinted on her stationery. After she had the house decorated, she sent me photos of the outside of the house, and the living room, which has remained essentially unchanged. A mix of Danish modern furniture, and antiques, decorate the house. The living room has a fireplace at its center. A white mohair rug, lies under a coffee table of simple lines, with a mosaic tile top. Her piano sets at the left, front of the room, with her father's gavel resting on top. Large windows surround the room, offering a view of the landscape beyond. A large picture window in the dining room frames the front garden, and the valley below.

Jane often wrote of working in her garden, and often decorated the birthday cards she sent to me with flowers, which she had saved and dried. She and Will hosted elaborate dinner parties, usually with a theme. Once it was a Mexican, with luminaries lighting the walk through the garden to the porch. Another time, it was a Greek theme, with table decorations brought from Greece by her friends, the Carlsens.

Marjorie Burke

The Hacienda in Bonita

~

For some reason, I began to save the cards and letters that Jane sent to me. The oldest note I have is dated 10/30/73. It pictures a darling child, identified as: "Petit Navajos, Eukabi, Old Albuq. N.M."

"Dear Marge - Thought you might like to have one of these snapshots taken after the luncheon, which was a huge success – just about the nicest we have had.

"Your note was darling and your notepaper hilarious! It went around so all could see and read it. Wish you could have been here – maybe next year. Love, Jane"

Jane wrote the above following an FBI luncheon for former women employees.

~

The following letter was dated 11/21/77.

Dear Marge:

I have a few moments before dinner, and if I don't dash off a note to you, fear you will not hear from me before you leave for

60

California! So glad to know you are really coming. Why don't you call me as soon after you arrive as practical for you so that we can try to arrange a luncheon date somewhere – just you and me? I certainly don't want to miss a good visit with you.

Nothing too much here to report. Will has had a lot of trouble getting work this Fall. It always seems to happen at the heaviest part of the year, such as Christmas, taxes, etc. Oh, well – in 1978 he will probably retire, and then we will know just how much money we have to pay expenses.

Our FBI luncheon was a big success this year. I secured Frank Price, the current national chairman of the Society of Former FBI Agents, to speak. His speech put a bit of new life into the bunch. We had about 25 present.

Just heard the other day that Helen is retiring Dec. 31st. If you care to send a letter, it should reach Miss Marguerite Hansen, Secretary to the SAC, no later than 12-19. I am sure Helen would treasure a letter from you. Lots of Agents have to retire in December, also, and they are having one big cocktail party at the Admiral Kidd Club on Dec. 29th. The following Agents are leaving: Mike Hennigan, John Flynn, Ed Miller, Bob Moore, Arnold O'Brien, Jim Scanlon. Others whom you would not know – 14 in all. We will be going to that party, as well as the Ex-Agts. Christmas party, which the Munoz have invited us to. That will be fun for us as I will know many of the people. Will, too.

I am sure you know about the complete re-organization the Bureau is doing of all its CCO (Chief Clerk's Office) operations. From what I hear, Kay will get the big job.

What do you hear from Wanda? If she ever complains that she does not receive letters about the X-B luncheons, tell her that the decision was made not to send out-of-state letters to anyone who has not attended at least occasionally. With the small treasury, every 13 cents counts!

Will be anxious to hear from you when you arrive. Much love, /s/ Jane.

I made a notation on the front of this card, "wrote 1-17-78," to thank her for lunch, during my visit to San Diego, which was probably at the Café del rey Moro in Balboa Park, since it was one of our favorites.

Frank Price was the Special Agent in Charge of the San Diego FBI office when I first reported for duty, and Helen was the Supervising Steno.

The retiring agents, Jim Scanlon and Ed Miller were assigned to the Oceanside Resident Agency, which covered Camp Pendleton. They made periodic trips into the office in San Diego, but I knew them mostly from transcribing their dictation from the Dictaphone. Robert "Bob" Moore had thick, wavy, almost white hair and wide, toothy smile. He worked the military bases, while Lou Munoz worked car thefts, especially those involving transportation across the Mexican border.

Kay Fox had been the Chief Clerk. She and her husband Jim bowled on the FBI league with me. Kay and I exchanged Christmas cards for years until some years after her husband passed away and she moved back to Iowa. I eventually lost touch with her.

Mention of the Admiral Kidd's Club always brings back the fond memory of my first real kiss, when Joe took me home. I remember planning what I would wear, and can still see the aqua dress with a belted waist, and the crystal, teardrop, earrings and pendant. I went to the party with two other stenos, Margo and Sharon. Margo was a big flirt, and I can still hear her saying, to one of the agents: "If you've got the money honey, I've got the time." Sharon was a religious fanatic who thought everything was a sin. (At a future party she reported some of us for drinking, because we were not yet 21, and several people were censured over the incident.)

~

Christmas, 1977, marked John and my 10th wedding anniversary. We flew out to San Diego, with our two children to celebrate. My parents were celebrating their 40th on December 31st. While there, we drove up the coast and visited briefly with Linda Anderson, who was living in Irvine. In a letter dated February 2nd, she stated that she enjoyed the visit, though brief, and was "glad to see" my children, whom she described as "really cute and very well-mannered."

~

A letter from Jane dated March 9, 1978, is on "stationery designed and drawn by my friend who was my Matron of Honor. The drawing on the front is of one of the oldest houses in Chula Vista."

Dear Marge:

Surprised to hear so soon? I have a moment so thought I'd drop a note before you leave for Boston. That was a great surprise and so glad you are both happy about it. Do you mean that John leaves 3-18-78 and that you won't leave until the house is sold? You said you hoped it would be by June. That is a long time in between. Let me know.

Talked with Anne recently and Nick had been to the hospital for the treadmill and some other tests. They said there is a "gray" area around the heart and want to do some more tests. If heart damage is found he would undergo surgery. Anne said Nick balked at that and decided he would try more exercises, diet, etc. first. Such a shadow to have hanging over you.

Saw Helen and her sister for a short time Sunday. She is really enjoying her retirement. She is quite a gabber, but an interesting one. Will and I drove up to see Lake Hodges Dam spilling over—I don't remember ever having seen such a sight in my life. Haven't had any rain for over a week until late afternoon today when it really began. Haven't listened to any weather reports today, so don't know whether it is just a cloudburst or the beginning of something else. I believe I heard that 9 reservoirs in SD Co. are spilling over.

Can't remember whether I told you that we have a new baby in the family – a little girl named Wendy Browne; 8 pounds, 3 ounces, and her mother is very tiny.

Will had a little accident at work a week ago – a heavy pipe hit him in the throat. There was so much swelling and so many bloodclots that the doctor couldn't conduct an examination, so he is going back today.

We may take a little trip to New England in the Fall, so maybe I'll be seeing you! I have another friend in Boston. All for now. Love, /s/ Jane. P.S. Doctor said Will's throat is all black, like a bruise. He goes back in another month. J.

My answer to the above was on 5-4-78. After nine years in New Jersey, we packed that many years' worth of belongings and headed for John's "Office of Preference." He had received his transfer to Boston and was sincerely happy about the transfer. So was I, since we'd be near family and I figured if our marriage was going to survive, this was our answer. Our son, however, was not happy at all! He had just signed up for Little League, which John wouldn't allow him to play the year before. He didn't think he was mature enough! John left for Boston in February, but the kids and I stayed on until July. So, Tommy was able to play baseball with his pals after all.

~

Anne's husband, Nick, grew up in Butte, Montana. While writing this book, and pumping friends for stories, Anne told me about the time Nick almost blew Agent George Strong's cover in Montana. Strong was on a surveillance, when Nick spotted him, but somehow Strong was able to signal Nick, and no harm was done. Strong was stationed there before his "disciplinary" transfer to San Diego. It was through a friend of Nick's - a "Lulu" - who worked for the Bureau, that Anne applied for a job. She had almost given up, after nearly a year of waiting, before joining the Bureau as a clerk. She eventually became the "code clerk" and worked in the vault deciphering secret communications.

~

"The Trossachs Loch Katrine" is pictured on a note dated 9-11-78. The reverse bears the following: "Judges Ltd. Hastings England."
9-11-78
Dear Marge:
Glad to know my letter reached you in MA and hope that crazy card did, too, so that you will know our trip is off. The

Neurosurgeon said a bus trip was the worst thing Will could do, and that if he went ahead with his plans, he would be ready for back surgery when he came home. He prescribed daily traction, heat, and massage as an out-patient in the hospital, and bed rest. He has been good about 50% of the time. Certainly has not obeyed orders, but I can't do anything with him. However, he does seem better. The doctor said it is a pinched nerve due to the bad disc in his lower back. Will wants to have surgery and get it over for we know it will be a recurring thing.

The main reason I am answering so promptly is to tell you I called Anne Sarris Saturday to chat. To make a long story short, they were coming home from a trip to Canada in a rented motor home and were staying with friends near Anaconda, Montana. Nick had a severe heart attack that night and was in intensive care in the hospital for five days. He flew home – they knew every stop was in a major city where there would be good hospitals and ordered oxygen for him on the plane. He is now at home. Anne said he is going to a cardiologist soon. One doctor told them that heart surgery was in the offing, as he didn't think Nick could pull through a third attack. Anne has to go to work, so I told her if she needed me, to call and I would stay with Nick, for he cannot be left alone. Thought you might like to send a note.

Also, went to the hospital in Chula Vista to see Arnold Orrantia last week. He is paralyzed on the right side and cannot speak, except for a few "grunts". Poor thing, it was heart-rending.

For some better news, the X-Agents invited our group to a joint meeting at the Police Range the end of August. It was a huge success. Wish you could have been there. Hope they make it an annual affair.

Sorry this letter is so full of illness. Let's hope for a better one next time. I'm feeling much better, thank goodness. Love, ----in a rush---- /s/ Jane.

P.S. Did I tell you I called Linda in Irvine and told her about the X-Agents' get-together? She said they planned to come, but she did not show up and I have not heard from her since.

Arnold Orrantia was a Spanish-speaking Agent. His partner's name was John Jones! Jane told me that she used to "sneak" back to the security agents' room, where their desks were, so she could practice the language. When Mr. Orrantia gave me a hard time about not being "cultured," Jane came to my defense stating there weren't too many places in San Diego to attend the opera or ballet!

A letter dated 11-21-78 from Jane reads:

Dear Marge:

I hope you will forgive me for not answering any questions, but I have so much to get accomplished this week, I thought I would at least get a short note off to you. I owe everyone, it seems.

So glad you like your new location. It must be beautiful there. You sound so happy.

I hate to tell you that Will goes in the hospital next Monday for back surgery 11-28-78. He had a myelogram about a month ago which reflected the definite need for surgery. The doctor said if he did not have surgery, he ran a good chance of being in a wheel chair in 4 to 5 years. All the nerves which control the lower extremeties are pinched in two places. He will be in the hospital about a week; then home, either standing or lying (no sitting) for 2 to 3 weeks. After a couple of months, he can gradually get into a car. Total recovery should take about 4 months. So, our holidays will be spent right here at home, but just so that he pulls through okay is really all the Christmas I want. It, of course, is serious and could result disastrously, but that is rare, and we have every confidence in both the Neurosurgeon and the Orthopedic surgeon who will assist.

I have not heard directly from Anne but understand that Nick is doing OK. I didn't want to worry her about Will, but will let her know when it is all over.

No special news from any of the FBI people other than Mr. Orrantia passed away about 6 to 8 weeks ago. He was in such sad shape, it was heartbreaking to see him. I feel so sorry for his wife, as she was one who had been sheltered by her husband – didn't even know how to write a check!

Please excuse this letter, but didn't want any more time to go by without some word from me. Really loved your last letter – just like you used to write. Almost as good as having a visit with you!

*Have Happy Holidays and write when you can. Much love,
Jane.*

~

A portion of a letter from Jane states:

*Am sure you remember Verdia Hollis. She called me to wish us a happy
wedding anniversary, and during the conversation, mentioned that the
week before she had had a kidney removed. She later wrote that the biopsy
revealed cancer in both the kidney and the tube. She was to undergo x-ray
therapy. She was making light of her situation, but it sounds quite serious
to me. I am writing and calling some of the girls who knew her and asking
if they will send a card, for she was always doing such things for others.
Wonder if you would send her a card or note? When you write Wanda,
would you mention it to her also? Hope she is doing OK. What do you hear
from her?*

Verdia was the office supply clerk who guarded every piece of paper,
rubber band, paper clip, etc. as if it was her own personal property.
We often joked about what a hassle it was to convince her that we
really needed whatever it was we were requesting. She was a sweet lady,
otherwise.

On part of a letter, which was only partially saved, Jane mentions
that she and Will went to Los Angeles for Saturday afternoon and
Sunday to celebrate their wedding anniversary. They had a drink at
a "fabulous hotel" with a revolving lounge. The paper is torn here,
but I can tell she is commenting on the price of the drink, which was
"$6.50!"

~

May 16th (1979 -- according to the envelope's postmark). I noted
that it was "answered 7-11-79."

Dear Marge:

*Thanks for your letter just before my birthday (March 7) and
also for the card. I see you are gradually getting back into the
business world, with your hours increasing at the job. Sounds good,*

but think you are so wise to be home with the children also. I took the pictures you sent me last to the luncheon May 1ˢᵗ, and everyone who knew you was happy to see them. You sound so happy in your present environment, and how nice that you and John's family get along so well.

I was so surprised to learn that you don't hear regularly from Wanda and that her Christmas card, especially, had no note. You are having a hard time with your correspondents!

Anne was at the luncheon. She looked thin, but well. Nick seems to be doing fine. I have been intending to go out there to have lunch with her ever since my birthday, but haven't made it yet.

I hope all signs of your fall have gone away and that you will not have a scar from the stitches. I had a bad fall when I was out walking last November and haven't gotten myself back in the mood to walk again.

How is the Boston Terrier? Imagine it is something to train a new puppy.

One reason you haven't heard from me is that we have been traveling! All of March and April, was spent either getting ready to go or catching up when we get home. On March 6ᵗʰ, we left for Green Valley, Arizona, 20 miles south of Tucson, to be with Will's cousin and his wife from Connecticut. They rented a darling little home there for three months. From there we drove on down through Nogales into Mexico, along the coast. Went to Guaymas, Hermosillo, and Los Mochis. From there we took the train ride over the Copper Canyon, spent the night in a lodge there, and returned to Los Mochis the next day. From there, home. We were gone almost two weeks.

The first of December we requested passage on the Delta Queen for a trip from Cincinnati down the river to New Orleans. Passage is extremely difficult to obtain, so we went to Mexico as it did not look as though our reservations would come through. Well, they did, so we quick like got ready and left April 13ᵗʰ for Akron, Ohio, where we spent the night with the former wife of one of Will's sons and his granddaughter. The next day we flew to Cincinnati and boarded the DQ. We stopped at Evansville, Vicksburg, and Baton Rouge and had 4-hour land tours at each place — all very interesting. *The Baton Rouge stop was unscheduled, so I called Verdia the moment we got on the tour, and she and Earl came to the boat at 4:00 p.m. and we had a nice visit. Am sure I must have written you that she had a kidney removed last year, which was cancerous. She is still having checkups. She looks well but quite thin. Wouldn't you know Verdia would come to meet us armed with an orchid corsage for me and a boutonniere for Will?*

Will took just a few pictures. When he gets some prints, I'll get a copy for you of the two of us, if they are good. Will has a beard and mustache (curled on the ends!) which I hate, but which he LOVES!

Hope all is well with you and yours – wish you would be coming this way soon. Any chance? Much love, /s/ Jane

P.S. I don't plan to go to the X-B convention, do you? Neither do we plan a trip East this year as we shot our wad in Mar/Apr. Feel one shouldn't even go driving around here any more, what with the gas situation as it is!

A photo of Will and Jane was enclosed with the above letter, with a notation on the back: "Life-saving drill aboard the Delta Queen, April – 1979."

Shortly after we were settled in our new home in Bolton, Mass., I began working part-time for the lawyer who handled our real estate transfer. I had not intended to work while Sarah was in kindergarten, but somehow was enticed to do so. I agreed because the hours enabled me to be home when the kids were out of school.

While Wanda and I had started off with a good exchange of letters, she became "bad" about writing and often would send a birthday card or Christmas card, signed simply, "Love, Wanda, Tom and Gina." She always said, "I love your letters -- they sound just like you talk." Her explanation for not writing: "Mine always sound so dumb!"

One winter's day, after picking the kids up from school, errands included a Post Office stop. My son called to me to "Come see" a photograph of a kitty posted on the outside bulletin board. Snow partially hid a small wire fence bordering a flowerbed. Eyes fixed straight ahead at the photo, the fence caught me at the ankles. I came crashing to the ground, my glasses cutting the area to the side of my right eye. Blood all over my face, which I tried to absorb in my mittens, I drove to a nearby doctor's office, with two upset kids in the back seat. The cut required four or five stitches – all this on the way to pick up our new Boston Terrier puppy, which John insisted we had to have. He was home so little that I knew the responsibility would fall entirely to me. Once I met "Barney," however, it was love at first sight.

~

8-3-79

Dear Marge:

Surprise? Less than a month from the date of your letter I am replying! The reason: We are expecting 3 granddaughters and some of the families to begin arriving next weekend, and I am desperately trying to get my correspondence and some other items in order prior to that. They will be here a week or ten days, but immediately thereafter I have a lot of work to do for the Sweetwater Woman's Club. The Fall always brings so much more work and so many more activities.

We are going to a beach picnic today with our group. I am taking a salad, the recipe for which I got from my friend in Hawaii. It is the oddest collection of items: peas, mushrooms, onions, pineapple, carrots, cheese, green peppers, water chestnuts, lettuce. All covered with a mixture of mayonnaise and sour cream with sugar, then sprinkled on top with grated cheddar and bacon. I volunteered to bring it – wished afterward I had not. It took me 2 ½ hours to cook and assemble, which included cooking ¾ pounds of bacon. Also, it cost $8.18! Think I will make it seldom.

So glad you like Massachusetts. I can't imagine having an address with no house number. Are you the only house on that street? You seem to be involved a lot with cooking for people – family I mean. Nice, though, that you all get along so well. Let me know about the computer company work – sounds good.

I have the following in bloom in the garden now: roses, verbenas, gloriosa daisies, tithonia, Shasta daisies, white and yellow marguerites, agapanthus, and a few phlox. Really looks pretty but does keep me busy, especially the roses, having to spray each and every weekend. Also day lilies, coreopsis, and pink lilies.

Re traveling and staying home: I am always happy to stay home; in fact, you sort of have to drag me away for more than two days at a time, for I worry about the safety of things, my flowers, the cat, etc. We recently spent two days with Will's oldest son who has moved in with his girlfriend. Both are divorced and both have 2 children. He has his quite often on the weekends. Hers are 8 and 11. We like her very much – she is a smart gal – but can't quite get used to this business of buying a home together, and especially when there are children involved, without the blessing of matrimony. They live in Redondo Beach. We went to the Huntington Art Gallery, the botanical gardens there, and had dinner in a Chinese restaurant where I had my first Seschuan (sp?) food, which is very hot.

Then last weekend a friend who is Manager of Jurgensen's Fine Foods, Westgate, invited us to the Huntington Hotel in Pasadena for a private wine-tasting, put on by eight wineries for Jurgensen employees and friends. These people always spend a lot of money on dinners and we wound up having to eat at the Huntington with them. It was only 5:00 p.m. and I had been eating cheese and crackers all afternoon and really didn't want a thing to eat, but what could we do? I finally ordered a seafood salad (which was no good) and just that salad cost $9.50! Well, it wound up that the 2 days and 1 night cost us about $100. I can't get over how much money it takes nowadays to have a little recreation.

Can't think of any special news of people you know. Nick Sarris seems to be holding his own, as far as I know; haven't talked with Anne recently. I am, as usual, battling the bulge and making myself starve occasionally, to not much avail! I imagine you are as thin as ever.

Time to get lunch, so had better stop. Hope your summer has been nice. Any chance you will come out for Christmas? Much love, /s/ Jane

Our house in Bolton was one of nine or ten along one side of a country road. House numbers weren't assigned until the 1980s. When the realtor drove me down the narrow, winding Long Hill Road, leading to Teele Road, to show me the house which John had selected, I thought we were in the sticks, for sure. We were definitely out in the country. It took some getting used to, especially when I became aware of the nasty black flies, ticks and mosquitoes. The locals warned me about the proper removal of ticks. "Don't try to pull them off, or their heads may stay attached," they warned. This could lead to real problems. "Try to suffocate them with Vaseline," I was instructed. One morning, while drying my daughter's hair, lo and behold, there was a tick stuck to the back of her head! Afraid that trying to remove it with tweezers would leave the feelers in and cause brain damage, I swabbed the area with Vaseline, and sent her off to school. It had turned into quite the gooey mess by the time she came home. I eventually learned that by grabbing the critter with tweezers, and twisting it, the whole thing would let go.

During the 1980s and 90s, the computer company, Digital Equipment Corporation, was in its heyday. If you didn't work for them, someone in your family did. DEC offered a program for mothers. I tried it for a short time, but just did not find the work interesting.

~

4-15-80
Dear Marge:
Was glad to hear from you – had thought perhaps something was wrong in your household. Remember the long letters I used to write? I just don't seem to have the time any more, or enuf to say! Right now I am going crazy with insurance forms, doctors, etc., and trying to do most of the yard work.

Will is much better but not thoroughly himself. The main difficulty is that he has no bladder control. The doctor told him he stood a 50/50 chance of being incontinent, and we still hope he will not be. These catheters are for the birds. He lost 20 pounds, and I think he must have gained back about 6 by now. He looked like death warmed over. The blood clot is not yet dissolved, so he continues to go for a weekly blood test and takes blood-thinning medicine, both to dissolve this clot and prevent another.

I don't see how you have time to do any redecorating, what with working and caring for that family! Guess it's just the diff in our ages – I used to accomplish much more. I have so many people to keep advised about Will, plus regular correspondence, that most friends are getting either very short notes or post cards these days. One day I put 17 items, including bills and checks, in the mail, and later that week 7.

I am trying my luck with some seeds this year – never have worked much with seeds – and believe me I am not having too good luck. I bought some pony packs of bright red begonias with almost black leaves, a pack of foxglove, and some impatiens. We had such a warm winter that a lot of my bulbs are not blooming and I wonder whether or not it could be that it did not get cold enough.

How did your St. Patrick's party turn out? You must have turned into quite a hostess. I understand we make much more of that day in the U.S. than they do in Ireland, according to Will's Irish cousins. I haven't done any fancy entertaining since the BIG party last October – the Delta Queen party – about which I must have written you.

The visitors have not arrived, thank goodness – just one: Will's missionary cousin who is my age and who was on her way home from two years in Japan. I wrote and asked her to stop, which she had not intended to do, since Will's condition was so uncertain. They are almost like brother and sister. She is a lovely person.

Boy, the New Englanders really do it up great with their Jack and Jill showers, renting a hall, etc. Everything these days seems to be done so that it will cost the most.

Thanks for all the birthday wishes. It was a sad one, since Will was in the hospital after the radical and feeling miserable, and I was alone.

No more time – this is a long letter these days for me.   Love,
/s/ Jane

As far as the "decorating," I was probably rewallpapering since most of the wallpaper in the house was not to my taste. Shortly after the Miss America Pageant that year, my son came home from school and commented, "Gee, Mom, if you were in the Miss America Pageant, your talent could be to put on country/western music and wallpaper a room!"

I had a St. Patrick's Day party for John's family -- 100 percent Irish on both his mother and father's side. Their hometown of Clinton, Mass., has a large Irish population, which celebrates March 17 in a big way. We often celebrated family anniversaries and birthdays at the "sign of the shamrock" known as the "Old Timers" restaurant. Sunday nights featured the "Jug of Punch" with whom we would sing along to the Irish folk music while enjoying either corned beef and cabbage or a roast beef buffet, hosted by a singing chef. The "Old Timers" is reputably where former Assistant Director William C. Sullivan wrote his book about his love/hate relationship with the Bureau/Hoover.

Showers, weddings, funerals, etc., are definitely done with more pomp and circumstance than we were used to in southern California.

∼

9-26-80

Dear Marge:

Since I have neglected you so, I will write you on my very special stationery. As you know, I love hummingbirds!

No, nothing is wrong. I have just turned into a terrible correspondent. I am not lazy, however! The only way I can explain it is that now (even after 10 years of retirement) there are so many classes I want to take, so much entertaining I want to do, so much sewing, etc. that I just don't get down to the typewriter to carry on my personal correspondence very often. You were very good to job me up with your sweet note, and I do appreciate it.

I was just typing up a recipe I have had on scratch paper and started to throw it away when I thought perhaps it might be something your family would enjoy. It is a very Mexican dish, although you seldom see it on restaurant menus. We have a Mexican boy working for us in the yard each Friday for awhile, and part of his pay is his meals – 3 of them. He is such a charming boy and so appreciative, it is a pleasure to cook something on Fridays that

I know he would enjoy. I also always furnished him with "salsa" (not sauce), and he loves that.

The X-B meeting this October has been postponed a couple of weeks so that the National Chairman, Ruth Wood, can attend. She will be in San Diego about 5 days on her way to the Agents' Convention in October in Honolulu, to which she was invited. I am having Ruth and the current Chairman of San Diego, Ina Beeson — who used to work in DC and never here — to lunch the Wednesday before, together with Kay Fox and Marguerite Hansen. The latter came from Washington at the time I retired. Then on the 29th, I am having another luncheon for 6 local friends. On the 4th or 5th, we are having a big garden party.

That party is to "christen" my new fountain, which was my birthday present in 1980. Will has about finished connecting it, and just for fun, and an excuse for a party, we are having a christening. I still haven't figured out how I am going to make Sangria and hors d' for 26 people, do the serving, and enjoy myself, but I have just one week now to get ready. Want to make all the hors d' myself, and am trying not to plan more than one which will have to be baked at the last minute. I hope Will takes some pictures — if any are good, will try to drop a couple your way.

Also, I enrolled in a class in Calligraphy at Southwestern College. It started last week. It is for only 8 weeks. I have never been able to print, and she started us on the Roman alphabet. Mine looked terrible. One of my main troubles was to draw a straight line, even with the aid of graph paper. What am I going to do when she takes the graph paper away?

On the second page of Jane's typed letter, she spoke of Will's ill health, his recuperation from "the removal of the lymph nodes in the pelvic area." She also wrote that she enjoyed a relatively inactive summer, which allowed her time to make some gifts for Christmas. She continued:

We are hoping to drive to Mexico in about a month, to leave the middle of December, if the doctors give their okay. Therefore, I have to have everything done for Christmas by the first week in December, and I have so many gifts to buy. It is not so much the money but trying to figure out what to give, especially to Will's family.

I do hope you get out next year – maybe you can plan it around the X-FBI luncheon? We would love to be in New England in the fall. You may recall we had a trip planned a couple of years ago, but had to cancel.

Our garden has been so pretty this summer but now the flowers are fading and soon there will be just the green outside.

Well, seems to me I have about run out of news, but do want to say I don't see how you work five days a week, run a house, take care of the children, and be company to your husband. You are a marvel. And on top of all you keep yourself so immaculate and cute.

Well, I have missed hearing from you (my fault) but definitely do not want our correspondence to drizzle down to a "Christmastime thing".

Would just love to be in New England – your card was a real teaser. I have a feeling you are sort of partial now to life in the East rather than the West.

Thanks again, Marge, for taking the time to write when I was the one who owed you! Hopefully you will get this Monday. Much love, /s/ Jane

Guess you knew George Strong died.

George Strong was the first real FBI Agent I ever saw. He gave a "career day speech" at my high school in an effort to recruit clerks and stenos for the Bureau. My business teacher suggested that I fill out an application. It was customary for the Bureau, under the direction of J. Edgar Hoover, to hire young women (and young men too) right out of high school who could be molded into properly dedicated employees. Thank goodness Mr. Hoover's capabilities fell short of actually creating us into his own image and likeness! The training we received, however, undeniably stayed with us all our lives.

Mr. Strong epitomized what I always thought an FBI Agent should look like -- tall, tanned and usually wearing a hat.

As far as FBI recruits, Jack Keith told me that when he worked in the Washington Field Office, agents "tilled the soil" of Pennsylvania,

Virginia and West Virginia each spring for young men and women to work at Bureau headquarters.

~

3-18-81

Dear Marge:

Many thanks for your nice little letters with both the Christmas and birthday cards. So good to hear from you and know all is well with you.

How nice that your folks were with you last year and possibly again this year. Just sorry that probably cuts out my chance to see you this summer, however! I'm so glad we do keep in touch, for you know that you and Anne are two of my most favorite friends – and it is flattering to know that someone that much younger wants to keep in touch.

Speaking of Anne, I talked with her recently. They had been informed by Grosmont Center that the lease for their cleaners would not be renewed due to some other development scheduled in that spot. When they finally found a new location and started a cleaners called "Mom's," they were advised the Center would have relocated them someplace near! They had to pay a month's rent ($1,000) to hold the store "Mom's" until they could move into it; consequently, Anne has been working six days a week, and she said she is so worried about Nick for he has been working much too hard. I hope some day those people have a break. Guess I told you that Sharon is now a Senior in high school, is president of her student body, was "Miss La Mesa" this last year, and on the court of the "Fairest of the Fair" at Del Mar last summer. She is really a beautiful, natural girl. Nick, Jr. has turned into quite a handsome boy, too. What a pair they are!

We had a fine trip – were gone 35 days – and Will drove almost 5700 miles. No car trouble and no serious illness, so we felt pretty lucky. We saw many wonderful sights and had some great food – some bad, too, of course. I fell in love with "Tortilla Soup" all over again. Also had a "Lime Soup" in Yucatan, which is similar to the Tortilla. I made it for guests when I had a Mexican dinner recently, and they loved it also.

Did you know they are having the X-FBI Gals' convention here in SD in October? I voted against it, for I felt there was not time to plan and do a really bang-up job; however, it was pushed through by the present group in power. Ever since the group went National, I think it has lost some of its close feeling, but perhaps I am wrong.

I wrote Linda about our last luncheon and she promised to come down, but didn't. I am not mad, of course. Just miss seeing her. Never have met her husband, although they live not too far away. Guess she told you her father had died.

Sandie never comes to the luncheons. Quite a few who used to attend have dropped out. Of course, we have Helen and Kay now, so that helps.

Our garden is a mess. We were gone when the weeds started growing, so lost control, and neither of us has had time to get at it. I have loads of seeds to plant but can't seem to get at that either. I am taking a 10-week cake decorating class at Southwestern College, taught by McMains, the present owner of Standlee's Cake Shop in Chula Vista, if you know it. It is fun, but I really don't bake enough to keep in practice once the class is over.

Am having our group of gals to lunch 4-10-81 (12 of them); then on Easter Sunday hope to have about 12 of the family here for brunch, so already I see April fading into the distance. We have been invited to share a mobile home in Palm Springs for 5 nights the latter part of April, so that should be fun.

Must run – was just determined I would get some sort of note to you today. I have developed the annoying habit of awakening about 4:00 a.m. every morning (no matter what time I go to bed) and can't go back to sleep. This morning I arose at 5:45 and got down to some much-needed letter writing. The other two are business letters, so I picked you first for social correspondence. I correspond with quite a few and always seem to be behind.

Much love, and write when you can – always great to hear from you. /s/ Jane.

P.S. Will went to Southwestern College and learned how to install solar heat. He thinks he will have it completed in another week or two. Sure hope so. Our last bill, just for the two of us, was about $114. We have cut down every way we can think of! j

During the 1980's after my dad retired, my parents drove across country in their 1979 blue Toyota, stopping along the way in Illinois and Pennsylvania to visit relatives. Once they arrived in Bolton, they stayed for two to three weeks. Returning home from work, I'd find them playing games with their grandchildren or making supper. I'd always have a project or two lined up such as wallpapering the hall, or ripping out tile in the bathroom. On one of their last visits, Tom was in high school. His rock band "Mayhem" practiced in the basement, and I worried that my mom and dad would be bothered by the noise. But when "Mayhem" practiced, my mother ran the vacuum and my dad would make his own noise swinging a sledge hammer to a barbecue grill (which had become rusted and was no longer of use.)

When I visited them in California, I often stopped by Nick and Anne's cleaning establishment in Grosmont Center, which was near to where my parents lived. Sharon is Anne's daughter, and the young lady who served as the flower girl at Jane's wedding.

Sandie Marchand succeeded Helen as Chief Steno. When she resigned to accompany her husband to the Los Angeles area, I wrote 30 page letters, to keep her up-to-date with the goings-on in the steno pool. I believe that sometime after my move to Washington, D.C., we lost touch.

∾

7-2-81

Dear Marge:

I have really lost track of "who owes whom" but feel it is probably I. Glad we both understand how it seems to become harder, as time goes on, for us to sit down and write. I seem to want to be active, either in the garden, the house, or going someplace!

First of all, Will is doing fine. He has passed his first two six month checkups OK, so we just have four more years to go.

I suppose you are keeping up your busy schedule. Don't know how you do it all. How old are the kiddies now? I lose track of everyone's children. Will's grandchildren are becoming teenagers now, all except the children of the youngest son. They are in South Carolina. Wish we could see them without traveling back there!

I have had another busy time lately. Was asked to speak to my sorority Mother's Day Luncheon about our trip to Mexico. Took me 3 days to prepare it, one to give it, and another to put away all my purchases I trekked along. Then about ten days after that, I was in charge of decorating for the June tea of the Sweetwater Woman's Club. I did it all in roses – it came out very nicely, I believe – but was a lot of work; however, the type work I enjoy!

The last big project was a Greek dinner party, I put on last Saturday. I made everything except the bread and olives. Had 10, including us. It seemed to go off very well, and we all had a good time, so that is what matters most. I had bought cards at a Serbian Festival several years ago to use for invitations – Greek figures on the outside. I typed the invitation, inside, similar to the enclosed. The Carlsens went to Greece and I asked them to bring me 10 Greek stamps – the enclosed placecard has one of the stamps on it, purchased at the Acropolis. I got the Greek alphabet from the library, and it was up to the guests to figure out where their places were. These represent our initials "G.L." Also had dinner napkins like the cocktail one enclosed. The table had mirrors down the center with crystal candlesticks, green candles, and the centerpiece was a cut glass bowl filled with olive branches, which had tiny olives coming on them. Also Baby's Breath mixed in with the olive branches. Turned out pretty well. White linen tablecloth.

I guess you know that the national convention of the X-FBI Women is to be in San Diego in October. I hate to say it, but just between us, I don't feel the interest in the group I used to before we became national. Then it was just fun, and now there is lots of work. I told them I would help with decorations, but would not be a Chairman. It would be fun if you could come. Think you would have to join the national first, however.

Incidentally, Linda came to the last luncheon. She looks just great – thin as always, or even more so – cute short haircut and nice clothes. She seems very, very happy. She is such a nice gal. Doubt she will come again as I was the only one there she knew, and I did not make the luncheon part due to a conflict with a baby shower. We had a nice, short chat, however. Guess you know her father died some months ago.

I finished the calligraphy class long ago, but haven't had time to touch it since then!

Hope all is well with your folks and that you will have a nice summer. We are fine. Much love, /s/Jane.

My kids would have been eight and twelve in July of 1981, and probably driving me crazy since it was mid summer.

Martin Carlsen was an Agent in the San Diego office during my time there. Jane had become very good friends with him and his wife, Barbara, and speaks of them often in her letters.

~

10-1-81
Dear Marge:
I guess from the middle of August to the first of October isn't too bad? Not as we used to correspond, however.

Loved your letter, and thanks for the clipping with the picture of John. He looks well and happy – you must be taking good care of him!

You are such a busy gal, I appreciate a long letter from you even more. Hope your parents' visit was a happy one for all concerned. It is nice for them to be able to get such a change.

I haven't heard from Anne for quite a while. The last contact was in June at Sharon's graduation. Anne said she received several scholarships. She is planning to go to Occidental College. She wants to be a doctor.

I don't suppose you knew an Agent by the name of Buck Torrens, did you? Just in case, will tell you that he and his wife Harriet were in an automobile accident about a week ago and she lived only 12 hours afterward. Such a loving couple – 45 years of marriage – no children, so it will be doubly hard on Buck. I went to the Memorial Service Monday in Rancho Bernardo. They seem to be having more and more Memorial Services here instead of funerals.

You may know that the x-FBI Women's convention is to be next weekend in SD. I may have told you that I voted against it, but the present "regime" railroaded it through, which I resented. It has had little publicity from either our local group or from the national group. I believe they have about 35 reservations at the hotel and approx. 95 for the main banquet, including the local gals. I am on the decoration committee. I suggested the Mexican paper flowers, as the tablecloths are to be gold. Will and I went down to Tijuana and bought about 100 flowers. Yesterday, I separated all of them and made very low bouquets, all different colors, with 5 flowers in an arrangement. Think they will look quite festive. The meals and tours are quite expensive, so I plan to go just to the luncheon and banquet on Saturday. That will total $37, plus drinks!

Yes, we went to Palm Springs, but I was in great pain from a ruptured vein in my back, plus the place we stayed had no air-conditioning, and it was 98 the day we arrived! So, it really wasn't too successful, I'm sorry to say.

Yes, Will installed the Solar heat. Between that and the fact that we also have a passive clothes drier (clothesline), our bill has been cut almost in half. Of course, it will go up again in the winter months when we have our no-sun days and I have to use the drier.

It's really strange that you hear from Wanda so seldom. Too bad, for you two were so close.

We have had problems again, healthwise. About 3 months ago, Will began feeling badly, so to the doctor we went, only to find he had a 40 degree drop in BP when he stood up, and also had blood in his stool. He went right from the doctor's office to the hospital for 4 days of tests. Guess you know I was worried. Once you have had that old CA in your system, you never feel really safe. Well, after much time and tests, they said the bleeding was due to an aggravated hiatal hernia. He knew he had that, but it had never acted up to that degree before. After he came home, he went *downhill, so finally the doctor gave him a prescription for strong iron capsules, and that seemed to solve the problem. He is about back to normal now.*

I was talking with Anne the day he went in the hospital, and had to hang up because I began to cry and could not stop. I haven't heard from her since.

Then the minute Will began to feel better, I came down with a respiratory infection, which I got over after 3 weeks. Then, Monday, at the Memorial Service, I caught another cold! So, I have been hibernating since then. When you get to be a senior citizen, you just don't seem to be able to throw off things as before. I remember that at the time my Mother became an invalid, I had not been to a doctor for an annual physical for 20 years! So, I guess I had my share of good years.

Much love, /s/Jane.

Buck Torrens was an agent assigned to San Diego when I worked there. His name was Marion, but everyone called him Buck. Former Agent Stephen Gaughan, called him "The Commodore," however, because he thought Agent Torrens looked like he belonged on a ship.

~

I made a note on Jane's envelope – her "La Casa de las Chuparrosas" stationery – "answered w/Christmas card 12-6-81."

2-23-82

Dear Marge:

Now I am the one to hang my head! As you said, it seems to get harder and harder to make oneself get down to letter writing.

I have thought of you and my other friends in the East and in Minnesota all through this winter. I simply cannot imagine what it must be like. I suppose the kiddies love it, though. It doesn't seem possible you will be 40 in October. I always think of you the way you were when we used to have "breaks" together, and also when you first reported for duty. What a beauty you were (and still are, I am sure).

I hope John is long since over his gallbladder surgery. How is your job coming with the large computer outfit? Would think it pretty difficult to get back and forth to work this winter.

You know, if you and I were now in the Bureau, we would probably have some type of administrative position with a great increase in ratings and pay. When I think of how hard we worked and how little they say the gals work in the office now, comparatively, it makes me a bit angry – and they get the money! Oh well, I am just happy I did not quit when we were married, as we really could not get along now on Will's retirement alone. Thank goodness, too, for Social Security. It is a boon to us. I just hope the Government comes through with our promised raise in April since they have taken away the October increase. You mentioned the "word processor" and needing to use it at work these days. Just how does it work?

You asked about Anne. First of all, I was really relieved to learn you felt I was not being super sensitive about her not calling me after I broke down on the phone when I told her about Will's condition. It turned out OK, but at the time it did sound frightening. When one has had cancer in his system, any inward bleeding usually means just one thing. Will is fine now but has to be careful to take all his medicine for the hiatal hernia so that the same condition will not pop up again. Of course, since he is still on the blood thinner that makes the situation even more serious.

Back to Anne. When I still had not heard from her at Christmas (the first time), I thought that perhaps Nick was sick again and that I had been harboring false thoughts, so one day I called the house and Nick answered. I asked if he was OK, and he breezily said, "Just great, doll". Anne was not at home. I inquired about Sharon also. I told him to tell Anne I had called. She usually sends me a birthday card, so we will wait to see.

Do you remember the reports you used to take from Mike Hennigan about Bompensiero, and Cosa Nostra? Well, you probably heard that Bomp was shot to death a couple of years ago near his home in SD. Now, Fratianno is testifying for the government in connection with allegations of mob control and infiltration of the fancy resort La Costa. Very interesting. Seems he went to a meeting with some of the mafia bosses some years back at which they plotted the murder of Desi Arnaz!!

I am fine except for having developed rather severe arthritis in my right knee, which is the leg I had stripped of varicose veins several years ago. Also had a light attack of phlebitis. This growing old is no fun, but so far I have managed to keep active as usual. Had a big dinner party for 10 ten days ago. I must admit, however, that I was in bed most of the next day! But it is all fun.

Well, that about brings you up-to-date. Hope all is well with you and yours. Do write when you can.

Much love, /s/ Jane

P.S. You are the only one I have mentioned this to, but we are thinking of coming East in October. We hope to take the Tauck Tour through New England and will probably be spending the 5th night of the tour in Boston, probably at the Sheraton Boston. Our meals are included and paid for, but I was hoping perhaps just you and I could get together for a chat after dinner. Perhaps it is too far for you to travel by yourself, but I thought I would mention it now just in case you have any thoughts. I went to the Travel Agent today and made a down payment for the tour beginning in NYC on Tuesday, October 5th. We do not come anywhere near you on our return. Hope we can work something out. jane

As far as the job with the "large computer outfit" – it was Digital Equipment Corp., which as I said before, just wasn't my "cup of tea."

With reference to taking reports from Mike Hennigan about La Cosa Nostra – I took a tremendous amount of dictation from Mr. Hennigan and others during that investigation. Bompensiero was one of Mr. Hennigan's informants.

Once when transcribing from a "bug" that had been planted, one of the "mafia guys" said he "had to take a leak." I had never heard the expression! (It was used recently on a popular weekly t.v. program. Oh, how things have changed since the 1960s!) My tour of duty with the FBI was educational in many ways! When an agent had dictation on a case having to do with the White Slave Traffic Act -- or anything to do with sex -- they requested a married steno – usually Jeanine Batis or Sandie Marchand! If those two were busy, the agent would have to settle for an "experienced," single steno.

During my lengthy telephone conversation with the ex-agent, Stephen Gaughan, he related the following story about Bompensiero. (During his assignment to the San Diego office, he often amused us with his tales of days as a Pinkerton Detective in New York.)

Stephen had just arrived in San Diego from Savannah. Being a "second office" agent, he was allowed to go off on his own. During a routine investigation of a certain Willie Cruz, who was running prostitutes to migrant workers, he checked out a lead. Cruz had listed Frank Bompensiero as a former employer from ten years previous, apparently supplying a phone number. Agent Gaughan dialed the number and Bompensiero's daughter answered. She then put her father on the phone. When Agent Gaughan inquired about Cruz, Bompensiero couldn't imagine that this was legitimate, so asked to talk to Agent Gaughan in person. A meeting was arranged, during which Bompensiero commented that he had just gotten out of San Quentin. When he inquired simply if Cruz was a former employee, Bompensiero was dumbfounded that this was all the agent wanted to know. Upon returning to the office, Agent Gaughan mentioned to some other agents having talked to Bompensiero. All of a sudden, agent "Dutch" Strahl jumped out of his chair and started yelling at Gaughan. He and other agents who had been assigned to work La Cosa Nosta were planning to develop him as an informant – unbeknownst to Gaughan, of course. Reportedly Agent Mike Hennigan managed to calm everyone down.

~

Jane and Will did make it to Boston – on my 40th Birthday, and I drove myself into the big city to meet them. We had dinner at a Polynesian restaurant within the hotel. Our visit lasted until midnight, and as feared, I got lost trying to get out of Boston, somehow managing to drive into the notorious "combat zone." Eventually I found my way to the Mass. turnpike and back to my quiet home in Bolton.

Jane mailed a postcard of the Red Jacket Mountain View Motor Inn, No. Conway, N.H., dated 10-13-82.

Dear Marge. We are in flight now from NYC to Atlanta. Saw Museums – Met and Natl History yesterday – both tremendous. Our guide who asked to be introduced to you approached Will the next day and wanted to know whether or not you are married! You really made an impression. Love, Jane.

I also have a note on stationery from the Quality Inn Palace, New Bern, NC, dated Oct. 24th which reads:

Dear Marge –

Just a note to thank you for making the effort to drive to Boston to see us, especially on your birthday and with your sister visiting you. It was wonderful to see you again, and see you looking so young and so chic. Motherhood evidently agrees with you.

Oh, did I tell you that the next morning after our dinner, our young guide approached Will to ascertain your marital status! I later warned him that should your paths ever again cross, he'd better take care since your husband was an FBI Agent. I also, another time, said something about our having visited late and he asked if you were a talker. (He's a great talker.) I said yes – you could talk and I didn't know who would win were the two of you together. He said no problem – if you were together there would be no talking! He certainly was impressed with you.

Also wanted to tell you that at the Bennington Museum in New England, there was a special wing devoted to the life and works of Grandma Moses. A picture of her on her 100th birthday showed her in a dark dress with a cameo pin at the neck. The gold setting for the cameo was exactly the same as the setting for the cameo I gave you, although her cameo was larger. Thought you might like to know.

There will be so much to do when I get home, I wanted to get this written while on the trip.

Much love, and hope to see you again before many years pass.

Jane

Some time before this, Jane had given me a small cameo pin, which belonged to her mother. She also gave me a beautiful silver serving spoon when I was married.

$\sim$

MERRY CHRISTMAS – 1982

And, now, we wish for you and yours the best of holiday seasons.

Love – Jane

The reverse side contains a handwritten note:

Dear Marge –You know all this but thought you might like it anyway. Thanks for your letter – always enjoy your missives. Best of Holidays and much love - Jane

~

A postcard, dated 10-19-83, reads:

Dear Marge: Please know you are thought about a lot and I realize I owe you a letter, but it may be awhile as things have gotten more complicated here. Will was all set up for rectal surgery, but over the weekend became ill and, to make a long story short, was operated on this morning for emergency removal of the gallbladder. So far as they could tell before the biopsies came back, there was no malignancy, for which I thank the Lord and hope the biopsies reflect the same. He was very thin to begin with and hasn't had any solid food since 10-15-83. He is, of course, being fed intravenously now. He is in a lot of pain. I am ready to go to the hospital for the 4th time today – he is semi-awake, so I come home in between to try to get some things done. Hope all is well there. Much love, Jane.

~

A letter dated 11-3-83 is written on notepaper with a hummingbird at a thistle.

Dear Marge:

This will be a quickie, just to keep in touch and so you will know I am OK. Things have been hectic around here since the middle of October, when Will had emergency surgery for removal of the gallbladder. The organ was so enlarged and inflamed that, even after a day and a half in the hospital being fed intravenously, (before the operation), the surgeon told Will he had a hard time getting the gallbladder out. He has a huge scar. Guess the recovery period will be pretty slow.

When I think of Christmas, I feel like going and hiding somewhere, what with the 100 cards we send out and about 35 presents to buy, wrap, and deliver. I love to decorate the house, but right now it looks like a HUGE task.

I could go on and on, but don't like to write blue letters and am really not in the mood to write a comical or chatty one. Just wanted you to know the reason you haven't heard from me recently. Don't worry – things will ultimately straighten out and I will feel much better in no time at all.

Much love, /s/Jane

PS. Will also had cirrhosis of the liver, which could remain stable or get gradually worse.

~

Stationery of gray with bright pink flamingos wearing silver roller skates dancing across the top, Rockette style, is dated 1-24-84.

Dear Marge:

Am writing on my favorite notepaper – it is called "Keeping in Touch"!

You were so good to write so soon – and, again, I am remiss! What with Will's surgery 10-19-83, Christmas, company, and now the task of fixing up his house in Chula Vista to rent, things have been very busy, and I found myself extremely tired after Christmas. Am back to normal now and trying to get caught up with my correspondence.

We went to the Doc today, and Will got a good report on his liver function. Am sure I told you that he has cirrhosis of the liver, having had yellow jaundice when he was 13. Of course, he was a great beer drinker when he matured, which irritated the condition. The liver is very bad, but the doctor hopes that with no liquor intake at all, it will stabilize; if not, there is nothing to be done. I heaved a sigh of relief today.

February will be taken up in part with getting together our figures for the income tax to take to the accountant. I don't even try to do it myself, as I don't know how to depreciate his rental, etc., and since I do everything else in a business way, would rather pay to have it done.

Went to the X-Agents' Christmas party at the Hotel del Coronado this year at the invitation of the Munoz; really enjoyed it. Mr. Keith came over particularly to ask about you and Linda. He would love to hear from you whenever you come out this way again. Do you have any plans, or are your folks going to visit you this year?

Thanks for the last pictures you sent of the children. They are really bright looking youngsters. Doesn't seem possible they can be yours – little, cute Marge who came to work at the FBI – so young, lovely, and INNOCENT! (I think!). I surely was at that age.

I have slowed down on the entertaining – big parties, etc. Last August, I developed an extremely painful foot. I went to the podiatrist and he took X-rays, only to report that I have spurs on both heels and that the one on the right foot is fractured. Consequently, I have to wear some acrylic inserts called either "appliances" or "orthodics" in my shoes from now on. Consequently, again, I can't wear sandals or any really stylish shoe, except perhaps occasionally just for a few hours, if I am going to be sitting most of the time. I also broke off a tooth today on the upper jaw in front, right at the gumline. Plus, next Wednesday, I have to have gum surgery – the periodontist will transplant good gum tissue from the upper jaw to the lower. Am not looking forward to it.

Other than the above, we are fine. Will has his good days, but mostly he just wants to sit. Guess that will be the pattern from now on.

Do you still hear from Wanda? Mr. Keith wanted to know about her also. There was little I could tell him, so you might fill me in and next time I see him will give him more of a report.

I never seem to have time to sew anymore, but last year I really suffered with our humidity, especially since I had not one real cool dress to wear around the house. Polyester pants are so hot. So, I bought some plain turquoise cotton and do hope to be able to get it done, using a simple pattern, before summer comes. Will enclose a sample if I do not forget.

Did I ever tell you that Helen Kilgore had a breast-reduction operation last year? You wouldn't believe how slim she looks now.

Can't think of any more news, and I'd better get started on dinner. Hope everything is great with you and yours. Write when you can and bring me up-to-date. Much love ----/s/Jane

Louis Munoz was a Spanish speaking agent who investigated ITSMV (Interstate Transportation of Stolen Motor Vehicle) cases wherein the cars were transported across the border to Mexico.

Mr. Keith was an Assistant Special Agent in Charge assigned to San Diego while I was there. He was well liked -- "southern gentleman" type. When *West Side Story* hit the movie theaters, several of the girls in the office raved about it, which seemed to astonish Mr. Keith.

~

A letter dated 6-8-84 is engraved with Jane's initials at the top.

Dear Marge:

It's been so long since you wrote me that I cannot locate your letter, so hope there were no questions. I have seen Anne – in fact, she came to the X-FBI Gals' meeting in May and looked just great. Her hair is a short cut and has quite a bit of grey in it, but that seems to make her even more attractive. She said Nick was doing just fine. They have had so much trouble, and she had worked so hard. The daughter is in college and is studying to be a doctor.

Guess you received a card from me when we were on our recent three-week trip through the Pacific Northwest. We had a fine trip, but ran into rain, rain, and more rain. Didn't bother too much except in Victoria and Vancouver, B.C., and on our way home down the Oregon Coast, which I had always heard was so beautiful. The first day we could hardly see the coast, but it did partially clear the second day and it was indeed beautiful. We had two nights in Vancouver, but Will was feeling lousy and so we didn't do or see much there, plus it was raining. However, in Victoria, it cleared enough for us to go to the beautiful Buchart

Gardens. We went late in the day, had a light dinner at their little café, then sat in the car for an hour or so (to keep warm), and went back to see the gardens when they are lighted at night. Really gorgeous.

The first part of our trip, we went up through the Gold Country – Sonora, etc. I love that section of the country. Two of our friends were there with their motor home, so we got together with them, which was fun.

We just received word that Will's youngest son, wife, five and seven-year-olds, are arriving on the bus Saturday from South Carolina. I guess they are planning to stay here at least for a few days. I am not geared to all those people around. Just hope I pull through without a migraine.

Do hope all is well with you. You are so busy and accomplish so much. Must take more time than 24 hours a day! Will love to hear from you whenever you can write. Love, /s/ Jane

1-4-85

Dear Marge:

I have been wanting to write you ever since I rec'd your card, with enclosed note. I can't tell you how sorry I am to learn that John is no longer living at home. I resent the fact (altho' it isn't any of my business) that he let you go ahead and fix up that room for him, sand, paint, etc., his desk, and then moved out! I know it has been coming on for years, but had hoped he would see the light and realize what a jewel he has in you and how hard you have tried to hold the family together. It is so sad, and I grieve for you. At this point, it doesn't sound as though a happy ending is in store, but we can always hope.

I just trust that, whenever he retires, you will come in for a good chunk of his retirement. Are you still doing reporting for the paper? You really have a talent for writing. If I have an extra copy, I'll enclose an article I wrote about San Diego at the request of the headquarters of the Society of Former FBI Women. Each issue of their newsletter features one city in which there is a local chapter, and I guess the next one will be San Diego. I had never done anything like this before and really "sweated it out", but headquarters seemed pleased. They probably will cut it down to some extent, but I left that up to them. One of my friends who has done quite a bit of writing, says I could probably sell it to a travel magazine, but I don't think I will bother.

We went to the X-Agents' Christmas party and saw quite a few you would know – Mr. Keith among them. He always asks for you. I probably won't see him until next Christmas, but should I, would you mind if I told him about John? The only person I have told is Anne, and I am sure you would tell her were you to see her. Hope that's OK. I suppose your folks know? I also hope you will tell the family how long this has been going on. Do you think you would ever care to live in SD again? Sounds as though you are in love with the East, and I know how much you think of John's family. I suppose if his new set-up is as he anticipates, he will be wanting a divorce one of these days. Oh, Marge, I am just so, so sorry about the whole thing. You deserve someone fine.

Will seems to be a bit better. He gained 2 ½ pounds in the last month, which is the first real gain he has made. Still is very, very thin and not much energy (especially to do any work!), but at least we are now hopeful that he can improve. Can't remember whether or not I told you his problem is a combination of cirrhosis of the liver and non-function of the pancreas. The two together upset the digestion of his food, and it seems everything had just been passing through without his absorbing the vitamins, minerals, etc. Our drug bill last month was almost $350. SAMBA has advised they will pay for no vitamins, minerals, shots, etc. We asked the doctor to write a letter explaining that none of this treatment, nor medications, is for preventive care but, rather, maintenance and/or improvement. Well, if the insurance won't pay, we will just have to. Medicare is no help at all in this regard.

Do hope 1985 will see some happiness in store for you, and that, somehow, things will turn for the better. Write when you can. I know you are a busy gal. Much, much love --- /s/ Jane

PS. Can you believe I will be 70 in March? Doesn't seem possible to me, and I DON'T LIKE IT!!

The reason I told Anne was that we took some special cleaning over to their cleaners yesterday. They are doing well, but can't get

*good help and are working about 10 hours a day each right now.
Worn out. Sharon is a senior, to be graduated in June; Nick, Jr. is
in his first year of college. j*
　PPS. How did Christmas go?

After years of trying desperately to hold my marriage together,
John decided to move out of our home in Bolton. It became apparent
that he was still involved with the woman from New Jersey, and was
making no plans to end the relationship. I was devastated to learn that
she had moved to Massachusetts. And yes, it was about this time, in
late 1984, that I had just finished staining all the new wood paneling
and built in desk in his study. I had also wallpapered the room, and
had it carpeted.

Thinking back now, I remember John had said to me, "You expect
things to be perfect." Funny thing was, I thought it was he who was
looking for perfection. It wasn't so much that I expected things to be
perfect – but I did expect his love to be undying and that he would put
as much effort into the marriage as I did. I was deeply crushed that he
would turn to someone else. I became depressed, and talked him into
going for counseling, which did not help. My friends, especially Jane,
became my sounding board. She allowed me to express my frustrations,
offered support, and kept assuring me that there was "nothing wrong"
with me, as I often claimed. In fact, she often chastised me for making
that statement.

I was writing for a local newspaper at the time – the Bolton
Correspondent to the Clinton *Daily Item*, reporting on Board of
Selectmen, Planning Board, School Committee and Town Meetings.
I also wrote many feature stories about local people, as well as feature
farm stories in the annual premium book for the Bolton Fair.

～

4-17-85
Dear Marge:
*First of all, let me say how shocked I was to read of that terrible
accident! I do hope the effects of the concussion have passed and that
you will have no lasting problem from the accident. I'm just so sorry.*

You said you did not think John was living with "the other woman". I wonder what happened? Have you ever seen her, know what she looks like, what age, etc.? I should think you would be most curious. I can't understand a father who can't "cope" with his son's growing up. What a strange person!

Re your desire to be employed as a writer. I am enclosing parts of letters from my friend, with some suggestions for you. I think her latest idea of your training as an Interior Decorator is a good one. You do have a knack for fixing up your own home and always seem to have lots of ideas.

We did see Linda – took her to lunch. Her husband was ill or we would have included him – just a cold or something. She looks great and is really an outgoing, sharp gal, as you know. They were planning a trip to Mexico, and she was going to call me for names of some places we had enjoyed, but I never did hear from her. Perhaps they just canceled the whole thing in view of the uproar of the Camarena case. Don't know whether that got any publicity in your area, but he was a Mexican – but US citizen – employed in the Government field of narcotics cases. He was murdered in Guadalajara. The man was from Calexico, I believe. I understand tourism in Mexico is down about 30% as a result of this case and some others.

I had not received your letter saying it would be OK to tell Linda about your situation, so I did not mention you. Let me know when you plan to be in SD so we can get together.

We are planning to leave Saturday on Amtrak for a little 8-day trip. Will stay over one day in Salt Lake, and hopefully hear the Mormon Tabernacle Choir. Then, on to Denver, where we will be four days. We will not stop on the return home. Will has never had a train trip, so we thought we'd better do it now, since, if the subsidy is taken away, Amtrak might fold up. And just a few minutes ago, I heard on TV that there had been an accident out of Denver and three cars derailed and went in the river! Well, you aren't safe in the air, on the highways, or in your home anymore!

Wouldn't you know – I haven't had a cold in years, but last Saturday night I came down with a dilly. I seem to be prone, every time I do get a cold, to have it turn into bronchitis. And we are to leave in 3 more days! I think I will call the doctor this morning and perhaps get some medication. The time we went on the Delta Queen, I left home sick with bronchitis and really did not enjoy the trip to the utmost.

I wanted to get this off to you before we leave, and May is going to be a mess – three different groups of people coming. You can bury me afterwards!

Will has picked up a little since the first of the year. He lost 30 pounds. Our medicine bills run between $300 and $400 a month. Then he takes four different shots a week, which are expensive. Don't know what we'd do without SAMBA. Hope you can keep it all your life.

Not much other news – just hope the enclosures will be of some help to you. Much love, /s/ Jane

PS. Sharon, Anne's daughter, will be graduated from college in June; doesn't seem possible! She was my flower girl!

The car accident to which Jane referred happened one day when the roads were slippery and I lost control of my car and skid head-on into a tree. The car was totaled. I was unconscious when the ambulance arrived, but remember someone asking me if I knew my name. When I woke up in Clinton Hospital, I called my kids, and my in-laws. Blood was caked to my eyelashes, and I had a cut on my hairline, which required seven or eight stitches. I suffered a concussion, which became aggravated by a sinus infection a few days later. I couldn't read for weeks.

John had a tough time dealing with his children as they were growing up. He usually maintained his sense of humor, telling our son on his 13th birthday that he would give him "six months to get through your teenage years!"

Jane sent me some advice from a writer friend of hers, since I was "toying" with the idea of writing a book about my mother's childhood days in an orphanage. A box of typewritten pages of "Tales from an Orphanage and Beyond," awaits completion. I decided to go to work for a wallpaper and paint store instead, and started attending Becker Junior College, where I pursued a degree in Interior Design.

96

8-25-85

Dear Marge:

To be "socially correct", this note should be handwritten, but I am sure you will excuse the type. Just wanted to thank you again for the lovely lunch and companionship. It is always such a treat to see and chat with you, and I thoroughly enjoyed our extended lunch. Just hated for you to spend your hard-earned money on me!

I haven't talked with Anne, so don't know whether you were able to reach her or not. No one ever hears from Sandie any more.

Well, you timed the weather right. It is in the 90's on our front porch. After our nice cool weather, it is harder than ever to take.

Do keep me posted when you can re your progress as an authoress and/or anything else of interest in your life.

Best of luck in all you do – you know you have an admirer in me! Much love, /s/ Jane

PS. This is short because we got pretty well caught up, I think! J

Jane thought that her note should have been handwritten, because she used personal stationery. I made a note on the envelope: "answered 9-5-85."

~

12-7-85

Dear Marge:

You did so well answering my last letter, I feel guilty in the long delay I have taken. I owe everyone – friends are even calling long-distance to know whether or not I am ill!

I am late getting to Christmas this year. We send out about 100 cards, and I like to put notes in some, letters in others.

I knew Anne would love it if you called her, for she is always so interested in your welfare. So glad you had a good chat and I hope you can see her next trip out.

Have you heard from Wanda? You said you hadn't been able to reach her at the time John wanted you to go with him to Myrtle Beach. Did you finally decide not to go?

I am anxious to know how the writing is coming. Have you ever tried to write anything about or for children? Your experience as a mother should prepare you for something along that line.

I feel sure I told you that George Strong and Orrantia had died, but just recently Buck Torrens died. I think he had a malignant brain tumor and I understand the end was pretty sad. His wife, Harriet, and he were in an auto accident five years or so ago, and she died the next day. He had remarried about two years ago. Mrs. Orrantia also was recently in an auto accident, and has been hospitalized for a couple of months now. Last I heard, they couldn't tell whether or not she even recognizes her children. She was in a coma for about 6 weeks, but now is out of that. No prognosis for the future. She has shown a bit of improvement; so sad.

This darn typewriter is skipping again at the first of the margin. I hate to take it in as they charge $25 minimum. Figure my friends can put up with the empty space!

Will has been feeling better the last 4 or 5 months than he has in 4 or 5 years, but now has had a pain hit him in the groin and back area. Kidney stones have been ruled out by two hospital tests, so now the doctor is giving him antibiotics in the event the trouble is inflammation. If that doesn't work, guess he'll have to go to a urologist. Always something!

I'm OK, for which I thank my lucky stars, both for my sake and since someone around here has to be healthy!

Hope things are fine with you and that you will have a fine Christmas and that something really nice and exciting is in store for you in 1986!

Much, much love -------- /s/ Jane

I believe the last time I travelled to South Carolina to visit Wanda was in 1975.

≈

A letter from Jane, dated 1-31-86, is typed on stationery with little hummingbirds in the left bottom corner.

Dear Marge:

This is a pretty fast reply for me – not quite a month since I received your letter!

I can't say I envy you that rock group practicing in your cellar; think I would go mad! I'm just too old for that stuff!

You said John told you he was going to New Jersey for Christmas Day. Who's in NJ? It didn't sound as though "the" girl lived there. You said John and she lived in the same town – surely John doesn't live in NJ?

It sounds as though you might as well carry on as the wife in order to get the support you are receiving, for how could you educate the children, etc. just on your own – and I am sure you want them to have an education.

Have you heard from the Ladies Home Journal yet re your story?

You mentioned having called your folks at Christmastime and that they both had colds. I don't know when I remember a winter with so much illness – if it isn't a head cold, it is the flu or bronchitis. I came down with the latter again (had it badly in May) two weeks before Christmas, and just this week have not had to go back to bed once or twice a day to rest. It always hits me so hard. I'm thankful I do not have to get out and shovel snow and/or walk on icy streets!

I imagine the astronaut disaster hit New England terribly hard. I don't know when anything has touched me so. I think, and know, that the whole country mourned.

A couple of years ago, I joined an organization that the Munoz had mentioned – "AFIO" – Association of Former Intelligence Officers. Although I was not an "officer," I found I was eligible. They have monthly dinner and/or luncheon meetings at which they have speakers. We are going to a meeting tonight at which the speaker is supposed to be excellent. We always sit with the Munoz and sometimes the Prices, so haven't really gotten acquainted with other members. Will doesn't care for it, but this time I just went ahead and made a reservation without checking with him. We have been only about four times in two years, and I figure that much won't hurt him! We have been "house-bound" for so long, it will be good to get out, and how nice not to have to get dinner for a change! I have gotten so much more done today.

I learned that the Historical Societies of California are trying to get together a record of California's heritage quilts, so I will be taking probably four quilts my Mother made in to the San Diego Gas and Electric Auditorium on 2-14-86 to show. The "most historical" quilt of the day is to receive $100. I don't think any of mine will qualify, but I thought I owed it to my Mother to show them. I am very proud of them.

I made a new friend recently – a darling young (to me) girl in her early forties who is the dental technician at my dentist's office. She had me out to see her home the day before yesterday, and then took me to lunch at Piret's in Grossmont Center. She is so much fun and makes me feel younger and peppier. I won't see her often, however, as she is very busy, working several days a week, taking care of a 4,000 sq. foot home, a daughter 20 or 21, and her husband. She does a lot of gardening and gourmet cooking. You should see that house! It is full of beautiful antiques. Her name is Sue Becker, her husband is a dentist, and she is a Junior Leaguer. Seems like every time I get together with my contemporaries, all they talk about is their aches and pains, and I come away more dejected than when I went.

We went to the X-Agents' Christmas Party this year. It was held at the Inn in Rancho Santa Fe. Very nice.

Incidentally, did you ever go to see the girlfriend? When you wrote, you were considering it. I guess it's OK now for me to mention her and John, now that he is no longer at home. If not, let me know.

Well, I'd better be getting on to some necessary phone calls. I hope by now the "ole stomach has stopped churning" and you are feeling more hopeful about life. It's not like you to be anything but bubbly. I'm just so sorry your life can't be that way for you deserve the very best.

With much love, /s/ Jane

My son, who played the drums from the time he was about nine years old, had formed a rock group, called "Mayhem" when he was in high school. The basement literally vibrated with such wild and crazy "songs" as "Black Heart Rosie," and "Party Hardy!" It was a trying time for us all!

With regard to Jane's questions about John's going to New Jersey, for Christmas, whether "the girl" lived there, etc. "The girl's" family lived in New Jersey and apparently John was going with her to be with her family for the holidays.

With regard to Jane's comment about my carrying on as "the wife," I feared that I would never be able to make it on my own if I divorced. In my most desperate times, I pictured myself as a bag lady!

The "girl" was 15 years John's junior.

I don't recall what I submitted to the *Ladies Home Journal*.

The astronaut disaster referred to, of course, was the Challenger explosion, with Christa McAuliffe on board – another occasion when most of us can remember where we were when we heard the news!

∼

The following letter from Jane is on notepaper with a drawing of the famous Hotel del Coronado "circa 1886" on the front. The letter is dated 4-8-86.

> *Dear Marge:*
>
> *Many thanks for your nice letter of 3-4-86. You are so good to write all that longhand! That was something about John going to spend Christmas with the girlfriend's family. Either the parents are extremely modern and broad-minded, or they feel that in time John will marry her. Can't understand any of the situation, anyhow. I wonder – does she work, go to school, or just sit home pining for John?*
>
> *The job you were about to start sounds good. You love to be with people, you have decorating ability, and I think you should be an excellent sales person. I do hope you enjoy it and that it will lead to something. Just don't earn so much that John feels he no longer has as much obligation to you as before.*
>
> *I had no idea you were interested in drawing. I would give anything to have the ability. Of course, I never had any instruction. Feel I could have done something in the art or craft field had I had*

some training. I feel a great void in my life there; also that I never had any children, particularly a daughter. Hope you and Sarah are close. Good for you to be taking both that and the literature classes.

Our only couple with whom we go places has illness. The man developed cancer a couple of years ago and it is now beginning to get crucial. He has extensive bone cancer and is now beginning chemo. We will certainly miss another couple with whom to do things. I know what you mean about being separated and not able to get together with other couples.

You asked about the quilt fair. It was a fun experience, although we carted 4 quilts from the car to the auditorium in a heavy rain! Everyone raved about all the quilts, particularly the "Mother Goose Quilt". I guess we did not win anything and I have been unable to find out who did get the $100 prize. Makes you wonder if that part was a "gimmick". Anyhow, I am glad I made the effort to wash and iron and get them ready; felt I owed it to my Mother.

Well, guess it's time to tell you that Will had surgery again – 4-4-86. He had two abdominal hernias which had been bothering him for about 6 months. He has a huge scar, six inches, on his tummy. He came home Sunday, 4-6-86. Guess he's doing OK, just so tired, weak, and sore. Naturally, this puts some extra chores on me, but I am canceling "social engagements" so I do not overdo and get too tired. As long as I can get a good night's sleep, I'm OK. I do not have to get up with him at night, thank goodness. We counted up that this makes his 9th hospitalization since 1967 when we were married, and I have had two surgeries, so think this should be the end!

This is my last piece of this stationery which was designed by an artist friend. I thought you would like to have it.

Do hope things are going better and that the new job has perked up your feelings. You are a wonderfully brave gal, and I love you. Always your friend, /s/ Jane

There is an added handwritten note:

"The snapshot is the only decent picture I have had in years. I was cutting the cake. They honored me as the founder of the local group."

Once my divorce was imminent, I decided to get a "regular" job. Writing for the newspaper didn't pay much and certainly came with no benefits. I answered an ad for a job at a wallpaper and paint store in Hudson, Mass., where I was a customer. When I went in to talk to the owner, he was out. As I looked around the store, I panicked. I knew nothing about selling paint, wallpaper and carpeting. I scurried home, only to receive a call from Joe as soon as I got in the door. He insisted that I was perfect for the job.

I took a basic drawing class at a local night school – something I always thought I wanted to learn. It didn't come naturally, but I stuck it out and was pleased with the results. I was also taking literature classes at Framingham State College.

~

9-1-86

Dear Marge:

Don't fall over with the prompt reply! We plan to leave 9-22-86 on a driving tour; first for one night to visit Will's son and wife in Prescott, Ariz., then on to Canyon de Chelly in Arizona, Navajo country. From there, into Colorado and Utah to spots we have not covered. I would like to garage the car at our most northern point and fly from there to visit friends in northern Montana for a few days. The man, Gordon Sands, went to school to my Mother when she taught a short time in Montana. He was only about 5 then. His mother was my mother's best friend. We visited them quite some years back, and Gordon and Will hit it off fine. They are not well, and Will is not well, either, so while we are still in one piece, I would love to see them. We'll be back about 10-11-86.

So good that you are close to John's family. You are doing great! Even sound better in this letter. I am thankful he gives you financial aid, although I think it should be more. Sounds as though you are really happy with that job. The man is lucky to have found you!

Those fortune-tellers are something. I went to one in L.A. in the early forties, who told me things about myself that were startling. Also, went one time with my Mother to the Spiritualist Church in SD. It was just after I had applied for steno work in the FBI. That gal told me amazing things, both in the past and future which were true. I was so impressed, I went for a private reading, which was useless!

No, I never did find out who won the $100 for the quilt. I tried a couple of ways, but nothing worked. However, I don't believe there was any dishonesty.

Will has recovered from his April surgery, but the combo of cirrhosis of the liver and pancreatis keeps him down most of the time. By that, I mean no pep and does practically nothing any more. He has lost weight recently too.

Our drug bill you wouldn't believe – anywhere from $275 to $525 a month! Right now I am arguing with SAMBA as they have been bouncing drugs which are on prescription, but really can be obtained over-the-counter. I got another letter from the doctor, and spent hours going back over my records, getting Xerox copies of everything, and then hours more composing the cover letter. It means at least $200 a month to us, so keep your fingers crossed.

The photo I sent you is really flattering – that is the reason I had a lot of copies made to send friends! It doesn't show any wrinkles or age spots. Wish I really looked that young!

The old eyes are still with me but much better. I went to three opthamologists before I found one who I thought could help me, and he has. The only problem is that he is at Scripps in La Jolla. He performed what they call a "Punctual Occlusion" which means he cauterized the opening to the lower tear ducts, thus enabling any natural tears and/or artificial tears to stay in the eyes longer. It has helped a lot. Instead of having to put in drops every 30 to 60 minutes, I do it, on a normal day, 4 or 5 times. If I get overly tired or am in air-conditioning, wind, or Santana, then I am much more uncomfortable and need to use more. Next, I had my eyelids "tucked" on 8-14-86. I looked horrible the next morning

– terribly swollen and black and blue. The discoloration is much less now, but I still have some swelling above the eyes. He may have to take one lid in a bit more as I think the right eye is a bit wider open than the left.

My kitty insists on sitting on my lap, and Will is across the breakfast room table staring at me, so it is not an ideal situation!

Can't think of any special news. Probably the minute I seal this letter I will.

I wish Linda would come out, or at least call sometime when she is here. I feel sure she must come down at times to see her Mother.

Oh, yes, about my friend who has written "A Little Death Music." It is to be published in Feb. or March in case you want to look out for it. I worked with her in the FBI in the early 40's. She left the Bureau and went with Army Intelligence, I believe, as a steno and was transferred to Heidelberg where she met and married a fine, smart young Army officer. She is very cultured, plays the piano beautifully, and has been giving lessons for years. It was a great surprise to find out that she is also a writer. I wish I knew whether or not she went to school and where, so I could "pick her brains" for you. I really wanted you to meet her and talk with her, but I wrote asking if the Carlsens could look her up this fall in their home in Paris, and she never replied to that.

PS. Am replying so fast as when we get home we may have guests and then suddenly Christmas work will begin.

My writer friend lives in Boston. They hope now that her husband is retired they can spend 6 months in Boston and six months in Paris. Quite a life, no? j

During the summer of 1986, I spent two weeks at York Beach, Maine, with my sister-in-law. One rainy morning, while doing our laundry downtown, Pat decided to pay a visit to Pauline – a card reader and fortune teller, located across the street. She was amazed by what Pauline had to say, and encouraged me to go. I was reluctant but went later on. Her revelations were incredible about the man to whom I was married. She said he was "mixed up" and would be suggesting a move back home. That week, when John came to see the kids, he did in fact make that suggestion. He came back for a week or so, but changed his mind.

~

12-31-86
Dear Marge:
On the last day of the year, I shall try to get a letter off to you! After Christmas, I had 11 thank-you's and general correspondence to catch up on. Am getting there, but slowly.

Have you made arrangements yet for a weekend with Wanda? Let me know how she is, if you do get together. Re: photos from our trip, there are none. They cost so much and we found we were looking at them once after we got home and perhaps showing them to a close friend or two, then burying them forever – so we quit taking snapshots. Also, it is a lot of trouble carrying around a camera as large as Will's. He bought two rolls of film before we left which are still sitting here.

You said you didn't know my mother had been a teacher. Yes, she started teaching in a country school at the age of 17. She had Norwegian boys of immigrant parents in her class who were bigger than she. Also, all grades in one classroom. She had to get to school during the winter early and build a fire. Then she boarded with a Norwegian family. My mother was born, I think, in Utah. Her father was an itinerant traveler, and they were traveling cross-country from Minnesota in a wagon. They stopped long enough for her birth. There were already a couple of other children. The family consisted of seven children, but only three grew to maturity. Her favorite brother died when he was 21. He was the only one who had an education. He studied dentistry. I never knew until about 10 years ago that he died from epilepsy.

Again, I am writing under a hardship – with my kitty cat on my lap – and he is sitting up and his head touching my left wrist.

You asked about "A Little Death Music." I don't know too much about it, other than that it is a mystery. On her Christmas card, she said she is considering making the locale of her third book in Paris. Think I told you that they have homes in Boston and in Paris, where they spend perhaps four to six months a year. Evidently, the second book is ready to be published. Her name is Joan Higgins. She said the book should be out in March of this year.

I think your idea of a book about your Mother's family sounds great and hope you will follow it up. You have a real talent for writing. I would love for you to be able to meet Joan and perhaps get some advice.

Thanks for sending the article you wrote re Christmas dinner; really enjoyed it. How was it received?

Wanda and I often talked about paying each other a visit.

The article I wrote "as a 20-year veteran of the kitchen," was actually written for Thanksgiving. It gave advice, from my experience, on what to do, and what not to do, when preparing a full turkey dinner, like remembering to cook the gizzard and such before adding them to the stuffing. If dinner is delayed, I advised, "Pour your guests another drink, set a beautiful table, and 'dazzle' them with a colorful, molded jello salad."

∾

The following correspondence is typed inside a lovely card with a picture of an exotic flower with hummingbirds. The back of the card says it is *"A Monograph of the Trochilidae or Humming Birds,* London, 1850-61, The Arents Collections, The New York Public Library, Published by The Metropolitan Museum of Art."

4-27-87

Dear Marge:

Thanks for the pretty birthday card and the thought. Was glad to hear from you – seems like a long time. You have many "irons in the fire," and I am glad you manage to do some of the things just for you – like writing, attending seminars, etc. Let me know how the seminar in April turned out.

I was happy to hear you plan a trip to SD again and hope we can get together for lunch.

This will not be a long missive, since we shall be meeting and also since I am beginning to get ready to leave on a 3-week trip around the middle of May. I am not too thrilled with the itinerary. We shall probably fly to Salt Lake City and then rent a car and drive through North and South Dakota and on up into Montana, possibly to Havre where we have good friends. We will have to go back to Salt Lake to return the car, so it will be some repeat scenery.

Nothing much to report from this end. Will is about the same, although better than he was several months ago. I'm having a few health problems, but keep going. The doctor asked me how old I am, and when I told him he said, "You are no longer under warranty." That made me feel real good!

I had the group of women who lunch together here last week. We have cut down on our food, and so I served a "liquid lunch" consisting of homemade carrot soup (does not sound great, but is very tasty), and a cold drink made of Kahlua, ice cream, half and half, ice, and almond flavoring. Didn't have to set the table. I miss entertaining, but I get so tired.

We are going to a new restaurant in Bonita this week and will meet the Carlsens there. It is a Basque restaurant, and we've found that food generally above average.

Am trying to get caught up on my correspondence before we leave; yours is the first. We are expecting a cousin of Will, his wife, and year and 6-month old baby to arrive in June. They won't stay with us, but will be in and out a lot. That will keep me out of mischief for a week at least.

Much love, and let me know ahead when you will arrive. /s/Jane

PS Have you been to the Boston Museum of Art? I love their catalogs and have ordered several gifts from there.

~

A postcard dated 5-26-87 of "Little Critters of Montana," simply states:

Marjorie and Jane, 1987, at the U. S Grant Hotel

Dear Marge - Hope your plans for a trip to SD are maturing and that I shall be seeing you before long! We get back about 6-10-87. So far the trip has been mostly good. Beautiful farm country all thru Montana. Love, Jane.

≈

8-11-87

Dear Marge:

I am delighted with the picture altho' I must agree with you that we two are much more fetching looking! It is really awful of cute you. Thanks so much.

It was a real treat to be with you that day, and wasn't it great we were allowed to sit and visit so long!

Did you get to Horton Plaza and did you like it? I think it most attractive, but I always get lost!

Relieved to learn you are checking with two attorneys and do so hope you achieve a terrific settlement. Keep me informed. In a rush, Much love, Jane

PS – How long does it take to get a divorce in Mass.?

PPS – Enclosed are bay leaves from my European Bay Leaf Tree. I meant to give you and Anne a big handful but forgot. They were just picked today. J.

Horton Plaza is a beautiful outdoor shopping center, painted in bright colors. It sets behind the historic Horton Fountain and park area where I used to catch the bus home from high school.

~

A postcard, dated 8-17-87, pictures *"Dancers Resting, ca. 1881-1917, Edgar Degas, French (1834-1917), Museum of Fine Arts, Boston."*

Dear Marge – I'm sorry but I guess I let the cat out of the bag! When talking with Anne, I mentioned how good the picture of you and me was and she said she had not rec'd one, but probably would so maybe you can send her a copy?

Sad news. Bill Fields is in a rest home, having suffered multiple strokes. He is classified as having "senile dementia." Isn't that sad. Hard to think of him in such a condition.

We may fly to Illinois for a reunion of the "Brown Clan" to be held 10-4-87. I'm not looking forward to flying into Chicago! Love, Jane.

Special Agent Bill Fields was full of fun -- always telling jokes and trying to embarrass the young girls. Mike Hennigan reminded me (during my fact-finding mission re this book) of the time that Mr. Fields asked me if I knew what virgins ate for breakfast, to which I naively replied, "No, what?" He kidded one of the male clerks, who was very thin, by saying, "If you stand sideways and stick out your tongue, you'd look like a zipper!" I believe it was he who bought me my first drink – a vodka gimlet -- at an FBI function, even though I was not yet 21! He also was an excellent dresser – a real Dapper Dan. Anne recalled (at one of our luncheons) how agents returning to the office after a day of firearms at the police range, looked in need of a shower and a change of clothes. Not Mr. Fields – he always looked fresh.

~

Sometime in the fall of 1987, I received a card with the following message:

> *Dear Marge –*
>
> *6:45 a.m.: I'm washing and getting ready to do my weekly shopping but wanted to get this greeting card off to you. I know it will arrive way early, but we are leaving 10-2-87 to return 10-9-87 and I did not want to risk not sending a card later.*
>
> *Am anxious to know how things are going. Know you are a busy, busy gal, but hope you can squeeze in a letter to me one of these days.*
>
> *Will and I are going to DeKalb, Ill., not far from Chicago for a small family reunion. I'm not relishing flying into O'Hare, but guess I can stand it.*
>
> *Will is about the same – just no strength or energy. I'm doing better now that the doctor doubled my heart medication.*
>
> *Surely was fun seeing you this summer. I see you almost as often as I see Anne!*
>
> *Much love – think of you often, Jane.*

≈

> *12-2-87*
>
> *Dear Marge:*
>
> *I hate to answer a letter with a letter enclosed with my Christmas greeting, but certainly could not send the card without a reply to your nice letter received early in November.*
>
> *I know you were upset over the changes imminent in your job. I hope it has all been settled by now and that you will come out ahead – both in enjoyment and salary. That is great you have enrolled in the interior design course. Do you think you like that more than writing? You have so many talents and interests.*
>
> *I am just as sorry as I can be that the divorce papers really hit home so very, very hard. I know you thought you were prepared; you even said so in your letter – but thinking one is prepared and facing the facts are two different things. My Mother was actually*

111

dying for three weeks, after six years of bed illness, but I went to pieces nevertheless when the time arrived. When you love deeply, what else can you expect? As I told you when we had lunch together, Will has hurt me by some of his remarks. I heard a talk show about women married to men with whom there was no communication, and the psychiatrist advised them to start living for themselves and thinking more of their own happiness than their partners. Just give up trying to communicate. I think I mentioned that for 20 years, I tried to kiss a good morning greeting. I have finally given up, and it is really easier, as each morning I do not feel "silly." I did not mean to get off on "me" – I have tried to follow the advice, but it is hard. I think, deep down, you still love John, and that is a major part of the problem. I hope something nice happens during the holidays for you.

It was good to hear you say that you feel ready to go out with someone else. We all need some male companionship, if we are normal. Will is very good about driving me places and h as always been willing to go to FBI affairs, etc., even though he may not relish them. We are hoping to go to the X-FBI Christmas party this December.

Did I tell you Bill Fields had several bad strokes and is in a rest home in North County? He does not know even his family now – they say he has Alzheimer's. It is certainly hard to think of him in that condition. Jim Fox has a small malignant spot on one lung and in the trachea.

I would love to write another page, but I am just getting started on my Christmas cards and, although December 2^(nd) seems early enough, we are expecting Will's youngest son, wife, girl 10, and boy 8, to arrive sometime in December. They have not told us when nor how long they will stay. You know I am an organized person, and this is hard for me to take! So, I am trying to get my Christmas work done before December 6^(th), just in case they arrive then. They will not stay with us. His other son from Prescott will be here for a week with his wife, and his son.

Ward has been working for us, fixing up the house which Will still wants to sell. That means I feed him for lunch and dinner – so

I have to do a lot more cooking than before. He does fix his own sandwich for lunch, however.

Hope you will write and tell me the terms of the divorce and that you are really getting a LOT! Do have as nice a Christmas as possible. I love you. /s/ Jane

Joe and his partner were battling, which left the future of the store where I worked, in question. I enrolled in an interior design program at Becker College in Worcester, MA.

After almost four years of separation, John took the initiative and filed for divorce. As Jane said, even though one feels they are prepared for such things, it was still hard to accept.

$\approx$

Jane enclosed a note with her Christmas card:

1987 was about the usual for us – a few weekend trips plus our yearly 3-week vacation. In late May we flew to Denver, rented a car, and drove thru Colorado, the Dakotas, Nebraska, and Montana, flying home from Denver. In October we flew to Chicago to attend a Brown family reunion in a nearby city. Everyone there was most hospitable and friendly, and we had a great time. Perhaps the most interesting part was meeting Will's cousin, John Browne, and his wife of Ireland who were in the U.S. on their first visit. They live on the same land and in the same house where Will's grandfather was born.

Other than the above, nothing special happened in our lives. We are just glad to be able to say MERRY CHRISTMAS and to send our best wishes that all is well with you.

Jane and Will

$\approx$

The following letter bears no date. The first part of the letter is missing, but its contents indicate a time shortly after Christmas of 1987.

I had a Christmas card from Anne, as you no doubt did also, in which she mentioned that Sharon is to be married the latter part of May. That will be an occasion I shall certainly enjoy.

Your folks have probably written how cold it has been for Calif. Our front porch has registered between 28 and 30 the last three nights, and I have lost a lot of plants. I can see prices on vegetables going even higher. Lettuce was $1.49 the other day, and some kinds $1.79. Everything in the produce line is already extremely high.

We went to the X-Agents' Christmas Party, which was held in the old Cuyamaca Club, San Diego. It was a lovely affair, although there were only 60 present. Ed Mari, the outgoing President, arranged it. I learned that Jack Keith is traveling considerably – baby-sitting the America's Cup. It seems that everywhere the cup goes, so does Mr. Keith. On an airplane, he is in one seat and the cup in the seat beside him. Think they said he has already traveled to 17 cities. Quite an unusual retirement occupation! Maybe he will come to Boston and you will see him!

Well, I am all behind on book and insurance work, so I'd better stop ranting to you and get on with that.

Best of all to you in 1988 – I was glad to note that you feel ready for a little male companionship; that is a good sign – and I hope he (or they) show up soon! Much love, /s/ Jane.

Ed Mari was one of my favorite agents. He sat next to another favorite of mine – Mike Hennigan. They worked stolen car cases.

❧

3-5-88
Dear Marge:
Thanks for the photos taken at our get-together when you were here. I agree: the one of Anne and me is OK but the one of you and me is no good of either of us. In that note, you mentioned you had appointments with two highly recommended lawyers, yet in your Jan. letter, there was no mention of those meetings, but you did say you had another appt. re John's transfer to D.C. I do so hope

you did not have to sell the house. I had wanted the settlement to give the whole thing outright to you. Perhaps it will help you adjust if John and his friend are not living so nearby. Am sure the children will miss him, but that business of seeing him all the time is making it hard for you to forget. This will be short as I have been in bed all week with bronchitis. Am desperately trying to get a few little things done today, as I'm getting behind with everything. And, of course, the woman still has to get up and get the dinner on the table. It surely hasn't been much this week, I can tell you. I do feel a bit stronger today, but have a nagging pain around my right breast bone which I hope is muscular and not something else! My garden needs so much attention, but I dare not get out there, probably for another week anyhow.

We hope to leave 3-24-88 for a 3-week trip to Tampa. We will visit a cousin of Will who lives near there for a week or ten days; then rent a car and drive south. I have two ex-bosses I hope to see – Joe Santiana and Richard Baker. Santiana lives in Tampa and Baker in Naples. Then there is an old boy friend who lives in Coral Gables. His sister is a life-long, almost, friend of mine. We have entertained him and his wife several times. I have never been keen on seeing Florida, but guess it is a beautiful state. Someone said it is boring – absolutely flat. Would love to get way down south, but we probably won't have time.

Did you hear anything from Anne re the engagement? I believe the wedding is set for May 28th, at the Serbian Church in SD. Sharon is marrying into a wealthy family, from what I can gather. I wish I had seen the clipping with her picture. If you still have it, would you send it to me and I will return it.

Well, Marge, I'm "pooped" and had better get back to bed for awhile. We'll be home around the middle of April.

Much love, and do keep me informed re what you find out from the lawyers, etc. /s/ Jane

PS. Didn't mean to address the env. that way – but am Scotch and didn't want to throw it away!

Jane addressed the envelope to "Mrs. John T. Burke." There was a possibility that John would be transferred to Washington, D.C., but that did not come about.

∼

A gold hummingbird, embossed on paper, decorates a letter dated May 31, 1988.

Dear Marge:

This is a prompt reply for me! But I do so enjoy your letters, and the last one had some good news in it – the remark your teacher made about there being nothing you could not accomplish. Maybe you should go into politics! You really ARE talented in many respects, you know, and seem to enjoy different types of endeavors. I wonder just what you will finally settle on.

Sad news that you won't get the house outright. Hopefully you have enough equity in it between you that your half will give you a nestegg to put away in case you need it in an emergency. When will Sarah be 18? I can't keep track of the ages of all these children of friends.

When the case comes to trial, I suppose you and John will have to appear in court together. I know that will be very hard for you. Just hope you win the Judge over and that you get the very best settlement possible.

We had a nice trip; stayed with Pearl, Will's first cousin's widow, near Tampa, for about 10 days; then rented a car and drove south. I think Florida is a very boring state in itself – the highest point is, I believe, 186 feet. However, there are lots of man-made attractions such as Epcot Center (which we loved and wished we had two days there instead of one), Cape Canaveral, Cypress Gardens, Edison's Home – a must, etc. I loved Key West – such a different place. I felt I was in the tropics for the first time. We saw a wonderful exhibit of gold and silver from the Spanish galleon "Atocha" recovered several years back. Also, I toured the home where Audubon did his bird studies of the region – rather, it is the house where he lived while doing the studies. I have always loved his work. I toured a home in, I believe St. Francisville in Louisiana, where he also lived. We had three good meals on *our time away from Pearl's (but very expensive, especially in Key West). We are spoiled, too, re motels as in the West you can, with luck, stay in a Motel 6 – but in Florida if you get a room for $65 you can feel reasonably lucky. Think it was the most expensive trip we have had.*

Everything is going up so, it scares me. The gal who cleans for me now wants $1.00 to $1.25 more an hour. I am sure if I don't give it to her she will quit. And I feel I should pay the gardener more. When you get to the point where help is a necessity instead of a luxury, they know they have you!

I went to a shower a couple of weeks ago for Sharon. It was in Anne's sister's home in Del Mar; a lovely little home, beautifully furnished. She, Patti, is a teacher and also does catering. She had a sit-down luncheon for 27. I couldn't get over the worth of the gifts she received. I gave her a goblet for a wedding gift which cost $37.50, but by the time I paid tax, wrapping and delivery charges, it came to about $48.00. Well, people gave her such goblets for shower gifts! They sent out around 225 or 250 invitations. The ceremony Saturday was in the Serbian Church in Pacific Beach. It was more centrally located than their Greek Orthodox Church in Del Mar, and their priest performed the ceremony. We got there at 2:30, which Anne suggested as the church is so small. The service started at 3:00 and was over a little after 4:00. However, it was very interesting. The priest "sang" part of the service, almost as a cantor in a synagogue. Beautiful voice. Lots of ritual in the ceremony. Anne said her dress (Sharon's) cost almost $1,000! She had four bridesmaids and a matron of honor, flower girl, ring bearer. The girls were all dressed in aquamarine satin, fashioned after the Bride's dress, which was white satin with a long train. Her brother, Nick, Jr., participated in the ceremony also. He is 6'4" and a handsome young man. He must have lots of girls after him. He just graduated from college, so now Anne and Nick will have it easier financially. She has just gotten a 5-hour a day job with the City of La Mesa, working on the switchboard and doing odd typing jobs. It is within walking distance of their home, so she is pleased.

Nick seems to be feeling very good these days. Anne, I feel, has aged, but it is no wonder, as she has had such a hard life. Incidentally, she did not know about the picture you sent that was in the newspaper. She wanted it, so I mailed it to her.

The reception was at the home of the groom's parents which is on Camino de la Costa in La Jolla. The house is built high above the sea, right on the edge, and each room has picture windows facing the ocean. You should see it! We toured her dressing room, closet, and bedroom. The dressing room, in addition to the square feet of the entrance thereto, Will estimated to be about 16 by 8 feet. Along two walls there are clothes racks (double) for garments (all full of very expensive garments). Another portion of the facing wall is divided into spaces to fit a large plastic box, and in those were sweaters. To the left on that wall were racks after racks for shoes and boots. There must have been AT LEAST 50 pair of shoes! The corner of the dressing room, adjoining, has windows of glass, and beneath the windows is a large, round, deep tub, so you can soak and look out at the ocean and not be seen. The bedroom is huge. Everything is beautifully appointed, needless to say. Five bedrooms, two kitchens, which adjoin, and a large room back of the big kitchen which was filled with all the equipment of the caterers. They had round tables for 8 on the patio, all decorated in bridal motif; we estimated about 250 people were served. In the patio when we arrived there was a bar set up where you could get almost anything you wanted. At the table were two unopened bottles of white (French) wine. The dinner was buffet-style. There was a band also. When it came 7:30 and the cake had not been cut, I was tired, and Will looked exhausted, so I thought we should not wait for the cake-cutting. The cake itself was in a gazebo on the patio, which gazebo was built to house the cake. Since the patio overlooked the terrace and was glassed in, you could see the cake from below.

You couldn't believe the huge pile of gifts on the dining room table. They were to leave Monday morning to fly to Austria and back-pack through the countryside, perhaps into Switzerland – air tickets the gift of the groom's parents. The groom is a tall, blond young man, nice looking, and seemed to have a lot of fun about him. We didn't even get to greet Sharon nor meet him. Every time that I located her, she was surrounded by others, so we didn't want to intrude.

I understand Anne's mother gave them their complete set of sterling silver for 13 – not including service pieces, which they did not want. Don't know what they are going to use!

Well, I must stop and work on dinner. I have rambled, but knew you would be interested in the details. I will tell Anne I wrote to you about the wedding.

I am sorry to learn that you are not planning to come out this summer, but understand. Do hope your folks are able to make it East. I am sure you could use their moral support, too.

Lots of love, and write when you can. /s/ Jane

PS As we were leaving, the caterers were serving up a variety of Greek pastries. Also, there were coffee cups out, and glasses for toasting the bridal couple. What a wedding!

In the driveway when we left was a 4-door white Mercedes, decorated with bridal ribbons. The license plate said "HIS/HERS". I wondered if that was a gift from the groom's parents?

The teacher's comment, to which Jane referred, was made after an hour's presentation for my "Design Materials" class at Becker Junior College.

Jane's amazement at Sharon's wedding stemmed from the fact that most people we knew usually did not have such grand weddings. The weddings we were accustomed to involved a gathering after the ceremony with a reception line, some finger foods, pictures, etc. The event generally only lasted a couple of hours, if that. That was California-style – unless, of course, you were wealthy!

My own wedding was a simple one, although I thought it was beautiful. The church was still decorated for Christmas, since we were married on December 30. Afterwards there was a simple reception – no sit-down dinner – no band – no open bar! My mother and father-in-law were wonderful about it though, stating "When in Rome....". They traveled from Boston, along with John's sister Mary Ann, and his best man, Bill Walsh. I always felt that my husband was disappointed with the wedding.

The Divorce

I wrote the following to Jane, keeping a copy for myself.
Tuesday, Aug. 2, 1988

Dear Jane,

Thought I'd type a letter for a change. It's so doggone hot, if I tried to write, my hand would be sticking to the paper. The humidity is absolutely unbearable.

Sorry I've taken so long to write. I think I found your last letter – dated May 31. I keep them all! I'm so disorganized at home (with working 40 hours a week) that sometimes I am not sure I've found the last letter to be answered. And my memory is totally unreliable these days!

Well, it finally happened. John and I went into court on July 25. The divorce will be final in 90 days. I can't believe it.

While the day in court wasn't bad at all, the weekend preceding it was horrendous. I had decided to go over to visit my mother-in-law on Friday, the 22ⁿᵈ, since Sarah was at her dad's. Tommy is always out somewhere! Anyway, I drove over to see my mother and father-in-law. They were putting up a package to leave on a friend's doorstep who was about to return from a trip to Ireland. They went off to do that (since it would only take a few minutes) while I waited at the house for them. I decided to go upstairs to checkout the room which John had helped his father strip of wallpaper the day before. It looked as though they did a good job. I stood in the doorway, though, thinking back to the time I first stayed in the room when John first brought me "home." I often do that when I'm upstairs in that house now.

Shortly, I returned to the den, and Ann and John were back. We sat down to visit, Ann and me. John's dad went into the living room to read the paper. I mentioned that the room looked good, and Ann said, "Yes John (her son, my husband) worked very hard. He had help, you know." She paused and my heart stopped as she added, "Jean came along to help." Well, it was like a bolt of lightening!

Ann continued to tell me that John had asked if he could bring her. It was his birthday, after all. As it turned out, both John's sisters also came and they all had a nice spaghetti dinner together.

I kept fighting back the tears, while she told me all this. I stayed for awhile, but found it almost unbearable. I left, gave her a kiss, told her I loved her, and then cried all the way home.

When Sarah returned from her dad's that evening, I told her that "Nan" had told me that she and the rest of them had met Jean. She said she was going to tell me, because her Dad was really in a good mood, and told her how well everything went, and how much everybody, including his father, who we thought would be standoffish, liked Jean. My heart was breaking. Sarah and I had a long talk. I cried. She cried.

It's so, so hard, Jane. Sometimes I don't think I'll ever get over it. But, now looking back, I think that night released a lot of tension, or whatever, which ultimately made Monday with the attorneys and finally, the judge, go pretty smoothly.

I am happy with the settlement; did better than I thought I'd do, although none of the "facts" really surface when you go through what is basically a "no fault" divorce – irreconcilable differences. The Judge did ask, "Do either of you have anything you'd like to add, anything you'd like to get off your chest?" Neither of us said anything. What would be the use now.

So all went fairly well for the rest of the week. My best friend here, Monique, was in Europe, still is, so I didn't have her to talk to. And Sarah was at the beach with her aunt, uncle and cousin. So I wallpapered my bedroom!

Like I said, everything was going well, until Sunday. That was the day of John's family reunion. I decided it was best that I did not attend, so John would feel free to go, and hopefully take the kids. He took Sarah. He also took Jean! I was hoping he wouldn't.

So, once again, when Sarah came home and told me about the day, the knot returned to my stomach, and I cried some more. It just seems that everyone is so g.d. willing to accept things. It hurts. And I keep needing reassurance.

Yesterday, I hesitated about going over to visit my mother and father-in-law. I hadn't seen them since that Friday night, July 22. I feel awkward now. But I went, and they were glad to see me. They are both so feeble. It's extremely hot and humid, and here they were trying to get the room which had been stripped of wallpaper, ready to repaper. Somehow, my father-in-law, who is very unsteady on his feet, pulled the carpet out from under the furniture. It was heaped in a pile. It's that thin indoor-outdoor stuff, with black foam on the back. The black foam had shredded all over, and stuck to the floor. Well, I picked it up and heaved it out the window, since dragging it downstairs would have made a terrible mess, and my sisters-in-law had just paid quite a bit of money to have the place cleaned.

I ended up having a nice visit with my mother-in-law. She told me about the reunion. And I told her how emotional I find the whole thing. She said she was curious as to what the feedback would be from the relatives about John's "friend."

Sarah had told me that Father Jim (John's first cousin, who is a priest, and who usually hosts the reunion which starts with Mass) had greeted Jean with a big hug. Apparently, John had brought her to meet him a few days prior. I couldn't help but feel that everyone is a hypocrit. Here, our church does not believe in living with a person (having sex) before marriage; commiting adultery, etc., and here John and Jean attend Mass, receive the sacraments, and it seems to be ok.

I realize everyone is happy that he is happy. Goodie gum drops! But again, the rejection I feel is unbelievable. Thank God I have my job to lose myself in.

That isn't hard to do these days. I've become the manager of the store, can you believe! I went from a part-time helper, running the wallpaper department, to a full-time, all around salesperson, and now to manager in 2 ½ years! I am now figuring and scheduling carpeting and flooring jobs, and generally overseeing all the operations. Thank goodness, Joe's son, Chris, is there to run the paint department and fill in anywhere else he is needed. Don't know what will happen when he starts college the end of August though. I think Joe is totally unrealistic when it comes to help in the store. I told him I'd be willing to "try" this, as long as I have the necessary help.

The rest of this letter I do not have; undoubtedly I only intended to keep the part about the end of my marriage.

It may seem odd that I would visit my in-laws when I was getting a divorce from their son, but they were very dear to me, and my sisters-in-law are two of my best friends. My mother-in-law once told me that she considered me a daughter, that there was no difference. We got along very well, enjoyed many of the same things, i.e. decorating! She was suffering with ovarian cancer, had been undergoing chemotherapy and was very ill. I not only lost my marriage, but I was also losing someone I loved very much. She died August 7, 1988.

~

Jane's answer is dated August 31ˢᵗ.

Dear Marge:

Please bear with me. I have a new typewriter and am not used to it!

When I received your first letter, I wanted to sit right down and answer it, but I have been so extra busy and tired, that I just could not work it in. It is now 7:50 a.m. I've had breakfast, hung the flag, taken out the trash, fed the cat, and now before I start any work, I will write you.

Needless to say, I am so terribly sorry and upset over the turn of events. The only good news was that you said you got a good settlement. Did you get the house? I surely hope so.

I think the thing which would have hurt me the most, other than John's remarks and seeing Jean, would be the reception your Priest gave them. I can't imagine! Guess the new mores of the country have also affected religion and its representatives. I think it was terrible also, that you were not allowed to sit with the family at your mother-in-law's funeral, for I know how much you thought of her and vise versa, from what you have written. You would have thought her daughters would have overruled John's wishes and had you with them, for I always understood that you were very close.

Is it good or not that your parents are there? I think it is OK for them to know what you are going through, even though I know it is hard on them. But you kept it all to yourself for so long, as far as they were concerned. Incidentally, I am glad that you let yourself "go to pieces", for if you kept it all bottled up inside you would no doubt long ago have had a nervous breakdown. Hopefully, by talking to friends and writing me (which I do appreciate and am flattered that you think that much of me, to want to confide in me), you will avoid any real nervous trouble. My Mother had a nervous breakdown before I was born, and I came near to having one during my earlier years in the FBI. Don't believe I ever told you about that. So, do let yourself go. I don't know your children, so don't know that they are subject to being "alienated". I mentioned it to Will, and he felt that such alienation would not be permanent – that they might feel that way at one time, but would get over it in time. I do feel you have a problem there, however, depending on how they react.

I think raising children in this day and age is a great and fierce responsibility. That scene with Tom must have been terribly upsetting to you. In the past, children would never think of speaking to a parent in that tone, and in those words. I asked Will if he thought you were right in stopping the girl from going up to Tom's room, and he did.

Things here are not good. Will seems to be going downhill, and it is very hard on him, and on me. I have just about everything to do here now. So far, he has been able to get the weekly trash ready for collection, take care of getting the car washed and repaired, give advice, and do just a fraction of the watering. We have a quarter acre, which must be watered thoroughly once a week. I have been learning the system he worked out to do it with the least effort, but even with that, it takes me all my spare time for two days to get it done. I do that Sat. and Sun. Monday I wash, do my weekly shopping, any ironing necessary, and get the meals. By the time Mon. afternoon comes, I am so tired I usually wind up just having to go to bed for an hour or so. Will's son Ward has been working for us as you probably know, and he gets his lunch and then I get the dinner for the three of us. Naturally, being just past 40, and working physically, he is a big eater, and I can't get by very easily. So with Will's diet and his many, dislikes, it keeps me hopping to think what to prepare.

Away from troubles: I recall some time ago that you expressed a dislike of Dukakis. Now I have gotten so that I really fear what would happen, should he be elected. I don't know your politics, but I am a Republican and do so hope Bush is elected.

Well, Marge, nothing special to report. Needless to say, we go very little. I am getting ready for a garage sale and going through just a few shelves in the basement and a bit in the house has put me so far behind with my book work, insurance claim work, correspondence, garden work, etc. It is to be 9-10. So much work, for so little money. Whatever is left I am just going to give to my church for it's big rummage sale 10-1-88. My head is in a whirl with it all. Will's minister cousin is coming for a week in November, his granddaughter from Ohio at Christmastime, and Will's youngest son, wife, boy 8 and girl 10, arrive about the first of November to stay in Pine Valley for two months while he is looking for work. He married a Panamanian girl and he has been in the Army for 20 years, but is getting out the end of Oct. I am in charge of a 50th wedding anniversary celebration 9-29-88. It will be a luncheon at the Horton Grand in SD, for which I am making the arrangements, then the group (about 20) will come here for wedding cake and champagne. I want to decorate the table and the house if I have enough energy. I just hate this business of having to rest all the time, as I like to keep going, and do to the best of my ability. Then there is Christmas coming. You see, I grew up as an only child, and am just not used to a lot of people around and confusion, and I hate to admit it, but it upsets me and makes me nervous. Oh, well, as my Mother used to say, "This, too, will pass away"!

Much love, and I do hope things will gradually quit hurting and that life has something really great in store for you. When the children are out of high school, perhaps it would be well to relocate if you still feel so upset and out of things family-wise.

Do write whenever you want to get things off your chest – I think of you very, very often. Much love, /s/ Jane.

PS. What does Jean look like? Is she attractive? Friendly to you? John's age?

When arrangements were being made for my mother-in-law's funeral, John called to tell me that Jean would be attending with him. This would be the first time I would lay eyes on her. He further said that I should not expect to sit with the family at the funeral. I was extremely hurt and started to cry, saying I thought it was completely unfair, when I had always been so close to her. John reminded me that she was not my mother. Everything he said made my heart ache, and I cried more hysterically. His comment was, "Get ahold of yourself!"

My parents were visiting from San Diego at that time. It was good to have them by my side at Ann's funeral, and at the house afterwards, where family and friends gathered. It was an extremely hot, humid August day, but I was determined to look my best. Most everyone shed their church clothes for more comfortable ones at the house, but I wore my royal blue nylon dress, pantyhose and heels the entire day.

I had expressed to Jane my fear of alienating my children because I was such an emotional wreck, while their father was happy and more fun to be with. Naturally, it was a difficult time for them.

~

I received a birthday card in October, which made reference to the 50th wedding anniversary luncheon at the Horton Grand, with cake and champagne at Jane's afterward. She said she was exhausted. The remainder of the card states:

Now, Will still wants to go on this two-week trip next Monday and I have everything to do to get ready, plus all the yard work.

Saw Anne Sat. at an X-FBI luncheon. She looks great – is working 5 days a week at the La Mesa City Hall where she is receptionist, telephone gal, secretary, etc.

Will about the same – not good.

The wish on this card is exactly what I hope for you in the year to come.

Love – and I promise to write as soon a I can. Jane.

The card read: "Happy Birthday, and may the year ahead bring you all the good times, all the dreams come true, everything you've set your heart on!" It was signed "Much, much love, Jane."

～

October 29th – The envelope is postmarked 29 Oct 1988. It bears a 25 cent stamp!

Dear Marge:

I am by no means caught up after our two week trip, but I know I owe you a couple of letters; also that this is a hard day for you, as was the 24th (I believe that was the date of the divorce). What gets me is where John receives all his money – to have kept two establishments going at once for several years, plus his own apartment, give you money, help support the children, etc., and still have enough money to build a house. It must be extra difficult for you since you did so much work to improve your present home and, I don't believe it was new when you bought it. I do so hope now that the divorce is final that you can really begin to get over this thing, for it seems to be ruling your life. Your job helps in a way to keep you busy, but it sounds as though your employer is taking advantage of your capabilities. I hope with the increased responsibilities, you are receiving an increase in compensation. I am not being nosey here. I wish there were something I could do which would really help you, but don't know what it might be. Perhaps in several more months if you don't begin to feel better, you might consider a psychiatrist; however, I have always felt that unless you get the right one it is better not to go that route and how do you know who the right one is? Don't you think that when your daughter is through high school, you might consider a move?

Sounds as though your relationship with your sisters-in-law will never be quite the same, and that will be harder and harder to take.

I'm with you when it comes to the new typewriters. The only reason I bought one is because I was not supposed to lift anything as heavy as my old one, and I had to wait until someone was

127

around before I could use it. I usually try to write letters in the early morning and Will isn't generally up until 10:00 and 11:00 a.m. I get along pretty well with letter writing on this typewriter, altho' it does seem to skip spaces at times, and at other times, there is no space between words. Also, in doing any form work or business letters requiring certain special spacing, it is hard to use, and slow. I can prepare insurance forms quicker by hand than on this typewriter.

Saw Kay Fox at the last FBI gals' luncheon. I asked her if she had one of the newer typewriters and she answered by saying she did but did not like it. Same with a couple other "old gals", so we are not in the minority.

We had a nice trip and nothing drastic happened, thank goodness. We drove up and back through central Calif. and were in the mountains a lot. Also, went through the little towns in the gold country. Spent the last night in Idylwild, which I have always loved, and Will has never cared for. The minute he gets home he starts to let down. He has an extremely heavy head cold and it seems to be going down, which is bad for him. I fear he will wind up having to go to the doctor.

Well, Marge, I have another letter I must get off this morning, and then I must go out in the garden to try to catch up somewhat with work from the two weeks. I can't balance my check book and I am far behind on the insurance papers. We have so many doctors' bills that it keeps me humping to keep current.

I do so hope things brighten up for you real soon. Much love, Jane

PS. (Always one of those with us!) Thanks for returning the book and for your comments. As I told you, I did not care for the style of writing. And, too, I am not keen on mysteries. I get to read so little that when I do I want a good novel or a story about real people. On the trip, I reread a novel my Dad gave me 35 years ago by I believe, Gwen Bristow, called "Jubilee Trail". I just loved it. It is a novel and is the story of a young, adventure-seeking girl, brought up in NYC, who falls in love with a trader. The story is laid before California joined the union and tells of their travel from NYC to California, via New Orleans and Santa Fe. It does not seem to be a well-known book. I had forgotten I had it and had tried at our library to get it, but there was no record. This is a long P.S.?

So, now adios for sure. J
I loved the long letter and was sorry when it came to an end!

Before John and I separated, he convinced me to refinance the house; thereby making it possible for him to build another one for him and Jean.

My employer and his partner were in a battle over the business, which resulted in his leaving the store. The additional responsibility thrown on me, on top of the stress at home, had me talking about seeing a psychiatrist.

~

A card, with a heart shaped sampler-type picture inside of a woman bringing flowers to the house and a tiny black kitty sitting under a willow tree, reads:

Dear Marge – I've been thinking of you so much and hoping all is well. Really enjoyed our lunch together – just sorry I wasn't as peppy as usual; I can't seem to be, for Will and his serious condition are always in the back of my mind. He's up for meals and occasionally goes on errands – otherwise, he's in bed all day.

I've been quite ill from a streptococcus infection, coupled with the bite of a Brown Recluse spider, whose venom is said to be more deadly than that of a cobra or other snake. Just lucky the fellow can't inject as much of his vile fluid. Was in the hospital 3 days and going to two doctors once and twice a week. Happened 5 ½ weeks ago. Think I'm almost at the end.

Sorry this is full of woe – hopefully my next letter will be better, but I did want to "touch base" with a favorite gal. Love, Jane
3-1-89

~

March 29, 1989

Dear Marge:

This is a prompt reply for me, but I am in the mood to write!

I was so sorry to learn of the trouble you are having with your knees. Believe me, I can empathize, as I guess you know I have had trouble that way also. It was at its worst just before we took our bus trip through New England. The doctor said he would give me a cortisone shot, and that worked like a miracle; however, he said he could not do that often. Luckily, the condition has improved, although I still get "achy" and very tired physically when I am on my feet a lot.

I did not mean to go into details about me, for it is you who are important and about whom I am worried. If it is not arthritis, Will suggested that perhaps you should see a Neurosurgeon, provided you can get a good one. He might be able to help. I imagine all those years standing in the store surely were not good for you.

Another thing: the loss of your job! That is awful; I do hope, however, that it is a "blessing in disguise". It seems as though you are due a rest; maybe that will help your knees. Did the fact that you were not picked for jury duty have anything to do with the fact that you had worked for the FBI? I have always wondered whether or not a defense attorney would pick me when he learned I had worked for the FBI for 30 years.

Incidentally, I did not pick this paper; it was a birthday gift. Anyhow, it is nice for typing.

Oh, when I was suffering with my knees, they would awaken me at night and I applied "Aspercream". It relieved the discomfort long enough so that I could get back to sleep. I don't know whether you can take aspirin or not but you might try it.

Have you gone to one of the group meetings you mentioned at the church where John's cousin is assigned? I hope you have and that there were some interesting men there. I think it would be awful to have to start all over again and, especially, to feel you could trust once more. Confidentially, I haven't had a real love life, but Will is a very kind and caring man, and I appreciate those qualities. I don't think he ever would have stepped out on me – but I fear I don't trust completely when I should!

I am so snowed under all the time with this house and garden and all the business, cooking, errands, etc. to do, plus spending a lot of time at doctors' offices – I seldom feel in the mood to write.

Will's son Ward, who has been working here off and on part-time for three years, plans to leave some time next week on about a five-year sailing trip in his trimarand. His cousin, Heather from Ireland, is going with him. She is about 26 and he is about 46, but they were seemingly just made for one another. They go from here first to the Marquisas (sp?) islands, which they think they will reach in four to six weeks. Then, all through Melanesia, around India, through the Suez Canal, the Mediterranean, up the west coast of Europe, and back to her home in Northern Ireland.

I have gotten so I hate to inflect my letters on my friends, as I seem to have nothing to report other than sickness. Will gets up anywhere from 9:30 to 1:30, eats only two meals a day. He dresses about 4:00 p.m., then goes back to bed, but does sit up with me, usually, to look at TV in the evenings. He is in bed almost all day, usually.

Easter, I went to church by myself, came home by myself, and he was still asleep, so I spent the afternoon working on income tax and other book work. Incidentally, you know the Fund over which I had control at the office? Well, I think only once or twice did I ever have to call on George Byrom to help me balance, and I wrote many, many checks. Well, now for the last four months, I have not been able to balance our checkbook. I have just taken the Bank's word for it, and added or subtracted as the case called for.

Must stop this rambling and get on to another long overdue letter to my friend in Mexico City. He lost his wife a little over a year ago, but seems to be dong very well.

Do hope things have improved and that your next letter will bring better news. Much love, /s/ Jane

My job at Hudson Paint and Wallpaper ended when my boss and his partner could no longer agree as to how to run the store, and decided to dissolve the business. The last few months were stressful, with distributors calling for money or holding orders, and customers upset when their orders weren't in. I decided to take a few months off to try to regain my sanity. During that time, I was summoned for jury duty, but nothing came of it.

Special Agent George Byron was an accountant.

∾

A postcard dated 6-28-89 reads:

Dear Marge – How good to get your letter! Sorry I cannot answer in kind at this time. Will has failed considerably – is in bed all the time, except for meals – does not read or look at TV even. I have so much to do, I just cannot settle myself to write letters, so I hope my friends will understand and accept cards.

Anne finally called me about a month ago! It was good to hear from her. So glad you have a new job – congrats! Much love, Jane

After two months of collecting unemployment -- something I had not done before or since -- my friend Monique told me of an opening at a paint and wallpaper store in Clinton. I called the owner, interviewed, and started working for Discount House of Wallpaper in May, 1989.

∾

Another postcard, dated 7-31-89 reads:

Dear Marge: Remember this tower? Many years ago! Thank you so much for your lovely card and nice note. Things here just decline steadily. Extremely hard physically and emotionally. Hope to get a hospital bed tomorrow and some help from Hospice. Think of you often. Much love, Jane

The card pictured the San Diego Trust and Savings Bank cupola. The back of the postcard states, "This arcaded tower atop the bank building is a prominent characteristic of the San Diego skyline. At one time, a lantern inside the tower served as a beacon to assist airplanes and ships at sea."

It is the building where both Jane and I began our FBI careers. Today it is a hotel and an historic landmark -- considered one of the finest commercial buildings ever constructed in San Diego. On a visit to San Diego after beginning this book, I obtained a sheet containing its history from the hotel clerk. It says:

"The San Diego Trust and Savings Bank Building was designed in 1927 in an Italian Romanesque Revival architectural style by master architect William Templeton Johnson, an individual who has been credited with shaping the character of San Diego during the first half of the 20th century. Johnson's work can also be seen in the Samuel Fox Building across the street, the Serra Museum and the Museum of Natural History in Balboa Park.

"Local legend has it that the crowning cupola was added to assure the structure would be downtown's tallest commercial office high rise."

The description goes on to describe the exterior which "features rich ornamentation including a Scotch Rose granite base; polished Briar Hill sandstone and terra cotta cast panels…bronze and glass doors; and a Spanish tile roof topped by a tiled and domed copper cupola."

"The interior features marble and bronze teller cages; arched clerestory windows and circular antiqued chandeliers. The magnificent lobby has a towering 32' high ceiling with original stenciling. The floor, columns, counters, pillars and walls were made from 19 different types of marble quarried from all over the world including the U.S., Greece, Italy, France, Great Britain and North Africa."

~

A note dated 8-4-89 bore sad news.

Dear Marge –

This will be short as I have many notes to write and things to do.

Will died August 2ⁿᵈ during the nite. My prayers were answered. I did not pray for him to get well for I know it was impossible, but rather that my strength would last so I could keep him at home.

For various reasons, the service cannot be until Aug. 10ᵗʰ – so long to wait. It will be a graveside service with only family and a few close friends.

> *It will be hard for me to write again very soon as I am swamped*
> *with everything there is to do. Love, Jane   Aug. 4th*

The "In Remembrance" note, indicated that William O. Browne was born in Chula Vista, California on February 18, 1913, and died August 2, 1989 in Bonita, California, with a graveside service to be held at the Glen Abbey Memorial Park on August 10, 1989, with the Rev. Harris Wood officiating. Private inurnment would be at Glen Abbey Memorial Park.

A copy of the obituary stated, in part: "He was an electrician, retiring in 1978 and a member of the International Brotherhood of Electrical Workers. He was a member of Chula Vista Historical Society and was a graduate of Sweetwater Union High School.   Survivors include his wife Jane; sons William F. of Manhattan Beach, Paul D. of Prescott, Ariz, Ward O. of San Diego and James D. of Chula Vista; six grandchildren; and one great-grandchild."

A thank you from "The family of William O. Browne" was also received acknowledging "with deep appreciation your kind expression of sympathy." Inside is a note from Jane:

> *Dear Marge –*
> *I am swamped with notes and business matters but did want*
> *to thank you for the lovely card and, particularly, your note. Wish*
> *you were near. Think you might be out this year to see your folks?*
> *Let me know if you do plan a trip.*
> *It is very lonesome in the house – really still doesn't seem*
> *true that I'll never see Will again. I'm not yet in charge of my*
> *emotions.*
> *Please excuse brevity – you are one of my very favorite people,*
> *you know.*
> *Love, Jane Aug. 19th*

∽

A Birthday card came that October with a picture of a beautiful Indian girl, entitled "Billxape, by Penni Anne Cross, verse by Pale Moon".

The verse: *May warm winds of happiness blow softly upon you, And may the Great Spirit bring sunrise in your heart. Happy Birthday.*

The back of the card contained the following message:
> *Dear Marge —*
>
> *I fear your card will be a day late. Since your day falls on a holiday this year; you probably won't receive it until Tues. I'm sorry!*
>
> *I am still writing "thank-yous", believe it or not. Have rec'd more than 30 memorial contributions and 140 cards, many of which required a reply. So, I regret to say I'm not able to get myself in the mood to write a regular letter.*
>
> *Remember the Carlsens? They have been absolutely wonderful to me — and continue to be.*
>
> *I do hope things are better for you. Please write when you can — I love your letters.*
>
> *Hope your birthday was a good one. Love, Jane*
>
> *PS. I loved these cards, so I bought about half a dozen. Hope I didn't send you one last year!*

∾

> *11-20-89*
>
> *Dear Marge:*
>
> *Thanks for your card and the note rec'd yesterday. It is so good to keep in touch. Sounds as tho' you like your new job. I hope it is a bit more rewarding financially and a lot more rewarding as far as your happiness is concerned.*
>
> *Nothing much new to report here. I am still trying gradually to get things done businesswise. Just wrote a follow-up letter re an insurance refund I should be due which they promised over two months ago. Also have quite a few things on which the title had to be changed. I have all my thank-you notes written for cards I received with special messages and for donations. I received almost 150 cards and, I think, about 32 individual contributions to different charities. People were really wonderful. I am still*

eating some things out of the freezer – it will be hard when I can't go there and jerk up a dinner.

That is the only thing I am enjoying about living alone – no cooking to speak of. I do try to prepare well balanced meals, however, and do not use the prepared food, such as Stouffer's, etc., for all those things are loaded with sodium – not good for people with troubles such as mine – heart, blood pressure, and varicose veins. Tonite, for instance, I am having some swiss steak which was in the freezer, fresh zucchini, a baked potato, and home-made apple sauce.

I have been invited out to lunch quite a bit by different friends, which has been a help emotionally. I am not quite as "weepy" as I was, but still break down when I see a friend whom I haven't seen since Will died. Going to church is about the hardest. I really don't go much, which is bad, but I keep up my contributions and interests there.

San Diego has been having what is called a Russian Festival. They have the largest number of Faberge Eggs ever assembled. They are on exhibit at the Art Gallery, and I expect to see them 12-6-89. There is also a wonderful exhibit of Russian folk art at the foot of B Street on the pier. I went to that last week with a gal friend.

Will's family has said they think I should remarry – but you know how that goes. Should I ever get to the point I feel I would like to, you also know how hard it is to meet anyone in whom you would be interested. It seems that the widowers have so many women running after them that someone who just stands in the background would not have much of a chance.

I hope to go to the X-Agents Christmas party, which is to be 12-17-89 at the La Jolla Beach and Tennis Club. I made a reservation at the same place for that night as I don't see well enough to drive at night, nor do I like to be out alone. The Frank Prices heard about it and have invited me to spend the night with them, which is very nice of them.

I, too, wish you were nearer so we could visit. I have joined several of the galleries and/or museums in Balboa Park. They have interesting lectures and exhibits for members only, but the ones so far that I want to see are at night. Now, if you were here I could pay your membership fee if you would be my chauffeur!

I guess I am getting along "as well as can be expected" – better than some – worse than others – but it is lonesome, especially at night. And in the evening I have been out twice to dinner at public places where there were couples, and almost broke down each time. That seems to be much harder than to go to lunch with a woman friend.

Well, now I am rambling, so had better get on to another letter. I have about four which I should have answered before yours, but just felt like a chat with you.

Do hope someone interesting comes along for you, as you have a lot of living yet to do. Thanks for being a sweet friend. Much love, /s/ Jane-

~

The new job was working out just fine, since the store sold exactly the same brands of paint, wallpaper, carpeting, etc. as the one in Hudson. With three years of experience, it was easy to fit in. I tried to change a few things, but the guys were pretty set in their ways.

~

At Christmas, 1989, Linda wrote of Jane.

"I haven't seen her in years," Linda said, asking how she was doing.

"We had a nice 10-day vacation to Mexico City in August. In November, we spent four days in Napa Valley – one of our favorite places – at a real nice B&B (Villa St. Helena)."

She reported that "the biggest event" was her confirmation into the Catholic Church.

During the year, she and her husband had seen "The Phantom of the Opera" and the French-Canadian, non-animal circus: "Cirque du Soleil.

PART THREE

The 1990s

January 23, 1990
Dear Marge:

Maybe you will despair to receive a reply so soon, but I had my typewriter out and time to write, so thought I would just do it!

I'm so happy to know you have a job you enjoy and lots of nice people with whom to work, and are fun to kid around with. One of these days there's just GOT to be someone who appreciates you.

I can't believe what you wrote about John's getting tired of his beloved! Now she is getting a small taste of what you went through. Wonder what the outcome of it all will be. Giving John as much credit as I could muster, I wondered whether or not his affair with Jean was a once-in-a-lifetime deep, love; evidently not! Wonder what age the newest one is? Probably works for the "B".

Sad news to report. Perhaps six weeks ago, Nick Sarris had another serious heart attack. He was in the hospital for weeks. He is home, but just now able to dress himself. Anne went to work full-time awhile back for the City of La Mesa. She was able to take off for several weeks when Nick first came home, but planned to go back last week on a part-time basis. She said Nick would never be able to work again – hopefully that will not be true. She really sounded blue. I know finances are not easy, and working only part-time will not bring in anywhere near enough for them to live on.   She is just too nice a gal for this to happen to – also too young to have this burden the rest of her life. Also, Nick has been such a worker, it will be very hard on him just to stay home. Let's

141

pray that does not happen. I'm sure she would appreciate a note from you, though I'm also sure you would probably not get a reply, especially now when she is so busy and so tired.

Is your daughter now in her senior year in high school? I suppose she is dating – hope the young people there are nice ones.

It is wonderful that you have such a good relationship with John's sisters; that speaks mighty well for you. Am sure they are a great comfort. And how is your son doing? Still living at home?

I guess I am doing as well as can be expected. I keep so busy during the daytime – so much paper work; still have not gotten all of Will's insurance papers settled, and some of mine. Now, I am working on a new will, and then it will be time to prepare income tax.

I have had a strong yen recently for sweets – something I did not have for years. Yesterday, I made a Shoo Fly Pie. Did you ever have that? It is a Pennsylvania Dutch dish – my Mother had some Pa. Dutch in her geneology, and this is a recipe she obtained from a relative. I got so hungry for some I could almost taste it – ate 3 pieces the first day! It is sort of like gingerbread.

Did I tell you I had joined three of the museums in Balboa Park? The Museum of Man, San Diego Historical Society, and San Diego Museum of Art. The latter, together with the City of SD sponsored a big "Russian Festival" here the latter part of 1989. They had, for one thing, the largest collection of Faberge eggs ever assembled. But the best was an exhibit of folk art from all parts of Russia. The things from Siberia intrigued me the most – such elaborate clothing – really looked like costumes. Beautifully embroidered, beaded, sewed, etc.

I had a nice note from Linda after she received my Christmas card in which I enclosed a note about Will; I had not written her – as I am not close to her as I am to you. She sounded really happy. I did not know she had turned to Catholicism. I never did meet her husband. Wish she would call me when she is in SD sometime.

That was a sad, sad thing about the loss of Pat's husband. Does not seem right that the happy people have to be parted.

Marge, it must be so lonesome for you, never having anyone to go out with. Even at my age, I am now wishing I had somebody to go to dinner, the theater, take a ride with, etc. While we love our women friends, it is just not the same as being with a congenial man. I had never thought I would be ready this soon for other companionship, but it seems I am, and you are so much younger, it is worse for you. I am not, however, interested in a "meaningful relationship" as they say – just a companion.

With this sad note, I will close. You are ambitious to keep up with classes – what about your writing? Much love, /s/ Jane.

Two Italian brothers, my age, owned the store where I worked. Their sons worked there, as well as a woman in her late 60's, who answered the phone and paid the bills. She was happy to have another woman around to help keep the men in line!

I was undoubtedly getting feedback from my daughter about John's relationship with Jean, since he took Sarah on Saturdays, while I worked. Sarah was in her junior year of high school.

I wrote to Anne occasionally, and when I saw her on visits home, she would always tell me how much she and Nick enjoyed my letters.

Although my relationship with my sisters-in-law had become strained following my divorce from their brother, we stayed close. When Pat called me to tell me that her husband died in the night, I spent the next day with her, going to the funeral home, picking out the casket, and so forth. It was a sad time.

~

The following undated letter from Jane makes reference to an upcoming trip in April of 1990. The notepaper on which it is written bears a sketch of a Victorian-style home -- "Built in 1894 by E. Gillette, Bought 1910 by Col. C. W. Darling."

Dear Marge:

It doesn't seem possible that your letter to me was written almost a month ago! Soon for me to be answering, but I have the time today.

Yes, you should get a new typewriter if yours is so old you do not like it anymore. I am not keen on this Smith Corona I bought about a year ago, but it was a matter of necessity, as I am not supposed to lift more than 15 pounds – and the old one was, I believe, about 25. I just wish the new one didn't ding-dong all the time. I don't pay any attention to it, as far as looking for mistakes, for it beeps at any unusual word – like "ding dong"!

Yes, I detest cleaning. I am so thankful that for the time being, anyhoo, I can afford to have a woman do the main cleaning. However, as you know, there is a multitude of things other than the regular to keep clean – windows, plates on plate rail, curtains, drawers, etc. and I hate to do even that much.

You are so ambitious to stain cabinets, paper the walls, and all that. I guess when I was your age, I might have done the same, but I doubt it. Your kitchen must be lovely with the new cabinet.

Glad you told me the next installment re your friend Paul. Why couldn't it have been someone you were dying to go out with! Always my luck, too. Keep me posted – as to whether the animal attraction won out!

Not much news here. Haven't been in to any Museum affairs since I wrote last.

Do you have a tabby cat, or what kind? Tabbies are my favorite – I think they have such good dispositions. Wish I could see your kitty and the kittens – and you. Do you think you will come to SD this year?

Did I tell you I plan to leave for about 2 weeks in Hawaii 4-28-90? Will take the 7-day around the island tour and then spend a week with a friend in Kona. She is a widow. Her husband was heir to the Seth Thomas millions and left her very well off. With that I shall close. Much, much love and thanks for the very nice birthday card. /s/ Jane

We always had cats in Bolton. One mama gave birth to a litter in my son's closet.

I had a cabinet with glass doors, built between my kitchen and family room. I stained it, and re-wallpapered the kitchen.

"Paul" was a customer of the store where I worked, who openly flirted with me. Nothing ever came of the flirting, however. Besides, my boss did not approve!

~

May 19, 1990

Dear Marge:

You will probably be surprised by this fast reply, since I returned home just a couple of days ago. Your letter was waiting, and I put it aside until after dinner so I could sit and enjoy it – which I did – but the contents touched my heart so that I got up extra early this morning to reply.

It is so hard for you – even at my age, I miss the company of a man, and you, really in the prime of your life, surely should have a lover and companion. You know, even though you and I are different in many respects, we are basically the same type people – moral, caring, happy disposition, dependable. (Need I go on?) Anyhoo, I don't think either one of us is either outwardly sensuous nor flirty. I think a flirty woman attracts the man soonest, but it is not in my nature to be that way.

I really DO think "there is a man out there" for you; however, the real trick is to find him. You did better than I – look how long it took me! The one real regret in life is that I never had children. I miss a family so. Will's sons are nice to me, but not overly so. A friend of mine who has two sons living in the area just returned from a cruise. One son was waiting for her at the airport, embracing her and telling her how much he had missed her, and how much he loved her. The other son and wife took her out to dinner, filled her refrigerator with frozen items and fresh veggies. The two sons planted a garden for her in the past and just recently added a sprinkler system. I had to ask Will's son in Chula Vista to meet me at the airport – the Carlsens took me in when I left. Well, my flight got in at 6:30 a.m. – which he knew – I had looked forward to having a young, 6'4" man meet me when I got to SD. He was nowhere to be seen when I came off the plane. I waited there quite awhile; then called his home. No answer. So,

I went to get my baggage. I waited until I was the last one, so struggled with 3 bags and my cosmetic kit and big hat and purse. Had to take them from the baggage area outside. He waltzed in at 7:05 a.m., mumbling something about traffic and getting lost – no apology or inquiry as to how my vacation went. I always have to pull conversation out of the whole family, even the kids. Due to my heart condition, I am not supposed to lift more than 10 to 15 pounds.

Well, enuf of my troubles. I am glad you have your lovely daughter. Even tho' you are tied down now, when you get older it will be a great consolation to have someone of your own.

I haven't talked with Anne – sent her a card. I hate to call her since she is so busy. Did I tell you that she had to accept work full time in order to keep her job? Seems they combined some jobs so that they did not have to pay health insurance for two. I guess Nick definitely will not be able to work again; so hard on both of them.

Re my trip: I went first to the "SS Independence" and took the 7-day cruise around the islands. We stopped at Kaui, two nights in Maui, and two stops on the big island of Hawaii. I took land tours each day. The first day at sea was busy unpacking and getting oriented. They seated me at a table with five Baptist ladies who were with about 35 other Baptists, from Alabama. They were so boring – nothing interesting to talk about. There was table after table of women – and the whole cruise was a geriatric one! (I am geriatric, I know, but I don't want to be completely with my age group.) I got so tired of seeing lots of old, feeble people creeping around. Some of the evening shows were excellent; others not so good. I did enjoy seeing the other islands, but I was so exhausted by the time I got on the ship that I had to give up two afternoons about 2:30 p.m. and go to bed; also one evening. By Thursday, I had gotten rested. I am not sorry I took the cruise, but at this point, I don't know if I would ever go on another one by myself.

The first weekend I spent in Honolulu and was entertained by my 50-year old friend, Maria. She and a friend picked me up Saturday afternoon and drove me around and took me to dinner. Sunday, they came at 9:00 a.m. and drove all around the island.

I took them to lunch at a beautiful spot called Turtle Bay. Is there one on the East Coast — seems I have heard of a Turtle Bay in the States? Then I had dinner with a couple of gals I had met on the ship.

The highlight of the whole trip was my stay with my friend Vashti in Kona. Her husband was very wealthy, and when he died a couple of years ago, left everything to her. She must be many times over a millionaire. She just knocked herself out to do everything to make my stay pleasant. I wish you could see the two hotels she took me to for brunch and dinner. I have never seen anything so lovely as the Mauna Lani Bay Resort Hotel, where we went for dinner Saturday evening with a friend of hers. We sat outside and dined at sunset — a perfect Hawaiian picture, with the waves lapping near us on the shore, a Hawaiian sunset behind swaying palms, trade winds blowing, and two Hawaiians playing soft island tunes. The food was out of this world. Vashti has a full-time man working for her. He does EVERYTHING, from keeping the garden, doing the housework, running errands, serving, etc.

Well, I must get out in the garden, which is a mess. While I was gone, they had temperatures in the 90's and all the flowers, of which I have many this year, burst into bloom. It will take me most of the day just to cut them and water, to say nothing of fertilizing. I'll probably not get to the latter. We are supposed to conserve water, and I hate to let my garden go, but guess I will have to cut down somewhere. At this time they are asking for a 10% voluntary reduction. I think they will probably also raise the rates sky high for use above a certain amount. My bill is already very high.

In closing, I will say that I was delighted to hear you are planning a trip home. Could you let me know about when you will be here so I won't get tied up with something else. (Not that I have that many invites, but I would hate to miss a good chat.) It would be a real joy for me if you could spend a night or two with me. I now have the extra bedroom and bath. It would be such fun to have you. Do you think you could get away? Please consider it seriously. I, too, wish you lived close. Guess I told you

I have become timid about driving, except around Bonita and Chula Vista – so not only your company but the driving would be a real boost.

When will Sarah be through high school? Wish when she is you could make a move someplace. Do you ever think of that? Much love, /s/Jane

I was becoming terribly lonesome for male companionship and wondered if I would ever meet anyone. I was busy with the kids, the house and the job, but there was a void in my life.

After Will died, Jane began inviting me to spend an overnight with her. Her guest room was decorated beautifully in blue, with an accompanying bath.

~

An American Hawaii Cruise postcard is dated 7-20-90. It pictures a ship in the harbor at night, with lights, and a Hawaiian scene in the foreground.

Dear Marge –

Thanks for your letter – so anxious to see you!

I'll be out of town the weekend of 8-25/26-90; busy on 8-20-90. A good time for me would be either Tues. 8-21 or Wed. 8-22 – spend the day, and night. Let me know.

Sorry to hear about your mother – do hope she will be OK.

Hot, hot in our area – guess you've heard about it from your folks. Much love, Jane.

About this time, my mother underwent a quintuple by-pass.

~

September 9, 1990

Dear Marge:

Many thanks for your prompt "bread and butter" note! I am so glad you were able to spend a bit of time with me. I enjoyed talking with your folks. I like them very much. I felt badly I had nothing really nice to offer them to drink or eat – I actually had no idea they would come in to visit, but was glad they did so I could get a bit acquainted.

I do thank you for giving me the very pretty vase. I shall think of you each time I use it. It says on the bottom that it is bone china!

Strange you should mention having been on the "downside" while here. I felt we did not have as many laughs together as we used to; however, I thought that perhaps I had gotten much more serious due to Will's death, and that perhaps you were bored with me! I hope that was not the case. Have you always had these ups-and-downs, or is it just since all the trouble with your Ex?

I was so sorry to read about your little kitty. As you probably know, I love kitties and hate to hear of anyone losing such a pet.

Re my Mother's story. Guess you know when I reached the end of it and saw that word "Adios", it really broke me up. I adored my Mother. We had such fun together.

I am sure you will hear from your folks about the heat wave we are having. Seems each day gets hotter. Thank goodness so far the humidity has hovered around 50, which is a big help. I just can't work in the garden when it is like this – everything will be drying up.

The Carlsens are leaving Oct. 4th for a month in Europe. I really don't see them very often, but do talk with Barbara a couple of times a month. I just know that, of my friends, they above all would be right here should I need any help.

Can't remember whether I had the results of my back x-rays before you came or not. If I did not, will say they reflected "deteriorating disc disease". The doctor didn't say much other than to come back in 6 weeks! A friend lent me a "grabber" which will pick up things from the floor (I have always been one to drop things easily), so I have been using it. It works to pick up a garden hose, etc.

This is a dull letter, but I am thinking of you and your darling daughter. She is SO CUTE, Marge – and sweet. I loved her profile; just sat there and sneaked looks at her when I could!

Let me hear when you can – and come again!! Love, /s/Jane

We had a little kitty, Nikki, who had been sick. We found her dead in the cellar on our return home. John was supposed to be checking on the house and the cat, but failed to check on her whereabouts when he did not see her.

While visiting with Jane, she shared a story written by her mother about her days as a teacher, either in Montana or Minnesota. She ended it with "Adios," which must have been the way she usually said goodbye.

≈

For my birthday, I received a hand-made card of seven little pages on lavender paper, decorated with dried flowers, such as Columbine and Pansy from Jane's garden. A thin silk ribbon tied the card together. Using gold leaf, she wrote: "My Garden and I wish you a Happy Birthday!" Inside, it said "To Marge - with love, Jane, Oct. 9, 1990."

≈

Laser cut butterflies dance across the top of the paper of the following undated letter. The reference to "George," indicates a timeframe of fall, 1990.

Dear Marge:

This is the last of some favorite paper given me. Your newsy letter came yesterday, and I hasten to answer. So sorry about your Mother; she looked so great when you were here. I guess one never knows about heart conditions. I am sorry you have to go to the expense of coming out again, but it is, of course, the thing you want to do and should do. I am marking your dates on my calendar and do so hope we can get together, at least for lunch. I know with such a short visit and the illness, you want to be with your folks as much as possible. You know you are always welcome, however, to spend the night.

I just LOVED your long, chatty letter and, especially, the news about "George". I think he must be sort of scared of getting involved with anyone, since you said he had been hurt also. And then the children take so much of his time, I am sure. Why do you object to the "Irish blood"? He must be a very cautious person

150

and want to proceed very slowly. Just try to be your own sweet self when you are with him.

So glad you liked the card. I made several, although yours was more complicated than any of the others. So, since I sort of slaved over it, glad you liked it. I am now enrolled in a Calligraphy class which meets in La Mesa each Monday morning. It is very difficult for me – others in the class just catch on immediately and do the most beautiful printing. Last week, I met a lady who does better than I, but not perfectly, so perhaps I can sit with her and not get such an inferiority complex. The class goes until the first part of January.

I saw June at the X-FBI gals' meeting, but did not recognize her at first glimpse. Her hair is the most unusual color – a lavender –and she vows she doesn't even use a rinse. It is also beautiful hair. She said she has people stop her on the street to ask what kind of rinse she uses. She has been on Weight Watchers for a couple of years and lost many pounds. She is very slim. I had forgotten she is so tall: 5'11". She has bought a condo and is now alone. Her boys left three years ago, so she has life to herself for the first time. She showed me pictures of them; both are good looking, but one is blond and looks like a Greek God. She said they call her every weekend. She said if anyone ever says "Life is no good after 40", they are crazy. She said she is dating three men and having a ball. She is only close to one, if you know what I mean. She's very vivacious and friendly. I hope when you come out you could get together with her. She said she would call me and get your address, but so far I have not heard from her. She also goes to exercise classes and night school.

Well, I have many things I hope to accomplish today, so I had better quit and start doing them!

I'll look forward to your phone call around the 7ᵗʰ of November, if convenient with you. Love,

As stated earlier, my mother had undergone heart surgery, so I made two trips to San Diego that year. Just before my trip in November, I started dating a fellow named George, who I met at church. A mutual friend kept trying to get the two of us together. His wife had an affair, which led to their divorce. He had three children, 16 and under. My reference to the Irish was made because of my unsuccessful marriage to an Irishman.

June worked as a clerk in the FBI office in San Diego during my time there.

$\sim$

Two little cut-out kittens pop off the top of a note dated Nov. 16th.

Dear Marge –

It's my turn to thank you for the get-together lunch and also for making an effort to visit me again. It surely is great to see you.

Hope your Mother is steadily improving. She looked quite tired, I thought.

Thinking back on what you told me about George and your times together, my feeling is that it is going to work out. Do keep me advised, Mrs. Flanagan! Love, Jane

$\sim$

The following letter is not dated, but I believe it fits in here.

Dear Marge:

Your welcome letter came the other day, and I was delighted to learn that you are continuing to enjoy yourself with George. I think, as it turns out, it was well you turned down your friend's offer to go with him a year ago – he is probably much more receptive to a different gal by now. He sounds like a very sincere, reliable person.

Any more news about how your "ex" is doing with his "live-in"? And do you know whether or not he has learned that you are dating? I hope it does not go down well with him!

I am anxious to learn how the office Christmas party turned out. You said you had asked George to go with you. I am sure the fellows you work with will be good, but I'll bet you take more kidding than ever now!

I'm so glad your Mother is doing OK.

Thanks for sharing a bit of intimacy with me; I had wondered but would never have asked. It really must be nice to have some warmth again.

I don't know what I shall do for Christmas; had thought I would get together with an old friend of mine, but she is upset about her brother, who recently underwent bypass surgery, plus a close friend who evidently is dying. So, I wrote a note to her today and told her not to worry about me, that I had had many fine Christmases and would make it a point not to be alone.

I have wondered, should something happen to your Mother, what your father would do. He seems so dependent on her. Although, sometimes, I think men seem to do better than women in that situation.

Well, I must close. Do keep me posted. Am just so happy for you that you are having some fun. And thanks for looking for the bittersweet. Love, /s/ Jane.

George accompanied me to the store's Christmas Party that year. We had a wonderful time. Christmas eve, he showered me with gifts and told me he had fallen in love with me. By Valentine's Day, 1991, he gave me a card, the front of which had two big red hearts and read "Heart to Heart." Inside was this note:

Marjorie

I can't believe how difficult it was to find the right gift and to let you know how I feel about my "Valentine." I did not want to be too frivolous, because I feel too strongly about you to do anything foolish. I did not want to be too serious for fear of sending you running away from a serious relationship. I guess we need to talk about where we're headed. I know I love you and my best times are spent with you – but they never seem to be long-lasting enough. Anyway, Happy Valentines Day, Love George.

We did have a talk, but only decided to continue as we had been and see what developed. But as seems to happen in my male relationships, it wasn't long before George's feelings seemed to cool and I became disillusioned.

❧

A letter from Jane, dated Feb. 15, 1991, is typed on plain white paper. The envelope bears a flower stamp, no amount, just an "F" – postage must have been going up again.

> *Dear Marge:*
>
> *Excuse the beautiful stationery! I have been doing a lot of paper work – income tax, etc., this afternoon and just don't have the pep to drag out a better piece of paper.*
>
> *I was delighted to receive your letter about a month ago and learn you are still seeing George and, evidently, becoming closer all the time. I told you I had a "special" feeling about him, Mrs. Flanagan. Incidentally, one of my Mother's best friends married a man named Flanagan.*
>
> *You did tell me that John and Jean were having problems, but I didn't know they were actually "broken up". What does he think of your having a man friend? Serves him right. He must be either a mixed up person or a selfish one who never should have married at all. I do hope John will be able to help you enough financially so that you can stay in the house once the child support stops.*
>
> *No, it does not sound silly that you both love one another but don't know one another well enough yet to think about marriage. Emotions are lots of times not based on length of acquaintance. When did you start dating? It sounds as though there really are a lot of problems with his children and his Ex. I wouldn't relish going into the situation, but then I am a lot older than you and that colors my outlook. What did he give you for Christmas? You mentioned his coming to the car when you were talking with Monique and "looking as cute as could be", carrying your gift. What does Monique think of the whole situation? If you ever have a snapshot, please send same. How does Sarah feel about it? And does she have a job yet?*
>
> *Yes, the war situation is just terrible. I pray it will soon end. I have been thinking about the oncoming heat there but no mention was made of it until just the other day I heard on TV that they felt the situation had to be resolved by some time in April, because with all the gear, gas masks, etc., the soldiers must wear, they would not stand the heat more than 20 minutes. I wouldn't put it past Hussein to have planted those people in the air raid shelter,*

which was undoubtedly in the same building as a communications center, just to raise the fury of the Iraq nation and the world. But I do feel so sorry for the general populace.

You know what I miss most in not having a husband or male companion? Just male conversation. After having worked 30 years with the Agents and being more used to male conversation than female, I miss those contacts terribly. Al Reginato stopped in to see me a couple of weeks ago. He came down for a retirement party, and I really appreciated his coming out here to visit -- for almost 3 hours.

I really have nothing special to report, and don't want to bore you with health talk, etc. Do keep me posted re "you and yours". Am so happy you have someone to go out with, and I am keeping my fingers crossed all will be for the best. You both must be the same type persons, and both deserve lots of happiness. Love you, /s/ Jane

PS Hope your Mother is doing fine.

After a couple of years of living together in the house they had built, when John and I divorced, John and Jean split up.

Monique and I have been friends for over 20 years. We were returning from lunch one day when George came bouncing out of his car, with a gift he bought in exchange for a massage pad he had given me for Christmas. The pad was to be placed in the bottom of the tub. It had to be plugged in, and came with all kinds of warnings. I was afraid I would electrocute myself!

Al Reginato was assigned to the San Diego FBI office after I left.

~

I received a postcard from Jane dated 2-18-91 with a picture of "Mau Mau (a cat) on a Carpet of Peacock Feathers" on the front. The card states:

Dear Marge – You were sweet to send me a Valentine. Will write one of these days but in the meantime – are you planning a trip to S.D? Hope so.

155

I saw 'The Marriage of Figaro' Sunday – SD Opera. V.G. Hope to see the movie "Hear My Song" – filmed in Ireland – a comedy with music. Supposed to be excellent. How are your kitties? Hope you had a nice Valentine's Day. Much love, Jane.

March 16th

Dear Marge:

I think I owe you a letter! Have been so busy with paper work: income tax, which is partially under control; starting to set up a Trust, prepare a new will and a new Durable Power of Attorney, plus the usual amount of paper work for the Mexican people.

Now to answer some of your questions. The house in Chula Vista is still in question. Jim says they will be moving to Texas after school is out. I hate to sell the house now, with prices so low, but also hate more the problems involved in renting it out. I know financially speaking for me it is a help to have deductions for taxes, etc., for the house, but I already have so much paper work.

How is your class "How to Get the Love You Want" going? Hope it gives you some help. Personally, I am not the kind such things appeal to, but I know they do help some. I think there is no reason you have had bad luck with men; bad luck just follows some. I had an old Great Aunt who never married. My Mother used to tell me that when she asked Aunt Martha why she never married, the reply was, "Those I wanted I couldn't get and those I could get the Devil wouldn't have!" And she was very religious – out of character for her to even use the word "Devil."

I feel you are on the right road to go ahead with your life, and Clinton sounds like an ideal spot. Maybe by now you have told George your plans and it has brought him to his senses. I have often wondered whether or not part of the trouble with his marriage was lack of personal attention to his wife. Maybe he gave most of his time and love to the children. You think of this before you marry him.

That was an unbelievable story about your having stood in line for three hours to give your condolences to the mother of the boy who died. Just like I think middle America must still be to an extent. Can't say I blame you for wanting to stay there instead of returning to Calif. Speaking of that, are you planning to come out this Spring? Do let me know, as I am sure you will.

The big news here concerns my other project which is keeping me busy: if all goes well, LeLa Letson, my friend whom I visited last Oct. in Arizona and with whom I worked years ago in the FBI, will leave with me on a trip, arriving in Shannon, Ireland, May 22ⁿᵈ. We will fly independently to Atlanta, spend the nite, and leave the following evening for Ireland. We will be visiting Will's relations in Muff, which is across the river from Londonderry in north Ireland. You probably won't find Muff on the map, but look for Londonderry. After spending about a week with them, we shall take the ferry to Scotland, rent a car, and drive around until June 6ᵗʰ, returning to Atlanta again, and home June 8ᵗʰ.

I am concerned about my health. My legs have been swelling lately because of my varicose vein problems. Went to the doctor Friday and he said I must walk at least every hour. Said if I don't, I will get blood clots. Nice thought! So, Lela and I have decided to get a hotel room and rest on arrival for a day before we meet John and Olive Browne who are to meet us and drive to their home, which will take about four hours.

I am going to ask a favor of you re the enclosed. Do not put any other message inside, and do not put a return. Please mail it to reach him by April 13ᵗʰ, which is a Monday. Would rather have it get there a couple of days early than late.

He is an old boyfriend. He called me a couple of weeks ago and said he had been quite ill. It happened that he called on my birthday, not knowing it was. So I asked when his birthday is. When I see you, will tell you more. He is married. Don't think I am starting an affair with a married man. It's just that I feel so badly this has happened to him and want to send a card. I think he will know who it is from, even tho mailed from your area.

The Woman's Club is having a fashion show luncheon in April. I am on the decoration committee — quite a bit of work. Also, the gal who is in charge is a great friend of mine. She loves history, etc., and is having several old-fashioned wedding gowns modeled. I washed my Mother's gown (which I wore) yesterday, and it turned out well. Now to iron it, which will be a job.

Did not mean for this to be so long, but lots to tell this time. Do let me know soon about the progress of your "affair" with Georgie. Lots of love, /s/ Jane

I had enrolled in the "How to Get the Love" class to try to figure out what I was doing wrong, since things were not going well with George. Reading Jane's Aunt Martha's comment, "Those I wanted I couldn't get, and those I could get, the Devil wouldn't have," reminded me of a comment I made to my daughter, that I thought sexual attraction was the work of the devil! Kidding, of course, but with my track record, I figure it has to be the devil who leads me into these devastating situations!

As far as "going ahead" with my life, I decided to sell the house in Bolton and buy a condominium in Clinton.

~

May 23, 1991
Dear Marge:
I loved your little note just to say you were thinking of me! More people should do that.

I'm happy for you (as you know) that you have someone, at long last, and especially someone who feels the same about marriage as you do. You never let me know how your children feel about the relationship – especially your daughter. She is so cute. Is she now working – will she go to college?

Last week I went to Borrego Springs with four other widows where we spent three nights at the El Zorro Resort. It is lovely. We had a cottage with 2 bedrooms, two baths, large living room, kitchen, and patio. It was $180 a night, but divided by 5, it all came to around $81 apiece. We took our food for breakfast and lunch and ate dinners out. I had to sleep with one of the gals, but we each took a sleeping pill and got along fine. It has been years since I slept with another female, and I don't think either one of us was looking forward to it, but it worked out fine.

Saturday, I am going to see the Calif. Ballet Co. for a matinee performance. I am not keen on ballet although I always enjoy it. A friend had two tickets given her. It is in Poway, but she will drive.

She is nice but a very serious person – someone I met through the Sweetwater Woman's Club.

I have been having increasing trouble with my eyes. Lots of headaches. It seems to be a combination of left-over migraines, poor muscle function, and the fact that my eyes do not work together – one looks one way and the other another way. I don't like to complain, but it is disappointing to awaken every morning and have an ache. I have been taking calligraphy at an Adult School Class in Lemon Grove. It is very hard on my eyes, so I don't practice much, and therefore am not progressing very fast. It comes so easy to some folks.

The only thing about your relationship with George is that I hate to see you have all the complications with an ex-wife and 3 children, plus his financial condition, which you inferred was not too lucrative. I am wondering how you will get along financially when John ceases his child support. Maybe Sarah will get a job to help. How do your folks feel about the Georgie deal?

Do you know, as time goes on, I have become more lonesome than ever. I was talking with another friend recently, whose husband has been gone about 4 years, and she said she feels the same way. I had hoped that feeling would improve. I hate these 3 day weekends, like the one coming up, so called this friend and asked whether or not she would like to out to dinner Monday night at Jake's Did I take you there? I feel I did—or rather that you took me.

Keep having fun, and I just hope your life turns out to be a most happy one from now on.

Much love, Jane

Things must have gotten back on course with George, based on Jane's comment, but, I cannot recall what I said about marriage. My children were not crazy about him, and my daughter became quite upset when I mentioned having him move in with us. Sarah graduated from high school in June, 1991. George attended her graduation and party. She had a job with an accountant, with no immediate plans for college.

~

June 30th

Dear Marge:

This is a quick reply, but I wanted to get a note off to you right away to comment on your present male relationship. I had very mixed emotions on reading your letter. I just regret that the person you met could not have been fancy free, with at least a moderate amount of money so that you could live comfortably without always thinking of money. You do seem to be very fond of George. And your doubts disappear when you are with him. What does your friend Monique think about the situation? She knows you so well and is on the scene, so certainly is a better person than I to comment. But perhaps she does not want to interfere.

I feel that George needs a rival. Then you would not always be home, awaiting his every call. I do think he owes it to you to take you someplace nice at least every other week. Maybe I shouldn't even say that much. Just keep me posted.

Naturally, I am delighted you are coming out again in August. And I hope again you can spend a night with me. I hope we have more fun than we did last time. We didn't seem to have a meeting of the minds as we always had done before. When you came out the second time, everything was as it used to be.

The main reason I am writing so soon is so that you will have a chance to think and let me know the answer to my query as follows:

I went to a retirement party Friday for Danny Morris – do you remember him? He took John Baker's place when John retired. There were a few Agents whom I knew and about four or five gals. Among the Agents was Joe Scallini. I was talking with him quite a bit and mentioned you. Told him you were divorced, had a rather serious boyfriend, and were due to visit SD in August. He gave me his card and said for me to let him know when you came and that perhaps we could have lunch. I don't know whether you want to see him or not, but if you do, I want you to look your prettiest. So, bring your most fetching, sexiest dress so that he will be sorrier than ever what he missed! His card says he is an Investigator.

Did you get an invitation to Linda's son's wedding the end of July? I never even met him, so I am going to just send a card. I wrote Linda that I would not be able to attend the wedding because my friend whom I visited for a week in Kona last year will be here. (That's the truth.) She will be here through the end of July and into Sept. a bit.

Will Sarah be with you on your trip? I imagine she will. I hope she has been able to find a job.

My friend Winifred has asked me to join her and two friends on a drive to Arizona sometime in October. We had a little falling out awhile ago. Things are better, but I don't think we shall ever feel the same toward one another as we used to. I considered her my closest friend and we have known one another since we were eight. I plan to go, hoping to stay several days with a former FBI gal who lives in Cottonwood, not far from Prescott. Other than that, I plan to be home all of 1991.

Thanks so much for taking me into your confidence regarding George. In case you're interested, I always had to talk over my serious boyfriends with at least one and probably more friends!

As they say, "Hang in there, Kiddo". Much love, /s/ Jane

Jane asked what Monique thought about the Georgie situation. She mostly listened, as she had been doing for years. I am sure I had her as confused as Jane.

～

For some reason I have a note I wrote to Jane, dated Tuesday, July 9th (1991).

Dearest Jane,

Just read your letter – it's 9:30 p.m. – went to the beach, well actually, took a ride to York Beach, Maine, today with my sisters-in-law. Beautiful day. I couldn't wait to reply to your letter, in particular, the part about Joe. I would absolutely L-O-V-E to see him! I know I'd be an absolute nervous wreck, but ... Unfortunately, I've sort of changed my mind about August and am leaning more toward a Sept. visit.

Sorry I burdened you with my Georgie stories. Believe me, any comments are welcome. I am having second thoughts about the relationship, but my feelings keep bouncing back and forth. I'm driving myself crazy. I'm trying to merely take one day at a time and enjoy the times we have together, keeping busy when we are not.

Will write at length later. Love, Marge

~

Jane's reply, dated August 14th

Dear Marge:

This is a fast reply, but if I don't write soon, you will be here! Am anxiously awaiting the date of your arrival. I was prompted to write so soon because I just hung up the phone from talking with Joe. You will recall I had told him you would be here in August. Knowing that you are anxious to have lunch with him, I called to say your trip had been postponed to September. He said he would be out of town part of the month on hunting trips. As a matter of fact, he is leaving this Friday for a week's hunting trip to Mexico. I am sure he wants to get together – that this was not a put-off.

Don't concern yourself that you are "unloading your troubles" on me. I am flattered that you think enough of me to confide your problems. I may have told you that when I was maturing (and even now) when I had problems I always had to talk with one, two, or three people about them. So don't feel upset with yourself!

I really don't like the sound of the George connection. I do think it sounds as though he takes you for granted. Maybe when you are away a week he will realize how much you mean to him. He is crazy if he should ever pass you by.

Although I don't know when we shall be leaving, it will be around the first of Oct. Confidentially, I am a little sorry I said I would go along. Three other women – all art teachers – all "intellectuals" – and much territory planned to cover in two weeks. I know with four people, there cannot be much luggage, but Winifred said to take two pairs of slacks – no dresses or skirts. I can't imagine living for two weeks with one change. Also, they are going to visit two other art friends, and they are all keen on Indian ruins, etc. American Indians never have excited me much, whereas I have always been most interested in the Mayan and Olmec culture of Mexico. So, keep your fingers crossed for me that there will be some fun.

Do you think you will be able to spend a night with me? I do so hope so. We just can't talk everything over in one lunch. And the lunch with Joe is not a time we could do that, either.

I do hope your doctor was able to give you some medication to help your depression. I was so fortunate at that time. The only thing which happened to me was bad migraines, and the fact that I developed high blood pressure. However, I don't think it was the cause of the latter. Getting married probably was! Will tell you about that when I see you if you are interested. Maybe I already have.

Did I tell you about turning down the chance to meet an interesting man? If not, will do so when I see you. I have kicked myself around the block every since.

I took my step-granddaughter in to Balboa Park with me a couple of weeks ago. We went to an exhibit at the Museum of Man, then I took her to lunch at the Café del Rey Moro. Last week, I asked the brother where he would like to go, and he wanted to see "Terminator II"!!! Can't you just see me? I had to sit through 2 ½ hours of it. He picked McDonald's as his choice for lunch. At least I got a break money-wise there. I can't believe how much it now costs to go to the movies and to buy popcorn and cokes. And so many people seem to go. You wouldn't think there was any poverty in the U.S. to see the way they go to restaurants, the movies, etc.

Well, I'll be seeing you before long, so shall cut this short. Let me know when you know about your trip – Keep me current! Much love, /s/ Jane

On my visit to San Diego that year, Joe and I had lunch and a very pleasant visit. Jane backed out, and I know it was because she considered herself a "third wheel." Naturally, I was curious about how I would feel when I saw him, his being my very first heartthrob and all. But it wasn't any different than a good visit with any friend whom I hadn't seen in over 20 years. I wanted to ask him how he felt about me way back, but I couldn't get up the nerve. After lunch, he asked, "Where to" and I told him that I better get back to my folks' house.

~

My birthday card that year was a product of "Leanin' Tree", Boulder, Colorado. "Happy Hands" by Vel Miler, is the picture on the front -- a beautiful Indian maiden sitting on a blanket, thrown across a log in the forest, stringing beads.

"Dear daughter Marge," Jane wrote – "or niece – or what-have-you! For I think of you as more than just a young friend.

"A Happy, happy birthday to you! The card doesn't say so but since you love 'words' I thought you might like it. I believe it is a series of cards styled with Indian photos and sayings."

The verse – by Virginia Covey Boswell:

"I wish for you the forest's peace, the scented air of pines;

I wish that you may always walk beneath a sun that shines"

~

A card with a picture of a "White-tailed Emerald", a type of hummingbird, dated Nov. 28th, contained the following message:

Dear Marge –

This is a short pre-Christmas answer to your recent note. Thought I'd better get this off before I get back to working on the Christmas cards I am trying to make!

Just came back from Thanksgiving dinner at the invitation of Winifred's brother and his wife who live at Lake San Marcos. Winifred and I spent the night at Quail's Inn Motel.

I never did have occasion to talk to Joe, by the way. Did you still feel the same way about him when you saw him again?

I am distressed over your worries with George's problems. I wish some man with no "past" would appear and sweep you off your feet. I feel like writing him and telling him what a fool he is not to "snap you up".

This note is just to keep in touch and tell you I love you and am thinking of you. Jane

~

Jane's Christmas card that year was handmade. On the front was a penned outline of the Holy City with the star of Bethlehem. The center sparkled with a little rhinestone. There was a little hummingbird flying over. This was on white paper, which was glued to a bright blue background.

Using her calligraphy, she wrote "The Chuparrosa wends it's way through skies of midnight blue to celebrate the Saviour's birth and bring good cheer to you." It was signed "Jane Esther Browne". She added a note: "I surely hope you have some merry times during the holidays! My best love, always, Jane."

~

The first letter of 1992 is dated February 8.

Dear Marge:

I hope I can get this letter in the mail today, but probably the mailman will come too soon. As always, I was happy to hear from you. Your letters are so wonderful – it is almost like having a visit with you.

That was some scene, after which George was served with a court order in connection with an assault and battery charge! Honestly, his life sounds more like a soap opera than reality. It is hard to realize people live that way. And then he had let his driver's license expire! Woe is me. Now on rereading your letter, I see that you believe his license was mailed to his old address and confiscated by Bob; sounds logical.

I don't understand a young, healthy man not wanting, as you say, "more out of the relationship." Gad, most men these days seem to have s— on their minds a lot of the time. Just doesn't seem normal, which I am sure you are!

Had upsetting news from Winifred. She has breast cancer. Surgery is scheduled for 2-12-92. I am very concerned, but she has a good mental attitude. She came to stay with me 3 days when I had my hysterectomy years ago, so I told her I would be up to help her. However, it seems her brother and his wife are moving in, which is really better as she is a great manager and cook. I'm not good in someone else's kitchen or house, I must admit. She will

165

probably need to have radiation or chemo, and I just hope that she comes out of it all right.

You mentioned in your letter that you might be out in February. Well it's here, and I've heard nothing. So, let me know.

I thought I might have a house guest in March – Pearl Hunt, the widow of one of Will's cousins – whom we visited in Florida several years back. Well, she is short of money and does not know whether or not she can swing it. She mentioned she would rather come in June – whereas I would rather have her in March.

Went to the first of the opera series – Die Rosenkavalier – or however it is spelled. Really wasn't too happy with it, but the others should be better. This one had only one piece which was tuneful. Others I know have been beautiful pieces – Figaro, Carmen and a Strauss, which always is lovely.

Don't think you bore me with your tales of George. I love to hear about it. However, I do wish "it were going someplace". Have you mentioned the annulment papers? I don't imagine, with all the uproar in his life, that the time has been appropriate.

Sorry this is not my usual long letter, but there doesn't seem to be much to report. Much love, /s/ Jane

The longer I knew George, the more trouble he seemed to get into. He had tremendous difficulty accepting his ex-wife's remarriage (to her old high school sweetheart), especially since they were living in the house George referred to as the "dream house" he had purchased for her and their three children. He apparently became so belligerent when he would return his children after his weekends with them that his ex-wife's new husband obtained a restraining order against him. He had to drop the kids off at the end of the driveway. Another time, when he had to appear in court, he was approached by an officer in the parking lot and asked for his license. At that time, his car was towed because he did not have a license and apparently there was some sort of warrant out for him. He always had a "reasonable" explanation, which I would fall for.

I had forgotten that sometime after we started becoming serious, George obtained annulment papers for both me and himself – which led me to believe he had some intention of getting married again.

~

April 30ᵗʰ
Dear Marge:
With two inches of wine in my glass and a piece of cheese loaf bread in my hand, I sit down to write to you!

Incidentally, this will be my "swan song" before I leave on May 20ᵗʰ. I get jitters when I think there are only 20 days left – and so many things yet undone. Guess I told you about being snowed under with so much paper work. It is now all done except making a new will, a new Durable Power of Attorney, and setting up a Trust. I just hate stuff like this, and having to do it all by myself, with no one family-wise to consult, is a bit frightening. So much "gobbledegook" legal terminology – I hate to sign things I don't understand, but believe I have the really important things figured out. It all has to be wound up before I leave, and I have letters to write still.

I have had six friends die within the last six weeks. Went to the last Memorial Service today. Can't get used to the new way they do things. It was held at the Sweetwater Woman's Club, to which the gal belonged. The husband wore slacks and a rather colorful top – almost like a T-shirt – very informal. There was no minister, not even a prayer – a couple of short speeches by members of the Club who knew her best. And the rest was eating the cookies, etc., which members provided.

Re your letter. I see you are back in your old feelings about George. NO mention this letter about selling your house and moving to an adjoining town. And yet, you say you do not want to marry him! Can't quite figure that one out, especially when you have said you do not want to have an affair. Don't think I mean to be critical – just am confused about how you REALLY feel!

And, please, I hope you will quit feeling there is something wrong with YOU. I find that an absurd statement. You must have turned John on or he would not have married you. (You said I could speak my mind – so I am!)

Thanks for mailing the birthday card to my one-time boyfriend. Don't know whether he figured it out or not. However, he called me a week ago Saturday (from a pay phone) – said he thought I was going to call him (I don't know where he got that idea); that he will be home this Saturday, and he hopes I will call him. I am scheduled to leave the house sort of early, so I will just call and have a short conversation. Good for my ego to know he still thinks of me, but what would it all amount to at this point? I never was in love with him, but liked him, perhaps better than most. Will tell you about it when I see you.

Hope you had a good time while your sister was with you. Did you talk with her about George, and, if she met him, what did she think? I imagine she would have brought up the subject of relationship had she been dating him. Let me know.

I return 6-9-92. The end of the month I probably will have a visitor for two weeks. Not certain yet. So, let me know when you expect to be here. Much love, /s/ Jane

I undoubtedly had Jane thoroughly confused about how I felt over George. It was definitely a roller coaster round of emotions – but that always seems to be the case for me when I am involved with a man. I always want things to work out and when they do not, I despair and cry on my friends' shoulders – sometimes I've even resorted to professional counseling, but never found that it helped.

My sister met him when I invited him to dinner while she was visiting. He was his charming, funny, best self – she seemed to be entertained, but never did say one way or the other what she thought of him.

I don't recall Jane ever telling me about her "one-time boyfriend."

~

A postcard, captioned: "Traffic Jam – Ireland," dated 5-24-92, pictured a bicyclist and pedestrians trying to make their way through a herd of sheep in the road.

Dear Marge –
Thanks for the lovely card and letter.
We arrived on schedule in Ireland and are now visiting Will's relatives in North Ireland. They have a lovely 6 bedroom home. Eating, eating! They really put out the food. Home 6-8-92. Love, Jane

∼

10-2-92
Dear Marge:
Excuse stationery; it is some which belonged to my cousin, so am trying to use it up after about 20 years!
'Twas good to hear from you, especially the part that you had had an offer on your house. Strange, but I am going through the same thing – with Will's house in Chula Vista. Lots of rigamarole, isn't it? I do hope both of your deals don't fall through. I had to come way down in my price and also pay $2,505 in termite treatment! I put in the counter offer that since I had reduced the price by $19,000 and had the big termite bill, I would not paint or do any other repairs to the house – and it needs a lot. Escrow is to close November 6th, so keep your fingers crossed for me and I will do the same for you.
As I am sure I told you, I went to the X-Agents' Convention in May. Stayed the 4 nights at the Sheraton on Harbor Island. Had a lovely room, and a good book to read when I got lonesome. Strange, but, as I am sure you will agree, sometimes it is more lonesome to be in a crowd as a single when there are lots of couples than to be at home alone in your own living room. I saw quite a few former Agents. Joe did not put in an appearance. I gathered he is not active in the local chapter, either. The thing I enjoyed the most was the 3-hour business meeting. Mr. Sessions was the main speaker, and at one of the breakfasts, the Attorney General spoke. I got quite a thrill out of hearing both. The food was good, and there were several tours. I opted for the tour to Tijuana. None of my friends will go down there with me. I lost a pair of earrings I bought years ago in Mexico and wanted to see about

169

getting a duplicate pair in TJ. Well, wouldn't you know, I was tootling along the last 20 minutes of shopping time and fell right in front of the Jai Alai Palace! Seems there was an irregularity in the height of the walkway, and I tripped. My glasses dug into the side of my right eye and then flew off to the left. I fell on my right side, so had bruises there. Got myself up and found the blood was running down my check, so went into Sanborn's and washed my face well with soap and water and got back on the bus. I think my guardian angel must have been on duty that day, since I broke no bones, and although I had a lovely shiner for the big banquet the next night, the glasses did not go into my eyeball, so I feel very lucky. I think the arthritis in my right knee is worse since then, but hopefully that will clear up.

Hope Sarah still likes her job and that it will develop into something permanent.

When I got to the convention, I immediately looked over the men in the room. There was only one who "appealed" to me. He was always alone – no woman. Finally I found his name and looked on the list of attendees and, of course, under the "Wife's Name" column – there she was! He lives in Escondido. He evidently felt the same way about me, for he was always looking at me. No point in getting involved with anything like that, however!

Well, I hope this birthday will be better than you had thought it would, without the former BF. I hope you aren't running into him every so often. I am sure that would hurt. Nothing more here. Much love, and Happy Birthday!

In October, 1992, our home in Bolton was sold. My daughter, Sarah, and I found it difficult to leave the house which had been our home since 1978, when she was but five years old. The nice new condominium was a welcome change, however, with no more big yard responsibilities, outside repairs, etc. It was a new beginning for both of us. She had just started a new job with the Massachusetts State Police, and I no longer shared anything with John's name on it.

～

Christmas 1992 brought the following note from Jane:

GREETINGS – ONE AND ALL –

Since I have a bit of different news this year, I decided to send a brief letter. In May, a friend and I flew to Ireland to visit John Browne, Will's second cousin, and his wife Olive. They live at Muff, across the river from Londonderry. The house in which they live was built by Will's grandfather. It is situated on 400 acres of beautiful Irish green countryside. I can't begin to tell you about Irish hospitality – you just must experience it to believe it!

A week later we boarded a ferry for Scotland, rented a car, and drove southwest since I was anxious to see the land from which my Campbell ancestors, the Argyll Clan, came. There we toured the great castle of the Duke of Argyll. He and his Duchess live in part of the Castle, but a good many rooms are open to the public. Next we drove up the coast and took a ferry to the Isle of Mull, a most unique experience. We spent several days in Edinborough and Glasgow, then home.

In September, I had a mini vacation when I attended the National Convention of the Society of Former FBI Agents which was held on Harbor Island in San Diego. I saw many of the Agents with whom I had worked over the years. It was a most enjoyable four days.

So, this brings to a close a short account of my 1992, but not before I send my very best wishes to you for a joyous Christmas Season. Love, Jane (over)

On the reverse is a handwritten note:

Dear Marge –

Happy to receive your letter today! Loved the snapshots – what a BIG house! How many square feet? Do you have an attic and a basement and are you happy with the house and change?

I'm glad you at least get out once in awhile with Ken. Maybe it will develop?

In a rush – will write when I can. I now am in the midst of Holiday rush and re-doing Trust and Will, etc.

Happy New Year! Much love, Jane

The picture to which Jane referred was of the condominium – but I only lived in one of the four condos in the building. She must have thought I owned the entire building!

Ken was an old friend – available for a movie or dinner once in awhile.

~

January 3, 1993
Dear Marge:

I never was any good in the File Room – consequently, I can't seem to keep track of letters I receive, receipts, etc. Now that I promised to return your pictures, do you think I can find them? I feel so badly. Surely one of these days they will turn up. Did I already send them?

The enclosed photo is from 1990, taken the day I left Vashti's home in Kona, on the Big Island of Hawaii. She had the wife of the man who does all her housework, gardening, etc., make this for me when I left. It is called a "Haku" and is properly worn as shown in the photo. I can no longer get into that skirt! I have gained 10 pounds since then, sad, sad to say. Christmas really ruined me. I made a batch of fudge and about 7 recipes of cookies. I gave most away, but naturally, had to sample quite a few. I had an "all chocolate" Christmas in the lots I gave most people. I did make one other batch by my favorite recipe, which was my Mother's called "Date Torts". Enuf of that except to say that I have developed a real sugar craving – for years the main craving was for pasta dishes. Now I am used to having sweets each day – I am becoming a "Chocoholic".

You need not return the snapshot. Maybe I already sent you one.

Really enjoyed our nice phone conversation. Letters are great, but there is nothing like conversation. I was surely interested in your "new beau". I thought afterwards that I should have commented on your remark that he is quite shy and perhaps waiting for you to make the first move. I think you should give it a try – maybe you have by now. Perhaps just a kiss on the cheek at the right moment would help, and there is the chance that some romance might change your feelings. Let me know.

I have been home three days straight, which is unusual. However, I have worked on my Trust restatement, gotten the W-2 forms and transmittal form to Social Security for the gardener and housekeeper, a couple of other letters in connection with their work, and some much-needed letters written. The re-do of the Trust, Will, and one other paper is taking a lot of time, plus trips to SD to the new attorney.

I hope you did not ask me any special questions in your call or Christmas card. If so, sorry but guess you'll have to repeat.

My next book work is to start on income tax. Really can't do much until Feb. after the W-2 forms come in, but I will go through my checkbook and make a list of deductions. I imagine under Mr. Clinton, there will be fewer, and taxes higher. I have put most of my savings in tax-free investments. Hope I have not made a mistake.

Sorry this is a dull letter – but there is nothing exciting to report. Isn't it awful, at my age, to still be missing male companionship?

Much love and thanks again for the call. Jane

The mention of a shy "new beau" is drawing a blank. We must have been talking about Ken, with whom I had gone out, off and on, over the years, with nothing transpiring as far as a romance.

~

2-28-93

Dear Marge:

Well, I declare, I get more confused and disorganized, it seems, as the days go by! I got out your last letter a couple of days ago to answer, and do you think I can find it now! Drives me WILD!!

I do thank you, first of all, for the lovely card. How nice of you to remember me that way – it means a lot, believe me.

When I received your last missive, I could hardly wait to sit down and read the latest re your new romance – and how disappointed I was that you wrote he was away! I had hoped

173

that you had taken a less passive approach, and that things had progressed. I can hardly believe it now, but do you know that Will and I dated for six months before he even kissed me? I am sure he wanted to, but felt I might turn him down. I really wasn't interested for months – just wanted him as a friend. But once we got together a bit – things changed! Just remember that! He wasn't an exciting person to live with, but I always felt he was the "Rock of Gibraltar" and would always stand by me and be there no matter what.

I swear life is so complicated now. Seems I have less time than when Will was here. I'm so swamped with paper work all the time, and seem to write letters to my friends all about the same time, because their replies all come at the same time, even tho' they may live in Ireland or on the East Coast. Incidentally my Irish hosts, Olive and John Browne, expect to arrive about 3-8-93 to visit their daughter and family who live in North County. I want so badly to fix up a really nice dinner, with best table setting, etc. for them, but that means 4 adults and 2 young children. The little girl is 8 and the boy 2 – and what a live wire! I get so tired, it seems, with extra effort. I would much rather have them at home than take them out – nothing to do with money; I just think it is a nicer way to entertain. They were so wonderful to me I feel I owe them a lot.

I didn't feel this year I wanted or was up to a long trip, yet hate to give in and stay home ALL the time, so I called a friend who lives in Northern Calif. and she is going with me on a week's cruise down the Mexican Riviera. I had originally suggested Alaska, but that entails a flight up to Seattle to begin with, and it is a very expensive cruise also. I thought a week seemed about right. I hope I get along OK and enjoy it more than the Hawaiian cruise. If so, perhaps I shall try to go through the Canal next summer.

Oh – we leave 4-18-93 and return a week later. I luckily have found a young man who lives in the area and does nothing but take ladies around who do not drive, etc. For pay, of course, he will pick me up at the house and drive me right to the ship in San Pedro. It will be cheaper than public transportation. My friend is flying down here the day before, so I am sure she will share that cost with me.

I had wanted to write another long letter today, but it is now 5:00 p.m. and I guess I will call it a day. Maybe tomorrow morning I can write my friend in Mexico City. A little gal who works in the office now has asked me to go to lunch with her, but we haven't been able to get together. She suggested it at the time of the last meeting of the FBI gals, months ago. I am meeting her for a Mexican lunch in Bonita.

I hope everything, in all ways, is going well for you – and that you won't be running into George a lot. Am sure it must hurt a lot to see him with someone else. Since you live in a small town, I imagine he knows you are dating.

Much love, /s/ Jane

PS. I looked again in my correspondence file and there was your letter, just where it should be!

I would see George at church occasionally, which was upsetting, especiaily at Christmas, when he brought his fiancee.

~

April 13, 1993
Dear Marge:
I should be doing things for my trip but did want to write you before I leave. Have had a lot of alterations to do on clothes, which I hate. Thought I was through, then last eve tried on a muumu I had made and found it would look better if it had more fit through the waist. Sounds easy, but to get it angled just right seems to take a lot of trying on! I still don't know just what clothes to take. A cruise calls for evening wear – then the "Island Night" the muumu. Also wraps, cool weather clothes, hot weather clothes, and shoes for the different outfits. Seems crazy to be taking a rather large piece of luggage, but with all those things, it is necessary. Leave 4-18; return 4-25.

Thank you for the card and for the thought of me. It is always so nice to know I am in your thoughts. I get so lonesome sometimes – do wish you were closer. Strange, but I have been more lonesome this last year than any time since Will died. Then I found out yesterday that my very best friends, on whom I thought I could rely in case of needing help, the Carlsens, are planning to enter a retirement home near Rancho Bernardo. That, plus another thing that happened to me during the last ten days really put me in a depression – not altogether out of it yet. Will tell you what happened.

A week ago yesterday, I went grocery shopping in Von's store in Bonita about 10:30 a.m. Toward the end of my shopping, I was in the produce dept. when I spied a very nice looking older man. A friend of mine was in the next aisle and I went running to her to tell her that I had seen this man who really appealed to me.

Well, just after that as I was picking out some asparagus, he came to my side to get some potatoes and started talking to me. I got very self-conscious and just kept raving about the asparagus! (How dumb!) Really almost brushed him away. Well, two times after that while I was still in that dept. he pushed his cart through, smiling at me more and more. I really thought it was just happenstance, never thinking I could be attractive to anyone. He did not have much in his cart, so checked out long before I did. I cursed myself for having such a load. Well, sometime later, I checked out. When I went out the door, he was waiting for me. He immediately came up and said a few words. I thought I detected an accent and said, "Are you Irish? to which he asked if I had thought that because he smiled at me. He said he was Scotch! We passed a few words on that, then he wanted to know whether or not I came to Von's often. I confessed I came every Monday morning, and he wanted to know what time. So, when I told him, he said then we would meet the next Monday, to which I nodded and he added, "And a cup of coffee, too?"

Well, by this time, he had me so flustered I couldn't remember where my car was! Marge, I thought I was all over anything like this. Very few men have ever had such an effect on me. I couldn't sleep all week for thinking of him. He had such an open countenance and was so genuine-looking. I could hardly wait until the next week. Well, after all that, he never showed up! I thought perhaps he would be there yesterday, but he was not.

It is just the strangest thing, which has ever happened to me. At first, I felt disappointed, then angry, then felt he had played me for a fool, and then depression, for I thought I was going to have some fun. See "P.S." Of course, he did not know my full name nor anything else about me, nor I of him, other than his name is Gordon.

Silly to go into all this in detail to you, but just remember – you don't get over not having a man in your life. Some folks seem to, and I have tried to make myself feel that way, but I was proven wrong. So, I do hope you have better luck than I. I can't figure why he tried four times to talk with me – and then never followed through. I wish I had never met him!

So, I leave Sunday on the cruise, which I hope will be fun. I honestly do not go on cruises looking for a man, for they are few and far between, and I think a lot of them expect more than I would be ready to give. But at least it will get me away for awhile.

Have you heard from your latest friend? Can't remember his name.

It seems you have had a terrible winter. We had almost 20" of rain from January through March, which, as you know, is unbelievable for us.

I do hope something good has come to you since you wrote. Please forgive me for rambling on about this. Write when you can.

Much love, /s/ Jane

PS. I also have always felt I could sum up a person rather well on first acquaintance; now that feeling is dashed for he seemed to be such a real person.

～

A postcard dated 7-10-93, picturing the San Diego Museum of Man, Balboa Park, San Diego, carries the following message:

Dear Marge –

Thanks for your letter. Don't know when I'll answer – am expecting some of Will's relatives to be in town all week, tho' not staying with me. I will be with them a lot, however.

Don't know what is wrong with me – I can't seem to get in a letter-writing mood! Am anxious to learn the results of your newspaper venture!

Love, Jane

❧

7-17-93 (I made a notation "sent short note 7-23".)

Dear Marge:

Well, I am writing sooner than I expected. Had intended to work in the garden today, but am not feeling real well, so thought I had better get down to some long-overdue letter writing.

I really feel so sorry about you and your "love life". I don't blame you for being blue about it. You are such a "catch," if only the men realized it. I have mixed feelings about your putting an ad in the newspaper, but I hope you meet a really nice man from it. (Realize on re-reading your letter that "they" put the ads in).

I have lost a couple of good friends recently. That is one of the hardest things about getting to this age bracket. You miss your old friends and, at the same time, feel you must develop replacements, and that is not easy to do. Lots of times I want to go out to dinner, but there is only one friend I have who wants to do that – but only very occasionally.

I spent the 4th with Will's oldest son and family who live in Manhattan Beach. I should not say "family" as there are just the two of them now. Peggy had been ill the two days before I arrived, so we did not do much except sit around and visit. However, the big treat was going to the Hollywood Bowl on the night of the 4th. The music was all by American composers – excellent. And, of course, the fireworks were magnificent. I went on the train to Santa Ana, where Peggy met me. And the dear girl drove me all the way home. She is a real smart cookie – has built up a computer business working from her home – working mostly in software – which doesn't mean a heck of a lot to me.

Have you seen "Sleepless in Seattle" yet? Everyone loves it. Guess I shall miss it.

I, too, love the "old songs"; however, "old" to me is not what it is to you. "Harbor Lights" was one of my very favorites. My best friend and I were dating two Navy lieutenants at that time and they left to join WW 2. It was a very apropos song for the times. Still makes me sort of weepy, thinking of my youth and those nice boys.

Hope you have heard from Ken by now, but guess you really don't care – he doesn't sound like a heart-throb. By the way, what did you say in your letter to the two gentlemen who had articles on the Dating Page?

Sorry I don't have anything more interesting to report. Do you think you will be out this way during 1993? I hope so. /s/ Jane

I had made a couple of handwritten notes on the above letter, stating "told her I was glad she had a nice 4th"; that I had "commented" on the movie, and had "commented" about Ken. I had been listening to some old record albums, with dreamy songs such as Frank Sinatra's, "Oh what it seemed to be" (It was just a wedding in June, that's all that it was, but oh, what it seemed to be…) and Nat King Cole's, "The Very Thought of You."

At the time, I was answering ads in the "Dating Page" – to try to find a male companion. I went out with one gentlemen for a short period, but he had much more time on his hands than I did, and was too controlling for me.

~

Sept. 15th
Dear Marge:
Excuse the long interval, but a couple of things: I always seem to be hunting for time, and I have not been in a letter-writing mood. Please forgive.

Two things before I forget: Do you still get "The Grapevine"? If so, I shall no longer send clippings from same.

Second, I did not have a response from Mike Hennigan to my note. Guess I shouldn't have "meddled" -- hope he is not upset by it.

I have been busy with reunions and anniversaries. My high school class recently celebrated its 60th reunion, and I was on the decorating committee; made six or seven centerpieces with red carnations, Baby's Breath, and leather fern. Now, the 70th founding of my State College sorority is coming up and I am on that decorating committee. That is the job I prefer, thank goodness.

The only thing I do not like is all the committee meetings – three just for the latter.

I went to the zoo Monday for the first time in years. Every time I go there or to Balboa Park, I think "Why don't I do this more often?" I love that park. Neighbors tell me I should not go there by myself. Crime here has escalated. I try to be as careful as possible. My windows all have locks, doors almost all have double locks, and I try to keep doors locked even during the day, but, of course, slip up at times. With the car-jackings, I always hate to think the thief would have not only the car but everything in my purse, including the key to my house.

I have no really interesting news to report. Oh, I did go to lunch a couple of weeks ago with two people with whom I worked in the early 1940's: Carl O'Gara a radio operator, and his wife, who was Dorothy Kevane, a steno. Also at the luncheon was Tom Evans, a radio operator, and a friend of his. I haven't seen the O'Garas since probably the early 1950's, so we did a lot of reminiscing. I fixed a pineapple cheesecake, and we came home for dessert and coffee.

Thursday, I am going to another luncheon which is a joint meeting of the Former FBI Agents and The Association of Foreign Intelligence Officers. The only ones I know who go to the latter are Frank Price and the Munoz. I usually let them know when I plan to be at a meeting, and they save a place for me.

Oh – re my reading with the psychic in Old Town. I may have mentioned to you that I intended to do this. Well, it turned out that she is one of two psychics who are called in by police departments when their leads play out. She told me so much, it is hard to recount. Among those items was the fact that money would not be a problem in the future (good news!); that she saw a change for me in 1994 to more space; that she saw no marriage the rest of my life, but that six months to a year, I would meet someone. Am wondering if I am to move to more space, but not marry, just what that means? She said I had psychic abilities and that I was very artistic. I don't know about that. She asked how old I was toward the latter part of the reading, and when I told her 78, she seemed incredulous – wanted to know what I did to look so young!

That made me feel good. I am supposed to have two trips, and she urged me to go on them. I don't feel I ever want to leave home again! Neither do I want to marry nor change residences. She really dealt with the future, not the past. Well, guess I had better stop so I can get this in the mail.

We have had a delightful summer and I hope it continues. Some of our hottest weather recent years seems to come in Sept./ Oct.

Oh, re my remark about an ad in the paper. Seems to me that you had seen an ad from a man or two in the paper and had answered same, asking that the recipient send a reply to the address of your friend, Monique, I believe. Did I dream all that up?

You asked whether or not I had any remarks about you when you first started with the Bureau. Well, I recall what a darling girl you were – peppy, yet demure, lovely to look at, a hard worker, good steno, loved your laugh, and how nicely you dressed. I recall especially one dress; I think it was navy with a white organdy collar – rather a large collar. I really didn't know you personally those years and did not realize you had been close friends with Pat Meaney and blonde Monica. Guess you were a pretty busy little gal socially.

Good luck. Hope your folks' visit and that you have a great time. Love, /s/ Jane

PS I need all sorts of new clothes but just Hate to shop. Haven't had good luck lately with mail order clothes.

The Grapevine is a magazine for former FBJ employees. I had never received it, but John made copies of it available to me from time to time.

~

Dear Marge:

I decided to write you a Christmas letter instead of sending a card. There's really not any special news to tell, but I want to greet you at Christmastime and hope you will have a really nice Christmas, with some happy surprises.

181

I had a very nice letter from Mike Hennigan, and will quote a bit of it: "I was sorry to learn of Marjorie McClintock's divorce. I always thought she was a very special and lovely girl. I recall she came to work for us right out of high school. I'll try and contact her when I get the opportunity. I've been dating a wonderful woman here for the past 2 ½ years, and we're making plans to get married soon. I hope we'll be able to travel to So. Calif. in Feb. and I'll give you a call. Thanks for thinking of me, Jane, and if you ever travel to this area, call me and come visit."

There was more, but not worth quoting. He had been taking care of his 101 year old Mother for six months and said that was the reason for his delay in replying.

I hope by now you have had some contact with your sisters-in-law, for I know how much you enjoy their company.

How is the book coming? I hope some day you do complete a story. One of my sorority sisters is an author and has sold several books. She is now writing one based on my sorority. When I see you I will tell you about it. Hope you will come out in 1994.

For the first time in years since Will died, I had an invitation for Thanksgiving – went up to Will's oldest son's home in Manhattan Beach. Went on the train and they brought me home. Now the Carlsens invited me for Christmas dinner; we probably will go out in mid-afternoon. I have spent 3 or 4 years at Christmas all alone. I try to pretend it's another day, but when the day comes, it doesn't really work that way!

I had two luncheons recently. One was for 5 folks, including the Carlsens. I used all my best china, glassware, and silver – nothing could go in the dishwasher. It took me 3 hours to clean up. Was bushed! Thursday, I am having 8 gals for Christmas dessert. I have done a lot of different little things to make it party-like. For instance, I bought some darling Christmas material and made 8 booties, which I filled with special candies, some from Hungary, others from Belgium. It should be fun.

This brings you up-to-date on my busy, but unexciting, life. I am just thankful I am as well as I am.

I do hope something special has come your way since you wrote November 6th – like a nice man! Love /s/ Jane

January 15, 1994

Dear Marge:

HAPPY NEW YEAR! I do hope it will be a better one all around for you, with some real happiness in store.

I really don't have much to write about, but didn't want any more time to go by without at least touching base. Christmas was a disaster for me. Strangely enough, it was the first Christmas I had looked forward to since Will died as I had five invitations the week before, and an invite also for Christmas Day. Well, wouldn't you know it, I came down with a very bad cold on Christmas week Monday, and on Friday it started to go down in my chest, so I got antibiotics. Had to cancel every darn invite and wound up, as usual, all alone on the 25ᵗʰ.

I keep so busy just running this place. Have had many repairs, necessitating finding workmen – and then inducing them to come to the house and finish what they started. So maddening. I don't work in the yard at all lately. If my good gardener ever leaves, I'll really have to think about moving.

I had breakfast this morning with a favorite young friend, and now am getting ready to go see "The Piano" with a neighbor who is quite a musician. Neither one of us usually takes time to go to movies, so it will be a treat.

Next week looks pretty free for me, so perhaps I can get caught up on things. I try not to turn down any invitation, as I don't want people to quit asking me, so I have been gone a lot lately – to club, to SD for lunch with a friend I worked with around 1937 in the insurance office. We lost touch for years, so it was lovely to resume our acquaintance. She lives in Pt. Loma. Her family had a big ranch in Descanso. I used to go up there and spend a weekend once in awhile. I believe she said the property originally had 15,000 acres. The oldest son inherited 12,000 acres, and the other 3 children received 3,000, but there are two houses on that portion. Imagine what 15,000 acres would be worth now! Think she said that some time ago, one acre sold for $10,000.

Well, Marge, I am just making up news, but I wanted you to know I think of you, fondly, of course, very often. Oh – Anne was so pleased to receive your card. She hasn't sent cards for several years to anyone. Nick is so bad. She really needs to go back to work, but doesn't dare leave him alone. I feel for her. Such a genuine friend.

  Hope I receive some news of joy from you!
  Much love, /s/Jane

~

June 15*th*
Dear Marge:
We really have been out-of-touch in 1994. I recall the birthday and Easter notes from you and was happy to be remembered. However, haven't had any real news from you and do hope it means you are so busy dating and having a good time, that you just can't find time to write.

  Am trying to catch up with my correspondence. I owe everyone. Finally got a note off to my little Belgium friend whom I've owed for five months. I just haven't been in a letter-writing mood for two reasons: busy, plus nothing specially interesting in my life to fill up even a page.

  This weekend will be the first different weekend I have had all year. A friend (female, of course) and I are driving to Lake San Marcos Saturday to attend the Scottish Highland Games there. We leave at 9:30 a.m. and probably return mid-day on Sunday. We shall be staying at the Quail's Inn. It is a little motel, not too expensive, right on the lake, and good food in the restaurant. This friend is my age, but a lot "peppier" and in better health than I. However, it is fun to be with her for those reasons.

  The X-Agents have extended an invitation for the X-FBI gals to join them at their July luncheon. They are having a speaker from the Border Patrol, so that should be interesting.

  I also go, when I can, to the meetings of an organization called "Association of Former Intelligence Officers." Lou Munoz sponsored me. I joined because they have good speakers – and that way I very occasionally am able to be in the company of men. There was such a nice man I met at the last two. He was such a gentleman. BUT, I found out he is married! Anyhoo, it was nice to talk to him.

I haven't heard from Anne recently. I paved the way for her to apply for work with the FBI – that was the first of the year – but as far as I know she has never sent in her application. Nick isn't able to work any more, and she says she has to find work somewhere.

Well, this is a dull letter – but at least it keeps us in touch.

Do hope all is well with you – how are your son & daughter doing?

Much love, /s/ Jane

In June, 1994, my son at 25, graduated Salutatorian from Franklin Pierce College in Rindge, New Hampshire, with a Bachelor's in Mass Communication. While he did not attend college directly out of high school, he went when he was ready – and excelled. He received numerous awards, including two from the president of the college.

My daughter had just turned 21, and was working as an Administrative Assistant at the Massachusetts State Police headquarters. She attended classes in criminal justice, eventually earning an Associate's Degree.

~

Sept. 29th

Dear Marge:

How's this for a fast answer? I was so pleased to receive your letter, but sorry to learn that the latest male friend was a disappointment. He didn't sound good enough for you. Better luck next time.

You sounded so much cheerier than some letters – what with the line dancing and the trip with your cousins. I was so close to Gettysburg one time, but did not get to see it; surely wish I had. I have been to several Civil War battlefields, however, which are most interesting.

What is the "Big E" fair? And what does the "E" stand for? There is so much going on in and around SD these days that it is impossible to take in even a part of it. The Zoo, during the summer months, was open in the evenings, and I so did want to go, but I do not drive at night. Also, the Wild Animal Park has a hummingbird exhibit, and now there is a butterfly exhibit. I understand one can walk in the latter exhibit and the butterflies may land on your clothing.

Incidentally, the line dancing is very popular here, but too strenuous for me.

Bill Curran passed away a couple of weeks ago. I went to his memorial service. They are Catholic, as you no doubt know. I was surprised to see how modern the service was. They had a young man playing the guitar and singing. One of the songs was not even a religious song. The priest had very little part in the hour-long service. One of Bill's brothers spoke; then Ed Mari, who evidently had been very close to Bill, spoke. They used to go hunting together. I don't know when I have seen Ed look so well – he really was handsome. His wife was there – I never "took" to her. His son is a doctor in the military and just returned from Turkey. I believe Ed said he is in the Air Force. The daughter lives at home and just landed a job with the Price Club.

One of my friends wants to introduce me to her brother who has just gone through a hectic divorce and lost almost everything. They had 5 children. I saw him one time years ago and he was extremely nice looking. He drove with Greyhound and retired from that company. I really hope she never pushes this, as some of the things she has said seem to me would become problems in any relationship. So, I go my un-merry way!

How is your daughter doing? Has she met anyone at all she might like? And what is your son doing?

You are lucky your relatives have traced your family as far back as 1774. Where did they come from to the US? The farthest back I know is the name of my father's grandfather.

The X-FBI gals' meeting is this Saturday, but I cannot go. Now I'm sorry as I hear the new SAC in SD is to speak. Incidentally, the FBI is having a new building put up – it will be somewhere in North County, and I think they expect to be moving around the first of the year. There are still 3 girls at the office who were there when I retired. The gals have so much more responsibility than we did – and are compensated accordingly. I think Patty, whom I knew, is a Grade GS-12 or 14.

I had a houseguest for 3 days last week – the gal with whom I went on the Mexican cruise 2 years ago. She lives in northern California; I met her through the Woman's Club.

On 10-21-94, the widow of one of Will's first cousins, who lives near Tampa, is coming for about 10 days. At the same time, Will's relatives whom I visited in Ireland will be visiting their daughter in Temecula. All these people know one another. My guest, Pearl, is a "goer" and I am concerned I cannot keep up with her. I cook so little now, I will feel it hard to cook decently! I usually just jerk up something, but sometimes I get hungry for some real cooking and then make a casserole.

So, I am now beginning to get the house in order for the guest. I would be ashamed if anyone saw my kitchen cupboards and drawers. Also, must wash curtains, etc. And, if I can find two men who could turn my carpet and my mattress, I want to have 3 rugs in the house cleaned.

Well, Marge, I'm just rambling. I knew if I did not write you immediately, I would get into all this cleaning and would not be able to write until after Pearl leaves, around the first of Nov.

Do you still have two jobs? Wish I had some exciting news.

Love hearing from you.

Jane

PS. Do you think you will take advantage of the low air fares and come to SD this summer?

During the summer of 1994, I dated a fellow who had been introduced to me by one of my customers at the store. He drove a truck and smoked pot! The relationship did not last.

In September, 1994, I joined cousins of mine, all originally from Pittsburgh, Pa., but then living in Illinois, Florida, New York and Pennsylvania, on a trek to an old homestead in Maryland. It had originally been the home of my grandmother's ancestors – the Ludwig Kamerers, who had come from Germany. A copy of a newspaper article, written by Dave Cottingham, but otherwise unidentified, states:

"He (Ludwig Kamerer) cleared this site for his house, felled the massive trees, gathered the limestone rock that would be fabricated into its walls. It was a small fortress that he envisioned, built over its own water supply, with walls two feet thick to make his home impervious to Indian attack.

"That was a full two centuries ago, and the house that Ludwig Kamerer built has survived the ravages of time, weather and events to this day. The datestone on which he so proudly chiseled the date '1774' and his initials is a solitary memorial to the resourcefulness and determination of that intrepid pioneer."

On our way back to Pittsburgh, we stopped at Gettysburg. It was nearing the end of the day. A photograph captured the monuments against the sky, streaked with bright pinks and purples as the sun began to set -- most awe-inspiring.

The Big E, to which Jane referred, is the New England States Exposition, which is held in Springfield, Mass., each September. I attended the Big E on several September Wednesdays (my day off) with my friends Monique and Wendell Smith, who would pack their car full of eager fairgoers early in the morning, so we could cram as much as possible into the day. Upon arriving at the fairgrounds, we would go over the day's program while enjoying a delicious, hot cinnamon roll and coffee.

Pairing off, some of us would head for the craft booths and exhibit halls, while others checked out the livestock. Wendell usually got the job of holding seats at the grandstand for some good ole' country/ western entertainment, after which we would make our way to the State of Maine Building for their famous loaded baked stuffed potato. This was timed to catch the daily parade down the avenue in front of the State buildings. It was always a great day – even when it rained on the George Jones concert.

I had taken up country line dancing, which I've continued to date. Originally, I traveled here and there, but settled on my favorite: the Bay Path Barn in Boylston, Mass.

The last time I attended the Big E was with a man I met country dancing, who taught me how to two-step.

When I returned from the trip with my cousins, bowling season had begun. I missed the first Monday, but when I arrived at the bowling alley the next week, a handsome young man by the name of David, smiled to greet me. He had always been on another team, and I had always been glad when our teams played each other. Now, it appeared that we were on the same team. Shortly thereafter, we began dating.

∽

Jane's 1994 Christmas note reads:

Dear Marge:

You are a tease! You just casually mention "David" – and leave me hanging. Where did you meet him – are you really enjoying his company – what does he do, etc., etc.

Guess it was the line dancing which did it – made a happy gal out of you. And then David came along at the right time. Tell him you must take some time out to write to an old, sick friend in California (ha, ha) who thinks of you so much and wants a letter.

Love, /s/ Jane

Christmas, 1994, was one of the best I had ever had. David was madly in love with me, showered me with gifts, including the most beautiful bouquet of deep red roses I've ever seen. I felt like a princess. He accompanied me to the annual Christmas Party for the employees of the store where I work. One of my co-workers at the time, who had a great sense of humor, helped me come up with gag gifts for everyone. He wore a Santa suit, and held the bag of "special" gifts, which I presented to everyone, complete with a note written especially for them. Afterwards, on the way home, David said he was "very proud" of me.

∽

A card picturing a hummingbird at a hibiscus flower "designed by Connie Keel" is dated March 2nd (1995).

Dear Marge:

I should have written you long ago, after that nice phone call we had, but really, there just isn't much of interest going on here, and you don't know my "old" friends, so nothing there to report.

Yes, in 5 more days I shall be 80. Doesn't seem possible. I don't have any plans for the day but usually receive lots of cards. I did get a surprise package the other day from Will's cousins whom I visited in Ireland. In it was a 7-oz. box of chocolates made in Dublin and a few hand-crocheted coasters. They have always been so thoughtful and nice to me, and here I am no relation. I'm happy one of their daughters is presently living in Orange county, and that way, when they come to visit her, I get to see them also.

I'm wondering whether or not you are planning a trip to San Diego this year – you mentioned you were thinking of it when we talked.

I really like the sound of your present friend. Guess I have said several times that I was not impressed with reports re George, but this man sounds almost too good to be true. The one main thing I like is how nicely he treats you and how thoughtful he is. I'm so glad you have finally met someone whose company you enjoy.

Do you go to many movies? I see very few. I heard the movie "Nell" was a beautiful one, but missed it. I would like to see "The Madness of King George" – also the one with Peter Falk, whom I like very much in his mysteries.

How are your folks doing these days? As I recall, they are not nearly as old as I, so they are probably more active. Your mother is a wonder the way she still sews. I almost hate to use the machine any more.

I really went overboard recently – bought 3 new outfits, rather expensive, too, at Nordstrom's. Have never spent so much in my life, but now that I do not feel like traveling, I decided I might as well have some nice clothes. Hadn't bought a thing except a sweater or two since my trip to Hawaii in 1990.

Well, I'm just making up news, so shall stop, hoping all is well in your life. Keep me posted on the romance – you know I am interested. Much love, /s/ Jane

When I first began seeing David, he stopped by the store where I work one day with a small bouquet of flowers. Another time, he handed me a card with a sweet note inside. He seemed genuinely interested in me. After one particularly endearing note, I asked him if he were "planning to sweep me off my feet – and then leave me in a heap of devastation?" He looked puzzled. After my experience with George, I surely did not look forward to more heartbreak. There follows an example:

> *19 Oct 94*
>
> *Dear Marge,*
>
> *Just a few words to tell you how much I've enjoyed the time we have spent together the last few weeks. You are a very happy and upbeat person with a positive attitude towards life, and you like country music!*
>
> *I've enjoyed our talks and I especially appreciate the way you tolerate my zanyness (is that a word?) You were a really good sport about driving to Bellingham to play mini-golf in the arctic air. You have a million-dollar smile and I like to hear you laugh. I know this is jumping all around the place but I guess the bottom line is – I want to say thank you for sharing some time with me. You are a ray of sunshine that has warmed and brightened up my life. Have a nice weekend and I'll see you when I get back from Maine.*
>
> *As always – David*

David had asked me to accompany him on a trip to Maine, where his parents were living, but I chose not to go. He returned with a brand new pair of bowling shoes for me.

I cannot imagine that I did not write to Jane between March and September, but the next letter I have from her is dated September 2, 1995. Of course, I was busy with a new man in my life! I am certain, however, that I kept Jane apprised of the progress of the relationship.

~

> *Dear Marge:*
>
> *First, let me say that I am forcing myself to do anything! We have had over a week of truly hot, humid weather, as your folks have probably written you. It really has gotten to me today. I should be out in the garden pouring water on everything, but I just am wilted with it all.*

191

Secondly, I was so happy to learn in your letter of August 3ʳᵈ that you are finally having a good time in life. It all comes at once, it seems, but it was great news.

Glad you are meeting other people, such as the man with whom you dance. I never was any good at anything intricate on the dance floor. I remember one time a man I met asked me to be his partner in taking lessons for the tango. Well, about the time it came time to dip, I was lost! That finished his interest in me, for which I did not blame him.

I imagine you are telling David about your dancing partner. Hope he's jealous!

Did you take your friend up on his offer to go to Tombstone? I recall that when we were on one of our driving trips, we went through Tombstone. I wanted so badly to stop and go to the graveyard. (For some reason, I have always like to roam thru old cemeteries.) Will was not a bit interested, so on we drove! Guess you know that Wyatt Earp had a business in San Diego at one time. I always enjoyed those programs on TV years ago. My Dad was a fan of the actor who played Wyatt's part. I have a signed photo of him – in case you ever want it, I'll pass it on to you. I can't remember his name off-hand. I think my Dad was in love with "Miss Kitty."

I, too, will try to keep in touch more often. I have turned into a lazy letter writer. It is no chore for me to write a short note of thanks, sympathy, or get-well wishes, but I put off longer letters.

I am so glad that before Will died we had the opportunity to meet his cousins in Ireland. They have been so very nice to me. One of their daughters just had a baby girl. Big, big smiles from all the family in 8 grandchildren, there is only one girl. They treat me as though I were their relative, and since I am so alone in this world, it is doubly appreciated. I recently sent her a pair of Indian made earrings. They were shamrocks, silver, with small pieces of turquoise in the center.

You will never know or guess whom I had a date with last night. My plumber! He is 40, as wide as he is tall (not very), dressed in a short-sleeve shirt and jeans. He has just gotten a divorce but is hunting a wife (not me). Years ago, Will found him and at that time he was struggling to keep his five children *cared for. He was with his wife then, of course. Well, since Will had so much trouble raising his four boys without a mother, he emphathized with Jerry and always called him for a plumbing job. I kept on with him for it is nice to know someone personally when you are a woman living alone. He said to me about a month ago that we'd have to go out to dinner some night. He has so little money, I felt guilty having him spend anything on me. Well, we went to the Hungry Hunter. He said to order anything I wanted, so I ordered a $15.75 steak dinner. However, I had no drinks, nor coffee, nor dessert. He loves to talk about his girlfriends. I knew there would be no hanky-panky from him. He is a very strict Mormon – will not engage in an affair -- does not drink, smoke or swear! I thought it was real nice of him to take me to dinner, as he knows I am lonesome.*

Monday morning is my exercise class, and with this heat, it is hard, but the instructor has cut down on the tempo of the exercise, so that helps.

Well, Marge, this is a most uninteresting letter, but I did want to reply to your good news missive and tell you how happy I am. It was great to see you. I don't know why June had trouble recognizing you. Guess I told you she dropped out of the X-FBI gals' group. The current president is pushing for a gala celebration of the 20 years we have been part of the national group. I volunteered to be in charge of decorations and favors, so must start planning same. Believe the date is around Oct. 14. I never have enjoyed the group as much since we went national.

Well, I was going to stop, wasn't I? Hope you're not completely worn out by the time you finish this. Much love, /s/ Jane.

My two step partner and I did travel to Arizona to visit Tombstone, which I thoroughly enjoyed.

While in San Diego, after Sunday Mass, my mother, dad and I were having breakfast at their favorite neighborhood restaurant. I noticed June at a nearby table, mostly because of her hair -- that it had a lavender color to it, as Jane described. I went over to say hello; she didn't recognize me at first. She said she worked for a local newspaper, which peaked my interest. We planned to meet for dinner later in the week. It turned out that she didn't write for the newspaper – just worked in the office.

∾

Jane's handmade birthday card that year had small pressed pansy-type flowers inside a lacy oval on the front.

Inside, the message read:

Dear Marge – I wanted to send a letter with your card – especially since yours was so interesting! I'm so glad you are having lots of "male attention" but sorry the way things seem to be going with friend No. l. Anyhoo, I wish you a great birthday and I hope to write before too long.

Love, Jane

∾

Stationery with kitty cats walking all around the edge, dated 10-27-95, bears the following typewritten message:

Dear Marge:

I can't believe it is well over a month since I rec'd your most interesting letter – always so much fun to read about your "affairs of the heart!" I hope the activity has continued.

Am wondering what David gave you for your birthday, and whether or not the fire has been rekindled. He sounded almost too good to be true, from what you wrote at first.

You said you wanted to have a talk with him re whether trying to re-kindle or let go. Am most anxious to see how that went and whether or not he remembered your anniversary.

Re the picture of the actor who played Wyatt Earp. That is correct. The mention of "Miss Kitty" was in error as far as any connection with Earp goes. Sorry I confused you. One of these days I'll box up the photos of Hugh O'Brien and James Arness and send them to you.

Re David's asking your daughter to accompany you two sometimes. I don't blame you if you are a bit jealous – I know I would be.

Did I tell you I recently had a note from a man I have known for years, acknowledging a note I had written him, complimenting him on being picked out as a "man of the year" by a San Diego organization? Years ago, I went out on a double date with him. He married, but is now divorced. Well, in his note, he asked for my phone number; said he was better at conversing than at writing. In due course – maybe 2 or 3 weeks – I sent a note with my number. Never have had a call! I did not realize until this happened how much I have missed going out to dinner with the opposite sex, and just the thought that I might have a break in this forced solitude was a lift. He has plenty of money and is a well-known businessman in San Diego. If I had my choice, I would prefer going to dinner with an unknown. Well, it is probably for the best. He's not one I would care to see too much of – so now I won't!!

We had a celebration for the 20th anniversary of the local FBI gal's group joining the national. It was a luncheon, for which I decorated.

I'm tired and making many mistakes, but wanted to answer your letter (which I loved). I was determined to get a note off to you today.

Much love and write soon! /s/ Jane

David began asking me if I thought my daughter would care to join us when we went out to dinner. At first, this seemed a nice gesture. Besides, I enjoyed having her along, but for Valentine's Day, I felt differently. Eventually, I wondered if she (who was much younger and prettier) was the reason he was dating me in the first place. The fact that the initial "thrill" had gone out of our relationship, on his part, didn't help.

Jane did, in fact, send me a photograph, autographed, "Best always to my friend Murray Campbell/ Sincerely Hugh O'Brien/ 'Wyatt,'" and also a photo of James Arness, who wrote, "Hi Judge/ Murray Campbell/ Jim Arness."

November 22, 1995

Dear Marge:

I really am not in a letter-writing mood, but I have wanted to write you for so long. I guess my "80" life is catching up with me, for the last six months I have found myself stripped of energy very early in the day. It is disconcerting, to say the least!

Your letters are so wonderful – I just love to receive them, especially when you write a long, newsy one. I have just re-read your last one and marked some parts I wanted to comment about:

You said Tom didn't want "just to go dancing" – and suggested weekends away. I firmly believe that it is a most unusual and seldom-found man who does not want to be "more than a friend." I think the women want just a man-friend many times, but if most men find you attractive enough to spend some time with, it always seems to boil down to the old sex thing.

Re your conversation with David when you had a phone call from Tom and decided to tell him. I think his remarks about not losing any sleep over it and also that there was no reason to belabor the point would really aggravate me. I can't figure him out, from what you tell me. Also, he does not lose any sleep over the lack of much physical contact in your relationship – that is strange. I cannot help but wonder, should you marry him, whether or not you would be satisfied in the marital relationship. He sounds a bit on the cold side, to say the least. Maybe I should not be saying these things ? ? ?

He did treat you nicely on your birthday, I must say, except that a card with some sentiment would have been preferred over a humorous one, I agree.

I think the comment by Pat about David's not being "wild enough" for you is laughable. I cannot ever think of you as "wild." Must admit I was surprised, however, to know that you even went out to lunch with a married man. To make you fell better – I had quite a few "dates" (innocent) with married Agents. Now – are YOU surprised?

There really wasn't much romance in my marriage; however, I always felt Will would be there for me whenever I needed him and that I could trust him without any doubts. That means a lot. And, he never asked how I spent our money, which was a blessing.

I had had my own money for such a long time, so it would have been hard to take if I had to explain what I paid for things. So, probably in the long run I was lucky.

Later. Just had a friend drop by, who talked and talked. So now my train of thought is broken.

Now re me. No, I have not heard from the "man-of-the-year" former friend. Guess that is all over, darn it all!

Re the luncheon. This was a celebration of the 20th founding of the SD Chapter of the national organization. I thought it rather silly to be celebrating before the 25th, but the current President seemed bound and determined to have it. I offered to do the decorations. I picked out a "patriotic" theme. In the center of each table of eight were three balloons – one red, one white, one blue. They were anchored to a heavy frog, which I covered with ferns from my garden. The President wanted each person to receive a "favor." Not having much money to work with, I bought a white scratch pad to which I tied a red pen and a blue pen, using red and blue ribbon. Then Chris Curran furnished some samples of shampoo and conditioner from a firm which one of her daughter's represents. I ordered white tablecloths and red napkins. The napkins were folded beautifully, and the luncheon was in one of the resorts on Shelter Island – a beautiful big room with large windows looking out on the water. The room really looked very festive when you entered it.

I was sort of honored – received a corsage and some sort of proclamation on a paper which the outgoing president of National brought with her. Patsy Cripps spoke of the fact that it was 25 years ago I had started the local group. So, I think it was a nice affair. The new ASAC spoke – he was so attractive – but looked so young!

Well, I am getting tired and my eyes are hurting for some reason. I thought I would be able to get 3 letters written this afternoon, but yours is the only one. I had a time with a cake I was making – will tell you about it another time.

Hope your Thanksgiving was a good one – did David celebrate with you? Sounds to me as though you are quite in love with him.

Good luck – and lots of love.

/s/ Jane

P.S. I'm to be with Will's oldest son and his wife for Thanksgiving. The cake is for then.

P.P.S. I'll enclose a snapshot taken at the luncheon if I can find it. J

Jane, with incoming and outgoing national presidents of the former FBI womens group, Shelter Island, Marina Inn, 10-14-95

As time went on, I realized that David never suggested doing anything together, so I took a few other fellows up on invitations. I did not, however, want to become "involved" with them, because I really did love David.

Pat – my boss' brother-in-law -- worked in the store where I do. He had observed the way I loved to dance and have a good time at a couple of parties and figured David was too dull for me.

Jane sent me a photograph taken at the luncheon to which she referred. It was a very good photo of her in a beautiful bright blue pantsuit.

∾

6-27-96
Dear Marge:
My, what a popular gal you are! I am so happy for you. I should say, "It's about time!"

Tom sounds rather dangerous. Isn't he the one who is married? You seem to like him a lot. I've forgotten – what do they do? Hard to keep up with you now.

And how is the modeling doing? I had no idea you were interested in that. I wish you luck.

Since you liked my kitty stationery, here's some more.

I have had my second cataract surgery since I wrote before. It was June 20th. I go tomorrow for my one-week checkup, then another in 3 weeks. Probably around the end of August, I will go back for a prescription for new lens. I am seeing better as far as the TV goes without glasses, but can't do anything close-up without them. The second surgery also did well but I got a black eye both times, and this time was terribly nauseated from the anesthetic. I'll be so glad when it is all over, but glad that I had it done now before I get any older. Each year now seems to make a difference, I hate to say. How are your folks holding up? They are not as old as I, however.

I probably told you that my friend whom I visited several times in Kona, Hawaii, has gone into the Casa de Manana Retirement Home in La Jolla. She has a darling little duplex right on the ocean-front. All her furniture is so beautiful, and she has excellent taste. Well, I am going to visit her Wed., returning Friday afternoon. It will be a nice break.

Generally, things are pretty boring here – but guess I can't expect anything else. It is awful not to have any family.

The San Diego Symphony, to which I have been going, the last few years, has folded due to financial trouble, so I have paid for the series of, I think it is, 5 operas, beginning in the spring. I can go in with the same lady who drove me to the symphony.

Do you ever hear G. Gordon Liddy who has a radio talk-show? I have gotten to like him a lot. He seems to have a wealth of general knowledge, and he is always so polite to his callers. He was an FBI Agent – jailed in connection with Watergate – I believe the only one who wouldn't "rat" on his fellow workers. Isn't this business of the FBI files something? Bet it would never have happened if J. Edgar had still been in charge. Seems as though the country is going to the dogs. I can't stand Clinton – maybe you are a fan? ? ?

Sorry, I don't have any exciting news, but do keep me informed of all your romantic episodes and your new modeling career.

Much love, /s/ Jane

I have no idea what I said to Jane to have her think that Tom was "dangerous." He was an older gentleman I met dancing. We took two-step lessons together and had fun visiting various country dance clubs. He had been married two or three times, but was not married when I was seeing him.

Somewhere along the line, I got the bright idea to take up modeling. I enrolled in the John Powers Modeling School in Worcester, Mass., and learned how to dress, and walk, and use makeup, etc. It was fun, but I decided it wasn't something I wanted to pursue. There's no way I was ever going to walk down a runway in a bathing suit – or shorts for that matter!

≈

Jane's Christmas, 1996, letter is typed on a note with a little mouse peering out from under a huge Santa hat.

Dear Marge:

How good it was to have a personal visit with you if only for a short time. You look great – and not your age! We are lucky – at least folks are kind enough to tell me the same thing.

I am wondering which of your many male friends met you at the airport? And is it snowing in your area? Guess you all hope for snow at Christmas. I would love to experience that once.

I think I told you all my interesting news, and since generally my life is pretty hum-drum, I do not have much to write about. I just finished a letter to one of my 3 favorite SACs, who lives in Florida. I met his wife only twice, but each year she writes me a long letter!

My card this year is very different from my usual ones. I bought them because it benefits the SD Zoo. Wish I could get to the Zoo more often, but I don't know anyone who has the time and inclination.

I was aghast the other day when I was in Fedco and one of the items on my list was a new ribbon for this typewriter. They now are $9.75. I think that is awful. I guess I shall never accept the current prices, after the years I lived when things were so much cheaper.

What did you think of that letter from Stan? You made no comment after reading it.

I always dread the holidays since I lost Will. I have spent most alone. Folks just forget that I am family-less. However, this year I am happy to report I had invitations to dinner on Thanksgiving, Christmas Eve, and Christmas Day. Helps make the season bearable. Seems as though the last year I have missed Will more and more.

I have had so much baking to do this year – and since I never bake just for myself – I have had several failures. I like baking but get so darn tired when I am on my feet that much.

Well, I'll be thinking of you and hoping you have a great holiday season, with many men! Ha, Ha! I guess David is still No. 1?

On that, I shall say "Adios for this time."

Love, /s/ Jane

I had been out to San Diego for a visit that fall. As usual, Jane and I had a wonderful lunch at a restaurant in La Mesa. She showed me a letter from a male friend from Minnesota, who had paid her a visit when he was in town. In the letter, he told her how much he had enjoyed her company. Now, I am sure I made some comment about the letter. But, I think I added something to the effect that, "I don't know what to say," since it was quite endearing. I remember thinking to myself, "Gee, how great for Jane, now in her 80's, to be the object of a man's affection." Apparently, I did not voice my thoughts.

$\sim$

A letter from Jane with a sketch of a kitty cat knocking over a birdcage, while two other cats watch, is undated. The contents indicate a time prior to February of 1997.

Dear Marge:

I really have very little to fill up a page, but will do my best.

About the only thing interesting is that I had a houseguest for two nites last week – my friend who lived in Kona, Hawaii, for years, and whom I visited there 3 times. Since there's not much in this area for two old ladies to do, we went to a movie one day and then rented another two for the second day. The first one was "Evita". I have never like Madonna, but I thoroughly enjoyed the whole movie and thought Madonna did a superb job. I always like movies based on real events. And, of course, I lived through most of that history.

We rented "Brave Heart" and "The Bird Cage". Even tho' the former was bloody and ferocious, it, too, was history and was an excellent movie. I did not care for the third. The story was the same as "La Cage Aux Faux", or however you spell it – and I had seen it twice before in different productions, both of which were excellent.

Recently received a letter from Will's wandering son, saying he is to be married 2-1-97. I never thought he would marry again. At present he lives on an island off of Hong Kong. The fiancée is Canadian.

Today is beautiful – not a cloud in the sky. We have had some much-needed rain recently, however.

Some day I shall have to buy a new typewriter because this one is getting harder and harder to type on. I like that it only weighs 15 pounds, however.

Referring to your letter, you said that your relationship with Ken is strictly platonic. Maybe some day it will be different. Will and I dated about six months before I was interested in him. It meant a lot that I had grown up about the same time as he did, and I remembered his family and his first wife. So, just keep having fun with him and see what happens.

Glad that David accompanied you to your office party. Strange the way he keeps hanging on. Sounds as tho' he wants to forget you but can't.

Well, this is about all I can think of to say so shall send a Happy New Year wish to you.

Much love, /s/ Jane

P.S. Are you doing any writing or modeling these days?

After a nine month break, David and I started seeing each other again, but I was also keeping company with Ken, who took me to see *Evita*. Ken was a male friend, who loved to go to the movies, and dine out at nice restaurants. I met him when he was on the Planning Board in Bolton, Mass. and I was covering the meetings for the *Daily Item*. We went out together, over the years, when we weren't dating anyone.

In the fall of 1996, David started coming around again. I had begun a search for a house to buy, having tired, after five years, of condo living, fees, assessments, etc. He accompanied my daughter and me on our Sunday rides to check out homes to buy. When my realtor showed me a duplex, I felt it was perfect for us, since we could live in the same house, but maintain separate quarters. David came along for the home inspection, after which we went for coffee. He said he thought it would be a good investment for me. I told him I would not buy the house unless he agreed to help me with the work that needed to be done. Subsequently, I asked him to move in with me, especially since things were heating up with us again.

~

4-4-97 -- an Anne Geddes card picturing babies as sunflowers:

You have probably moved by now, but I am sure this note will be forwarded.

You are so strong, the way you go from one residence to another. It sounds like a good idea for both you and your daughter to have your own "quarters." I'm sure young women these days don't want to live with "mama" forever. I'm not typing this time as there is so little to tell, I couldn't fill up a page on the typewriter.

Now that I don't entertain, every dish I have to cook for club, etc., seems like so much work. I did find an easy dessert. I'll enclose the recipe just in case it appeals to you. Good for a group, potluck, etc. I served it with cool whip a few strawberries "on the side."

Remember Helen Kilgore? She lives in Rancho Santa Fe. She is having the next x-FBI gals' luncheon 5-10 or 11-97.

I'm never invited any more to the x-Agents' meetings. Really miss seeing those fellows who were such a part of my life for years.

You seem to be getting deeper and deeper into your relationship with David. Wonder what he has against marriage.

Did you decide to stay with your present job? If so, I do hope they have given you a good raise! I'm supposed to go out tonite with some gals to a nursery near Flinn Springs. It's so cold and windy I almost feel like staying home.

Hope to hear from you before too long re your new home and your "old" romance.

Much love, Jane

P.S. You asked about Stan. He calls me every Sat. and sometimes in between and we talk for an hour or so. However, this relationship will never amount to anything.

Jane felt this way because Stan was married, although his wife had been very ill for a long time.

I had given thought to going to work for Home Depot since the atmosphere at work was tense (due to bickering between the male employees). Besides, I had only been given two raises after eight or nine years there, and only one week's vacation.

～

May 16, 1997
Dear Marge:
This will no doubt be short, as there just isn't much to tell you since you don't know folks I do. The main interest lately, however, was the garden tour I worked on which the Woman's Club gave on May Day. It really was nice but so much work, especially for the gal who had all the clever ideas and also carried out a lot of them all by herself.

May is always a busy time. There's the Woman's Club monthly meeting; my FBI group, which you will remember I started about 27 years ago, meets the first Sat. in May, and my sorority from college holds its spring luncheon the first part of May.

It sounded from your card that you possibly are planning a trip here. You also said you'd tell me about the move "in the very near future." It will be great to see you, as usual, and we can discuss our mutual "love lives". Ha, ha on my part. The phone calls continue every Sat. and sometimes a brief one in between, but the Sat. calls consume anywhere from one to two hours. Don't know what in the world we talk about. He writes a one to two full page typed letter every week and expects one from me. That does not really thrill me, but it seems to be very important to him, so I try to abide. However, he has the word power, which I do not, on top of that, he loves to write letters. He may come out the end of Oct. to visit. I really don't know just where I fit into his picture, but guess I'll find out some day.

Well, sorry there's not any news. Just wanted to keep my promise to write soon. Do hope all is well and that I'll be seeing you.

Much love, /s/ Jane.

The "move" to my present address was complicated. As the time drew near for the closing on my condo, April 30, it became evident that the tenants in the house I was buying were not moving. Arrangements were made to hold my belongings on the moving van for an extra day, until I could at least move into my daughter's side of the duplex. I didn't actually close on the house for two stressful months.

∼

A birthday card, dated Oct. 3rd thanks me for my letter which she will "answer one of these days."

You sound busy – but happy! You told me about your brushes, your wallpaper, your paint, etc., but – NOTHING about your relationship with you know who.

Stan arrives 10-25-97 for a week, so I'll be busy getting ready.

Much love, /s/ Jane Happy, happy birthday.

∼

12-6-97 – A card "designed by a child who is a patient at M.D. Anderson Cancer Center," bears the following:

Dear Marge:

I guess you must still be busy refurbishing your new home. You are so smart to know how to do so many redecorating things. I hope you still have help.

Do you continue in your same job? Stan was here for a week in Oct. and we had a thousand laughs. Right now I have a stepson visiting for several weeks – so I have to cook again!

Have your happiest Christmas yet! Love, Jane

~

Another Anne Geddes card, picturing a little girl in flowered pants and hair ribbon, checking out her navel, is dated 3-20-98.

Dearest Marge:

Thank you for sharing the beautiful "Spring's Dream" card with me. I love it too. Sometimes it takes me several years to let go of a favorite card.

"The visit" went very well. Stan is really a wonderful man and treated me like a Princess. I can't analyze my feelings toward him. Maybe if he were free, it would be easier, but in the back of my mind, his status is always there. I know I am not in love, but do think the world of him. We did many things: "The Follies" in Palm Springs, a day and night in Borrego, apple pie in Julian; two movies: "As Good as it Gets" and "The Apostle." Don't miss the latter – it is stupendous. A play at "The Old Globe"; The Lambs' Players in Coronado, production of "The Secret Garden"; lunch at Peoke's Restaurant in Coronado; Valentine's dinner in the Crown Room at Hotel del; then birthday dinner at "Mister A's" in San Diego. Guess those are the highlites. Oh, also went to the opera – "Madame Butterfly" his last night.

So, you see, we were busy. We both were very tired after he went home. Consequently, I came down with a bug for about 10 days, but am ok now.

Marge, I worry about you and your status. I want you to have lots of love and affection and trust you don't have to wait much longer for it. I don't want to inject my feelings in your relationship, but do so hope things improve.

Sunday, I lost my best neighbor friend who lived across the street and who was always here immediately to help me if something went wrong in the house or garden. The services are today – I just hope I don't get emotional. He was such a fun person, too.

Now I have stepson Ward with me a few days, so have to cook. Stan calls every day – glad I don't have his phone bill to pay. Please write soon. What happened at Home Depot?

I love and admire you – if that helps at all.

Jane.

After just a few months of living with David, I came home from country line dancing one Thursday night to find that he had gone to bed in the spare bedroom. The door was closed. I tossed and turned the entire night, angry that he would make such a move without discussing it with me. When I confronted him in the morning, he brushed it off by saying, "It just seemed silly for me to try to be quiet every morning, while you slept." I had a feeling this meant the end of any intimate relationship.

Home Depot didn't work out for me. I returned to my old job after 10 days.

~

The following letter is undated, but due to reference about my sister's visit, repeat of news about neighbor's death, etc., it was written in April, 1998.

Dear Marge:

I do love your letters and your beautiful penmanship. I don't think CA schools teach same any more.

I have good news and some sad and some just upsetting.

Good first: Stan continues to call every evening at 7:00 and talks for about an hour. He wants to come out again for a week but family plans don't leave much opportunity to plan. Pretty soon I'd think the family might guess that there is something in CA other than the weather! He has plenty of money, so I don't worry if he spends some on me.

When a letter comes from you I can hardly wait to open it for your letters are just like a chat with you.

I imagine your sister is with you now. Please remember me to her. I hope you will discuss your relationship with David with her. I just can't imagine his not even hugging and kissing you. You deserve lots of affection.

Bad news: My wonderful neighbor, who was always here to help me when anything went wrong in the house or garden, died suddenly March 15th. He was only 64. So much fun. No one has ever had as contagious a laugh as he. Also, he was my Successor Trustee – so now I have to re-do my Will and Testament and find a new successor Trustee. Wish you lived nearby and could be that person.

Upsetting items: I had a partial new roof put on about 2 months ago. Now, I have another leak – in my bedroom. My typewriter is on the blink and just to clean and oil it is going to cost $55 – about half the price I paid. The soil in front is washing away with all the rains. Then a neighbor who lives in the Valley below informed me that he plans to build a 2-story large house at the foot of the house to the east. I fear it will interfere with my view. If it does, it will certainly de-value the property. And all the heavy duty equipment which will be hauling in soil to build a 6 foot plus pad for the house.

More other little things have gone wrong, but I won't bore you with them.

I was in bed Easter – an awful cold -- I'm still trying to get rid of.

You were so right to have left Home Depot. I have known a couple of folks who couldn't stand working for that concern.

Keep me posted. Wish you were coming for a visit. I understand American now has a direct flight from Boston to San Diego.

Much love, Jane.

My sister visited in April, 1998. David had been vinyl siding the house. One day when Donna and I returned from an outing, David was running around outside in the rain, trying to stop water coming in at the back of the house. He had demolished an overhang on the mansard roof, after which I had problems with leaks along the back of the house – a problem which has taken seven years to fix.

The only comment I recall my sister making about David was that it was good to have him help me fix the place up. When I complained to her about his lack of affection, she said, "Maybe, you should just let him do the work on the house, and then have him move out." Easy to say, but difficult when I felt I loved him.

After just a week or so at Home Depot, I decided it wasn't for me. Working different hours each day would be difficult since I was having so much trouble sleeping. It also would be a problem scheduling appointments of any kind. I felt totally thrown into things, with little training, especially on the computer.

∼

June 27ᵗʰ (1998)
Dear Marge:
I was so happy to receive your letter yesterday – felt almost like a visit.

I was sorry, however, to learn of your bouts with depression. I think the counselor sounds like a good idea and I hope she can help you. (I think a little "loving" would help too)!!

It sounds as tho' this house is more work than other places you have lived. If I didn't love my house, garden, and view so much, I'd be long gone. In an almost 70 yr. old house, it seems there are always 2 or 3 things in need of repair.

Right now Ward, my stepson, is staying here and fixing up. He is a great help but also a great expense as I have to pay him quite a bit.

I talked with Anne recently. She now has 2 grand-daughters. She quit her job and is taking care of her son's daughter all day and, I guess, doing all the housework, cooking, etc. I'm sure she gets paid. She sounds good. Nick is still having heart problems – but no worse than usual.

You asked about Stan. He calls every other nite now and we usually talk an hour – mostly on his part. He was here in Feb/March, as I had written you. He hopes to come back sometime in Oct. He is a wonderful man, and I think the world of him and we have such fun together. However, I am not in love with him – really wish I were – as I feel he is in love with me. Maybe I'd feel differently, if he were free. He is so good to his wife and still loves her.

Have the Valerian tablets and the Chamomile tea help you sleep? I surely hope so. What did your sister think of your staying indefinitely with David?

No more news re the house being built down in the valley. Am keeping my fingers crossed.

Re Stan again. I know that if something happened to him I would be devastated.

The reason you are getting such a quick reply, is that I am trying to keep up with my correspondence as it comes in since I am scheduled for knee surgery July 15th. My doctor is in La Jolla, so the operation will be at Scripps Hospital. I'll be in the hospital about 4 days; then will go to a rehab place in Del Mar for as long as it takes. Up to 3 weeks. I understand the therapy is very painful and I'll need some for 6 weeks. The Doctor said I probably wouldn't be completely free of pain for 6 months.

I decided to have this done now since Ward will be here and can help me when I get home. Can't drive for a month and will be using a walker.

I do so hope you will keep feeling better. I think of you very often.

Much love, Jane.

By the summer of 1998, I was so distraught over the situation with David that I sought counseling. We had worked together on house projects at first, as I planned. It soon became evident, however, that he would rather work alone. I became increasingly frustrated with his shutting me out and when I tried to talk about our relationship, he'd clam up. Dwelling on the problems with the counselor only made me feel worse, so I quit going after a couple of visits.

∼

8-16-98

Dear Marge –

I would have called you after receiving your last letter, but wasn't sure either your daughter or "lover" would be within listening distance.

I am just so sorry things are so rough for you. You are too good a gal to have all this uncertainty and trouble in your life. I know several women who are about your age and they seem to be having lots of emotional upsets – going to shrinks – going to marriage counselors, etc. I'm so thankful I never had to go through such times.

I'd like to be frank, but hate to put my thoughts on paper. If you would drop me a note as to when would be a good time and day to call, I'll do so.

I'm waiting for the physical therapist. She comes 3 times a week. Then, on my own, I have 13 exercises to do 4 times a day, and then a half hour of icing after each session. My knee is still very swollen and painful. However, the doctor said that my operation was so difficult that it might take me longer to re-coup. I must soon be able to drive as my stepson can't stay forever. He has been a great help.

Much love – and let me know about the phone call.

Love, Jane.

I continued to beat myself up for not having discussed our "relationship" before asking David to move in with me. I assumed we would have a "normal" live-in situation. It started out that way, but as time went on, it was more like having a handyman on the premises who did not communicate with me or show me any affection, although I was cooking for him and doing his laundry.

~

9-16-98 a.m.

Dear Marge –

I have an appt with a dermatologist at 1:40 p.m. today, but will at least get a letter started to you. I've been wanting to write ever since your last missive arrived.

First of all, I had a visit last evening with Anne. She said she had gone to the doctor as she hadn't been feeling well for some time.

She has very high BP, so the doctor put her on medication. Also, he found that she has two cysts growing on one of her kidneys. He didn't know whether or not it was malignant, but will take tests. He is also Nick's doctor.

Her good news was that friends from Butte, Montana, had talked them into going with them on a 3-week tour of Greece. The doctor gave her and Nick both the ok to go on the tour. They leave tomorrow. I'm just so sorry she has this kidney problem hanging over her while she's gone. She has had such a hard life – she deserves much happiness now.

I assume from the tenor of your letter you have decided to keep going as is with David. I couldn't stand his reticence to talk. It would drive me up the wall!

Do you suppose, by any chance, David might be ready to leave but doesn't want to hurt you by suggesting it?

Of course, I don't mind your "complaining" – which it really isn't. I am concerned for you and just so wish you could find a really fine man. Please don't stop confiding in me.

I guess there has been no time for you to even think about writing. Do you still have the desire?

Thanks for sharing your beautiful "Iris Spring" note card with me. I, too, hate to part with a special card, sometimes keeping them for years.

Should something happen to me, I wish you could be here to get my stationery collection. I have whole cabinet full!

Well, it is dinner time, so I'll say "Adios" for now. I am so happy we are in closer touch. Also happy I have heard from Anne again. I'll keep you posted re her health condition.

Much love, Jane.

By this time, my relationship with David was such that there was very little conversation between us. I continued to allow him to live in my house – trying to make the best of things – even though, deep down, I wished he would leave.

$\backsim$

212

10-4-98

Dear Marge:

Just finished my second set of exercises for the day – what a bore! Takes abt. 1 ¼ hrs. I see my surgeon Tues. Hope he will say I can discontinue them.

So glad to be in better touch. I always love your newsy letters even tho' the news doesn't always make me happy.

Your last letter was certainly on beautiful paper. I feel complimented!

The card is one I made from some paper cut-outs my stepson brought from China. I made quite a few for birthday greetings this year.

I hope you are content "just making the best of it." I hope things improve.

I seldom read the obituaries, but for some unbelievable reason did so today. There was the notice of Anne's mother's death. I believe I wrote you that she and Nick were leaving for a 3 week tour of Greece. Well, I called her this a.m. and the son answered, saying that Anne is still in Greece. There was some family eninity toward Anne and I just hope they didn't hurry up the services. The mother died Dec. 2ⁿᵈ; the funeral is the 6ᵗʰ.

Ward, stepson, is still here. I have a feeling he may leave the end of Nov. to pay a visit with friends he left in Hong Kong. I gave him notice a month or more ago that Stan would be visiting 10-18-98 for two weeks so I would need the bedroom. I asked that he leave by Oct. 9ᵗʰ. That will give me 3 days to get the room, bathroom, and rest of the house in some kind of order. Last visits, the house was spotless, but this year I just haven't had the strength to clean drawers, wash curtains, and the many extra things.

We are driving again to Borrego Springs to spend 2 or 3 nites in that super resort "La Casa del Zorro." He is renting a little house with L.R., 2 BR and 2 Bath. Everything there is A#1 and the dining room excellent. The rest of the visit will be more quiet than last Feb. I'm not up to too much and I think I wore him out that other visit.

Well, it is now 6:00 p.m. and I have things to do.

> *Look forward to your next letter. Hope your birthday is GREAT and that David will remember you well.*
> *Much love, Jane*

The birthday card she made was on bright green paper with a paper cutout of a fanciful horse.

∾

3-19-99 – written on a chocolate-colored card, decorated with a lace cutout.

> *Dear Marge:*
> *Thanks for your first birthday greeting, the card, and your missive – all welcome.*
> *Do you like this notepaper? Don't say "yes" unless you really do. I never know when I "create" something whether or not it would be pleasing to others.*
> *On 2-19-99 I unexpectedly entered the hospital on an emergency basis. It was a Friday a.m. and I went to my Internist for a heart problem; he sent me to a cardiologist who wouldn't even let me drive home. I had an angiogram where they found a blockage in an artery of the heart. He then performed an angioplasty (the "balloon" procedure), put in a stint, and sent me home the next day.*
> *I'm beginning to feel more like my "old self" – should – since I am taking 5 medications for my heart!*
> *Tomorrow, "Legoland" opens in Carlsbad -- something new to see.*
> *Looking forward to seeing you this spring, and hearing from you sooner.*
> *Much love, Jane*

∾

6-7-99
> *Dear Marge –*
> *Thanks for your letter of May 5th. Your two "travel" books sound so interesting. I do wish I had the eyesight to read.*

I have gotten so lazy – once I do the "just-do" things around the house and yard, I have to force myself to do any of the extras, such as bits of mending, letter-writing, certain shopping which should be done, etc.

I'm all over the effects of the angioplasty and am feeling as well as 84 years allows.

Today I had a nice experience: my step-grandson, who rec'd an appointment to West Point last year, is in Calif. for just a few days. He had 3 weeks off from the Academy. He drove out from his home in Texas with a young oriental man and a girl from the same town. Jimmy, the grandson, took me to lunch. The other two were at lunch also. I tried to help with the bill but he wouldn't let me and I know he has very little cash. Such a nice boy – 6'3".

We have had a very cold (for Cal.) spring – about 60 during the day. I love it – much more invigorating than 70/75 – but you know how Californians cry when the weather isn't just to their liking.

My favorite stepdaughter-in-law just underwent surgery to remove a malignant tumor in her breast. She has to have 6 weeks of radiation, but won't know until Monday the extent of the cancer and whether or not she will have to have chemo. I'm very worried about her.

I haven't talked to Anne recently. She called to thank me for her birthday card and at that time both she and Nick were having health problems.

I loved your writing paper with the beautiful envelope lining – and ink to match!

I still have phone calls from Stan, but his 84 years caught up with him in a hurry, so I really doubt he will ever be able to come out here again. So – nothing of great excitement now in the offing.

I'm glad your life is, as you say, "contentment" and hope it continues. Maybe you can talk with your new boss and then be able to plan a trip West.

Love, always, Jane.

I had been on a kick, reading books about folks traveling across country, by car, on foot, etc. It all started when I read *Blue Highways* by William Least Heat Moon. Then I saw Bert Herzog on the *Millionaire* – the year it debuted and everyone was glued to the t.v., trying to answer the questions. Bert mentioned that he had written *States of Mind* about his travels with his wife. Then it was *Travels with Charley*, by Steinbeck, and a few others.

In the spring of 1999, the store where I work was sold. I was hoping to negotiate better pay and vacation with my new boss.

~

9-30-99

I'll bet this note will cross one from you to me! Thanks for the darling card you sent after your visit.

Things the same here. The Society of Former Clerical Employees' Natl. Convention is in process now in SD. I plan to attend the luncheon this Sat.

My main reason for this note is to tell you that Anne called yesterday. She was in her daughter's home in Del Mar, taking care of her daughter and two new grandchildren, born Sept. 17th. Anne said the combined weight was almost 14 pounds, even tho' they were born almost a month early. Sharon also has a girl under two – so Anne did everything except nurse the newborns! Sharon nurses them every 3 hours – both at once.

At the same time, Nick is sick and has to go to the hospital next week to get a new defibulator inserted. Quite a dangerous surgery. Anne said. So, of course, she is worried about him too. Her life seems always to be full of problems.

Hope all is well with you.

Love, Jane.

~

11-16-99

Dear Marge:

This will be just a "quickie" to thank you for your two notes. I'm so happy for you that you have a new kitchen. It all sounds most attractive and convenient. Now, I hope your roof has been fixed as it is near rain time, I should think.

There's nothing interesting in my life to relate. I just wanted to touch base before it is time for a Christmas communication.

One item: I have to buy a new dishwasher — to the tune of $800 plus. I never liked the Maytag I have now, so am trying a Kitchen-Aid. I had that brand at one time and loved it. What brand did you install?

I plan to have 7 gals (incl. U.T.) to lunch Dec. 11th and am already stewing about it. I finally bought my Christmas cards but that is as far as I have gone. I have been cooking (candy) to make to ship out. Haven't had time to sit down and try to balance my last two bank statements! Don't know where the time goes. I try to walk 20/30 min. every morning. I feel fine in the mornings, but am too tired in the afternoons to get much done. Yesterday I got ambitious and fixed a recipe I saw in the paper. It was a mixture made for stuffing a Portabello mushroom, wrapped in foil and baked. If you like that kind of mushroom, you might like it

Happy Thanksgiving!

Love, Jane

P.S. Do you remember John Baker, a SD clerk? He died Sunday.

David tore out my kitchen ceiling while I was in California that August, and installed a wooden one. It was something I had mentioned, but as usual, there was no real discussion before he installed it while I was away. I spent Labor Day weekend brushing polyurethane on it. I had purchased cabinets, which he put together and installed, after having removed the old ones. I also had a dishwasher installed, which necessitated moving the refrigerator. And, had a new floor installed.

John Baker was the clerk who wrote Jane the long letter when she retired.

∾

The Christmas card from Jane that year was designed by "Hessa, age 9," as part of a "Children's Art Project, making life better for children with cancer."

Dear Marge:

Nothing much new here since I wrote. I have an invitation to Christmas dinner at Bill and Peggy's. I think she plans to serve on Christmas Day.

Then a friend invited me and I believe she has her dinner Christmas Eve, so that works out fine.

I am just beginning my cards. I sent at least seventy and I like to write a note on almost all, so it is a big job. As I think I probably said in my letter, I just can't keep up with life any more!

Do hope your Christmas is GREAT, with lots of nice things happening.

Love, Jane.

≈

12-29-99

Dear Marge:

Thanks for your card and Christmas note. I hope your kitchen will be finished early in 2000. I find it increasingly hard to push myself to get anything done. It is now 11:30 a.m. and all I have done is walk for abt 20 min., visit 20 min. with a neighbor, make my bed and pick up in the living room!

I wrote Anne that I was sending the snapshots to you. Please return. Isn't little Krystine beautiful? She reminds me of Sharon at the same age.

Anne said that Sharon nurses both babies at once – can you imagine? I wish I could see Anne once in awhile – she's such a good friend – as are you.

I had perhaps the best Christmas since Will died as I was invited to a friends' for dinner Christmas Eve and another on Christmas Day. Still a lonesome time, however.

My luncheon was OK altho' I don't think they liked the soup. It was a recipe I got out of the newspaper for Mexican Clam Chowder. It calls for a can of Mex. flavored bean chile and I guess the seasoning was too much for most. However, they loved my salad (made with butter lettuce, apples, walnuts, raisins, and a dressing I made from walnut oil). For dessert I served a lemon cake made with lemon curd and whipping cream. I finished off with a piece of special after-dinner candy.

I still haven't lost the 5 pounds I gained some months ago and am uncomfortable since it all went to my hips and my slacks are tight! Ugh!

There have been so many gov't warnings (inc. the FBI) re Y2K – I'll be relieved when it is over, and hopefully, no disasters.

Yes, Linda has a wonderful life. She finally called me abt 3 weeks ago but I wasn't home. She gave me her tel. number and asked me to call back. It took her ever since your visit to call, so I have not tried to reach her. She said she would call again, but has not done so.

How did your framed message to your children turn out? What a lovely gift! Well – Happy New Year! Love, Jane

For Christmas that year, I wrote a one-page letter to each of my children, remembering special occasions spent with them as they were growing up. I selected paper with a shoreline background for Tom, and a cloud background for Sarah. Each was put into a special frame.

~

2-17-00 (Postcard made by gluing a closeup photograph of a brightly colored flower to a plain card.)

Just received your note on the cute notepaper. Am delighted you are coming West again. I have marked my calendar. Am sure you will let me know our get-together date. Am glad Linda is finally coming down. Thought you would like this snapshot of an unusual plant in my garden.

Love, Jane

~

Note dated March 19th

Thanks for the card from Balboa Park and your note. I'm so glad we had some time to visit after the luncheon.

I felt embarrassed after I asked if Joe was the reason you left S.D. It's your story – and if you don't want to go into it – that's ok.

What a great marriage Linda has! I guess she and Jeff are close now.

I'm anxious to learn about your mother. I am sure it was hard for you to leave her. I don't want to call your father.

Love, Jane

The day after my return to Massachusetts, I received a call from my dad that my mother had passed away. The last night I was with her, she had gone to the hospital for a Catscan. She was extremely weak and frail, but sat up on her bed and visited with me the morning I was leaving. She commented that the shrubs outside her window needed to be trimmed. I never thought she would be gone in less than 24 hours. Rather than turn around and fly back out, I told my father that I would wait a couple of months, and then come back to be with him. My sister lives nearby, wasn't working at the time, and was able to assist him with paperwork and arrangements.

~

March 29th
Dear Marge –
I said this morning I would not be writing for awhile – but your life is so mixed up right now, I felt I must write.

I think you made the right decision to delay your visit. It gives your father something to look forward to and give you the chance to stay longer.

I will let Anne know when I send her birthday card.

Know I am thinking of you – with sympathy and lots of love.
Jane

No matter what decision I made, it would have been approved by Jane.

~

5-8-00

Dear Marge:

Since you like special stationery, I am sending you one of my very best. I ordered it from "Gump's" in S.F. You can see their mark on the envelope. I've had it for years but save it for special friends.

I loved your letter all about your "Western Room." You are something! I had forgotten about the photographs. I'm real pleased that you could use them – and how happy my Father would be!

So far the Millenium hasn't been very kind to me. I think I wrote you that I was in the hospital April 19/21ˢᵗ with a heart problem. Just getting over that when I had another fall – last Tuesday. Fell flat on my head on the sidewalk and wound up in emergency. Now I am getting over that – a cut to my head – lots of blood, etc., but no broken bones, for which I am thankful.

I feel for your Father – it's no fun – I know.

It will be great to see you again, so I know you'll call me when you arrive.

Love, Jane

After the death of my mother, I immersed myself into decorating a small room in my house, western style. Jane had given me autographed photos (to her father) of James Arness and Hugh O'Brien, which I hung on the wall. I also had framed black and white photos of my mother, dad, sister and me on family vacations to the Grand Canyon, Yosemite, Lake Arrowhead, and such. When I go to that room, I reminisce about those days long ago, when I lived in San Diego, with my mother and dad.

≈

7-1-00

Dear Marge

It is well over a month since you stayed with me – and I am worried that something is wrong.

You are usually such a good correspondent! I hesitate to call your Father in case you are ill.

Please let me know.

Love, Jane

≈

221

7-16-00

Your second letter came the same day I mailed a note to you. There's no news here since then so I thought I'd use this birthday gift notepaper to write you.

You probably know that, from what you have told me, I am not a "David fan"! I believe you not only love him but must be in love to put up with all you do. Maybe you should tell him to pay everything over the 6 to 800 he originally quoted you!

Don't worry about writing me your troubles. I just wish I could do something to help. It makes me feel good that you think enough of me to share your problems – so keep it up. Love, Jane

When I came home from my trip to San Diego this time, David had torn out the fireplace wall in my living room, hauling away all the old brick, etc. The place was "under construction." We had talked about possibly installing a gas fireplace. He said that it would cost about $800. On my return, he informed me that the gas fireplaces run about $3,000. I was stunned, and had not planned on such an expense. I asked what my options were. "Either put in the fireplace, or I can close up the wall." I did not wish to lose my fireplace all together, so I felt I had no choice but to spring for the gas insert. Once again, he had decided to take on a large project while I was away, without discussing the matter.

~

7-17-00

Dear Marge –

It was good to get your letter of June 28th. I was concerned about you!

Yes, my birdies are gone. They flew away one morning before I got up. I was so disappointed I had so wanted to see them leave. I fear I would have shed a tear or two.

But now I have another family in the nest. I think it is the same kind of bird but a different mother. Really fun to have them around.

I also have the beautiful yellow and black orioles flying around. They really devour the H.B. syrup. You probably have many more pretty birds where you live. I have always wished we had chickadees. I think they are so cute.

Congrats on winning the wallpaper contest. What a shame it wasn't a cash award. Thanks for the photos. The snapshot of Linda and me turned out quite well. Yes, "scrapbooking" has been very popular here too. You get so much done – I can't seem to keep up with life anymore.

I am sending you Linda's address on the last page here. I believe the postage is 60 cents for the first half ounce and 40 cents for each add'l ounce.

I had been watching for your bread and butter letter or would have sent it earlier. I haven't heard any more from Linda, have you!

I'm in the throes of dental work – had to see three different kinds of dentists before they all decided to piece the darn thing.

Out of space – Hope all is well. Love, Jane

While I was in San Diego and visiting Jane at her home, she pointed out a nest of birds she had been watching from her back window.

After my mother passed away, I put together a special scrapbook, with photos and cards depicting her life. Once finished with her album, I began one for each of my children of their young lives.

Linda was touring Europe with her husband, after she retired, and had left an address in Spain where we could write to her.

∼

8-23-00

I am writing you on my newest letter paper. Even tho' pretty, it is not easy to write on.

I'm sorry that your mail box has not had a letter from me since yours of July 25th arrived. I owe everyone with whom I correspond. Part of the trouble is that my life is so dull, there's not much to impart. However, things have picked up a bit recently. My friend from Arizona was in town recently, house-sitting her daughter's home in Bonita – so I was invited there for a barbecue one Sunday, and then we had lunch together after that.

Tomorrow my friend Winifred, her brother and wife, and possibly the Carlsens are coming to take me to lunch. They all live in a very fancy retirement home in Rancho Bernardo. Then Saturday, I am going with Bill and Peggy Browne and his daughter and fiancee' to lunch. Everything happens at once.

I do so love to receive your letters – I should answer more promptly.

I wish Anne would call me once in awhile – I would like to know how things are with her.

I imagine your father has told you about our problems with the high electric rates. My bill was over $200 and I know the next one will be more. I had air-conditioning put in abt 3 years ago ($4,000) – haven't really needed it until this year – and now I'm afraid to have the extra expense. On top of that, my water bill was $388! I'm so glad I saved when I was young. But I hate to see the money go for those things. I just hope my 1988 car will last as long as I do!

I have been cooking a bit more recently – just get so tired of jerked up meals – but when I spend time that way, other things suffer. I feel fine in the mornings, but about noon or one o'clock, I get so tired all of a sudden, I have to sit for an hour or two. Yesterday, I was not only tired, but weak and had to go to bed. My blood pressure was 104 over 59, which seems a bit low to me, but guess it's better than high B.P.

Our weather is cooler today, thank goodness. We are so dry – wish you could ship a supply of your rain here.

This isn't a very interesting letter, for which I am sorry. It's always so good to hear from you – your letters are almost like a visit. Much love, Jane

~

11-22-00
Dear Marge:
On re-reading your last letter, I noticed you had been to a restaurant called The Old Mill. When I was in New England

many years ago, Winifred's attractive, single, male cousin took us to such a place – right on a stream of water. Thinking back, I now believe he had his eye on me. I mentioned that my next stop would be Washington, D.C., to which he replied that he had plans to go to Washington at the same time. At this, Winifred immediately spoke up and told him that I was being met there by a boyfriend! Of course, I never saw him again. Winifred had told me he was looking for a wife. I think she herself wanted him!

Glad you had a birthday card from David.

I had a note from Linda yesterday. They have rented a small house, in Laguna, five min. from the beach for six months; they move to Oregon for 6 mos. to decide where they want to settle. She was so good sending cards, which I thoroughly enjoyed.

I have an invite out for Thanksgiving, thank goodness. My best friend in the Woman's Club, Ginny Brown, moved to Ariz. She and her husband came over to visit their daughter who lives in Bonita – and hence I got an invitation.

I keep so snowed under with "things" – I can't seem to keep up with life anymore – and it frustrates me. I now have Christmas – and haven't made much headway. The most time-consuming is writing notes on most of the 80 cards I send. At least I have my cards.

No more news. Hope all is well. When are you coming West again.

Much love, Jane

The Old Mill restaurant, in Westminster, Massachusetts, has been in existence for over a century. Its beautiful setting, with rushing water, has been enjoyed by my family on many special occasions.

During her tour of Europe, Linda regularly sent postcards to Jane and me.

∽

Christmas, 2000
Dear Marge –
I hope the holidays bring some special happiness.

I had a card from Linda – very nice note, too. It set me to thinking: You had mentioned you might be SD bound one of these days. Wouldn't it be great if we could get Linda and Anne to go to lunch with us while you're here? Anne probably would have to come on a Sat. I think Stan will probably be here some time in Feb/March – so I'd be busy for abt 2 weeks.

Think about it and whenever you plan to come to SD, I'll contact Linda and Anne – if you agree.

Love, Jane

❧

2-28-01
Dear Marge:
Sometimes one just has to quit doing the necessary things to make room for other things, such as writing a favorite friend.

I probably have written to you before on this paper. I know it is computer paper, but it was so pretty, I couldn't resist.

I haven't heard any more from Linda. Guess in a couple of months they will be moving to Oregon. I believe she has a brother there and a sister here. We finally got some rain. Need more. It was so good to see that wet stuff come down.

Your letter is dated 1-23-01, so I am doing pretty well in answering.

It's always something going wrong in a house. I hope your garage door problems are solved by now. Must have been quite expensive. Speaking of expensive, my gas and light bill last month was $331+ -- and they say both rates may go up. Stepson Ward and I replaced almost all the lights with fluorescent ones. I do not use any light in the kitchen until about 4 p.m. Have cut down on other lights too, including 2 flood lights outside. One outside I am keeping as it is sort of scarey when one is alone to have everything pitch black outside.

I'm sorry about the water damage in the store. Has the owner said any more about selling? If so, maybe you could just continue with the new owners. I'm so thankful I worked for the gov't and have reliable monthly income. Our raises aren't much, but anything helps. I feel so sorry for folks on a fixed, low income, *and for all the small business owners, a lot of whom have already closed. They say the flower business in Calif. is in dire need of relief and that that industry may be driven out of Calif.*

I hope your father did not develop bronchitis – I well know how severe that can be.

I had a nice surprise Christmas card from Donna – please thank her for me. I have some more shoes she might be able to use. You mentioned you were thinking of coming West in March. Keep me informed about that. Stan's wife died about two weeks ago after 12 years of illness. He is grieving terribly. They evidently had a wonderful, long marriage, and he loved her deeply. His health is such he does not think he will ever be able to make the trip to CA again.

I'm OK physically – of course, there is always something wrong. I have noticed a big difference in my energy since a year ago. I have been going to bed from 8 to 9 but just get too tired to enjoy TV after that. But, I am lucky to feel as well as I do – 86 come March! Love, Jane

After purchasing my present home, I scraped and painted the 100-year-old wooden garage doors. In time, however, a hinge broke on one of the doors, for which we could find no replacement, and a row of panels on the other door split. So I had to buy new steel doors.

∽

4-3-01

Dear Marge:

Loved your chatty letter of 2-28. I thought I was answering it soon and here it is over a month!

I'm glad you did not come out in March. I have had bronchitis most of that month – am almost over it now.

I dropped a card to Linda the other day and told her you hope to be here in April or May. She will probably be in Oregon by that time, however.

Guess you have had lots of snow. Hope your roof was OK.

Do you have a new phone number, if David moved his phone to the apt. house? If so, please let me know.

I have managed to bring down the electric bill somewhat, having replaced almost all my light bulbs with fluorescent ones and giving up two outside lights. I also turned down the thermostat on the 2 water heaters. The gas bill doubled, however, and they are talking about a water shortage this summer!

You asked about Stan. He still calls every 7 or 10 days. He's having a hard time with his wife's death. They had a wonderful marriage of 63 years. He says he knows he can never get back to Calif. due to health problems. I haven't told him, but it would now be hard to have him here any length of time. My strength has failed a lot in the last two years.

I still hope you can spend a nite with me. Just re-read your letter and see I have your new phone number.

About this time, David informed me that I would have to get a new phone number as he was moving his phone over to an apartment, which he owned, where he was supposedly setting up an office.

~

This notepaper was given to me by a neighbor who created rather weird ceramics.

Thanks for your birthday greetings. I had a surprise party at a friend's home – about 20 ladies! Will tell you about it when you come out in April/May. If your sister comes out, I might have a pair or so of shoes if she would like them.

Hope all is well with you and that you are having some fun.
Love, Jane
P.S. Does David still answer your phone calls?

~

4-6-01
Dear Marge:

I wrote to Linda and told her I hoped she would still be in CA when you came out. She replied that they are moving to Oregon the last week in May. She wants to get together again, so would you let her (and me) know as soon as you do just when you will be here. Hope to see you soon. Love, Jane

I travelled to San Diego in May. Jane arranged a wonderful luncheon at her home, which included Linda, another former FBI gal, Jan, with whom Linda had remained friends, and Anne. Somehow, Jane and I got the days wrong. I was busy sightseeing with my dad and sister, while she and her guests awaited my arrival. She tried calling the house several times, but I never got the message until late in the day. I felt just awful, especially since Jane prepared a special lunch for our reunion. I stewed about it for the rest of the visit.

When I returned home that year, David picked me up at the Manchester Airport. My flight was over two hours late, due to thunder and lightening in Chicago. Once we got home, he informed me that he had moved back to his apartment. Again, no discussion.

~

6-11-01

Dear Marge:

I'll at least start a letter to you, altho' I have no interesting news. I find that my penmanship is changing. I can't seem to write as well as I used to.

I am having a battle with squirrels – they like the grain the birds toss out of their feeder. Ward bought a trap and we've caught 3 so far. I still have 4 others – and I understand it is breeding season! They are so destructive – almost destroy a large Baby's Breath plant. And now are eating leaves and blossoms of my mini roses. Ward probably will be leaving in several months to roam the world again. I have been feeling so punk. I really don't see how I can carry on without him.

My filing system isn't working. I cannot locate your last letter; however, you sounded as tho' you are coping quite well. It has always seemed to me that you have a fear of living alone. Altho it's no fun, there are balancing factors.

I haven't heard any more from Linda other than a Xerox copy of a joke. I thought by now she would be sending her Oregon address. Have you heard? Maybe she and her husband are just visiting at present. I have so many sick friends, keeps me busy.

I finally got thru one long tape furnished by the Brail Institute. It was a murder mystery by John Laraleroire (sp?) The name was

"Guilt". I always fall asleep as the voices lull me to sleep. When that happens, I have to rewind the tape to find the spot I fell asleep.

After about 14 chiropractic treatments, I quit and went for 6 physical therapy treatments. They did help but I don't know how long the benefit will last. (Problems with my neck.)

So far, I haven't undergone a "rolling blackout" and hope I won't. They last from 1 ½ hrs. to two. My bills are scarey.

Do you have a favorite frozen choc. chip cookie? I got some Nestles' but wasn't too impressed.

I have arranged an FBI speaker for our Sept. meeting of the Woman's Club. The current president of our FBI group helped me. The agent will speak on "Telemarketing in San Diego". I'll keep you posted.

I hope you have had some interesting invitations and doing as well as possible in your "new life".

Love, Jane

Write soon — I love your letters!

Author, standing at the doors of the former San Diego Trust and Savings Bank Building, 6th and Broadway, San Diego, 2003

10-5-01

Happy Birthday! I hope it will be a great one. I'm sorry to send this card instead of one I made. I am behind in everything – having been in the hospital three days. Am better, but not doing much. Thanks for your card. Love, Jane

~

A week or so after Christmas, 2001 --

"Leave it to you to worry about Jane," Anne quipped, when I called her, explaining that I had not heard from Jane at Christmas, and was unable to reach her by phone.

"I'm so glad you called, though. I'll see what I can find out."

While I waited for Anne's report, it dawned on me that Jane had been complaining about not feeling well and being tired all of the time. Not receiving a card from her at Christmas worried me. I prayed that nothing serious had happened to her. It's funny how we assume that people we love will always be there for us.

I started reading over Jane's old letters, wondering why I had felt compelled to save them. Soon, her motherly sort-of love became evident. She was always so supportive, and complimentary. I believe, now, that her constant bolstering played a part in my eventually reaching a point where I no longer doubt myself. No wonder, I continued to write to her.

She felt the same way about Anne, and kept me posted over the years about her troubles. "She's had such a hard life," Jane would say, and often expressed that we deserved "so much more."

There were similarities in our lives, which I hadn't really thought about before reading over the letters. Jane and I had been transplanted in our early childhoods from our native states, and were raised in strict households. We began working for the FBI in San Diego exactly 20 years apart, and shared a love for the Bureau and its people. We both married in 1967, and then lost our husbands about the same time – mine through divorce in 1988, and she when Will died in 1989. In 1992, we were involved with selling homes, mine in Bolton, and Will's house in Chula Vista.

We even took similar falls – mine outside the Post Office in Bolton; hers in Mexico. Both of us were "domesticated" to a point. We always enjoyed our homes, and in her case, her garden. We loved having dinner parties for friends, which involved setting an elegant table, despite the amount of work we felt it entailed.

We both detested house cleaning – and paperwork, especially of a legal nature. But we both enjoyed corresponding with our friends.

We shared a love of little things like flowers, beautiful stationery, and kitty cats.

Of course, there was the "Scotch" in us. I always understood her need to be frugal, as I was the same. Some folks mistake frugality for being tight or stingy, but, to me, Jane was one of the most generous people I have ever known – and it had nothing to do with money.

Among my "souvenirs" is a photo of me and Jane taken at an FBI luncheon in the early 1970s. It is probably the only time our hair was the same length – long and similar style. Even our dresses were alike – although mine was bright and high-necked; hers was more sedate in color, but with a low neckline!

∾

A few days after I called Anne to check on Jane, she called back to report that Jane had been hospitalized with pneumonia and ended up having surgery to remove part of a lung. She went to see her, and had a good visit. She said she was doing well.

∾

Shortly thereafter, I received the following short note, dated 1-29-01.

> *Dear Marge:*
>
> *Thanks for your card and note. I have not been able to write since the pneumonia attack and it is still hard to control the pen.*
>
> *I am very slowly recuperating. I had extensive surgery and was in the hospital 4 wks and 1 day and then in a rehab place another week.*
>
> *Hope to hear from you soon.*
>
> *Love, Jane*

∾

We have just celebrated Christmas, 2004. Jane is still writing, much shorter notes now, but still on beautiful cards or notepaper. She telephones me on occasion, especially if she hasn't heard from me in awhile. Her latest call was to advise me that I would be receiving "something" in the mail from her daughter-in-law.

"Want to know what it is?" she asked.

"Of course," I replied.

"It's an invitation to my 90th birthday party. I know you won't be able to attend, but I wanted you to have the invitation."

"Guess what?" I said. "I will be in San Diego for your birthday. It just so happens that the kids and I are making the trip out the first part of March. Tom wants my dad to meet Hannah!"

Hannah is my first grandchild.

~

When good friends find themselves apart,
They still are close, at least in heart,
Because their friendship means so very much.
They think about each other still,
Because they care, and always will.
That's why they need to always stay in touch.
For the truest friends can understand
That friendship really can't be planned,
It simply happens – when two people give.
It's built of sharing, joy and smiles,
And crosses time, and even miles –
A gift to cherish every day you live.
Amanda Bradley

This message came on a birthday card from my friend Wanda in 1993.

Printed in the United States
73648LV00005B/26